THE BRONTËS

Modern Critical Views

These and other titles in preparation

Modern Critical Views

THE BRONTËS

Edited and with an introduction by
Harold Bloom
Sterling Professor of the Humanities
Yale University

CHELSEA HOUSE PUBLISHERS ◊ 1987
New York ◊ New Haven ◊ Philadelphia

© 1987 by Chelsea House Publishers, a division of Chelsea House
Educational Communications, Inc.

    133 Christopher Street, New York, NY 10014
    345 Whitney Avenue, New Haven, CT 06511
    5014 West Chester Pike, Edgemont, PA 19028

Introduction © 1987 by Harold Bloom

Printed and bound in the United States of America

∞ The paper used in this publication meets the minimum
requirements of the American National Standard for Permanence of
Paper for Printed Library Materials, Z39.48-1984.

Library of Congress Cataloging-in-Publication Data
The Brontës.
  (Modern critical views)
  Bibliography: p.
  Includes index.
  Contents: Artistic truth in the novels of Charlotte
Brontë / Inga-Stina Ewbank — The tenant of Wildfell
Hall / W.A. Craik — Charlotte and Emily Brontë /
Raymond Williams — [etc.]
  1. Brontë family.   2. Brontë, Emily, 1818–1848—
Criticism and interpretation.   3. Brontë, Anne, 1820–
1849—Criticism and interpretation.   4. Brontë,
Charlotte, 1816–1855—Criticism and interpretation.
I. Bloom, Harold. II. Series.
PR4169.B76   1986   823′.809   [B]   86-14761
ISBN 0-87754-687-8 (alk. paper)

Contents

Editor's Note

This book gathers together a representative selection of the best criticism available upon the writings of the Brontë sisters—Charlotte, Emily Jane, and Anne. The critical essays are reprinted in the chronological order of their original publication. I am grateful to Jennifer Wagner and Susan Laity for their erudition and insight in helping to edit this volume.

My introduction centers upon both *Jane Eyre* and *Wuthering Heights*, considering them in relation to Byron's influence, particularly upon the characterization of Rochester and Heathcliff. The chronological sequence begins with an overview of Charlotte Brontë's novels by Inga-Stina Ewbank, who finds that they take as their crucial concern the emotional and intellectual needs of women, and represent those needs by an authentic psychological realism.

W. A. Craik, in one of the best of the all-too-few studies of Anne Brontë, convincingly demonstrates the aesthetic validity and strength of *The Tenant of Wildfell Hall*, a strength I also find in it despite its inability to match the passion and originality of *Wuthering Heights* and *Jane Eyre*. In a comparison of Charlotte and Emily Brontë, Raymond Williams, the eminent Marxist critic, finds in them authentic continuators of Blake, though they reflect social conflicts and class unrest more obliquely than he does.

Rosalind Miles, describing the dynamism of Emily Brontë's poetry, emphasizes its function as a representation both of mystical experiences and of the less benign aspects of nature. Nature is again the focus in a distinguished reading of *Wuthering Heights* by Margaret Homans, who shrewdly observes that Emily Brontë "must repress literal nature by not naming it directly, in order to write."

Charlotte Brontë's *Shirley*, through a strong exegesis by Sandra M. Gilbert and Susan Gubar, becomes a convincing repudiation of the myth of Mother Nature in a post-Romantic and wholly mercantile England. Its companion novel, *Villette*, is explored by Janice Carlisle as a study in problematical memory, resembling the quasi-autobiographical mode of Thackeray's *Henry Esmond*.

The narrative art of *Jane Eyre* is described by Rosemarie Bodenheimer as a highly self-conscious performance, intensely aware of its status among other fictions. In this book's final essay, J. Hillis Miller deconstructs *Wuthering Heights* as a structure of repetition, relating this structure to Freud's version of the Sublime as the "Uncanny." Though Miller sees the novel as a psycholinguistic pattern of paired oppositions, he still preserves a clear sense of its force, though perhaps at the expense of its pathos.

Introduction

The three Brontë sisters—Charlotte, Emily Jane, and Anne—are unique literary artists whose works resemble one another's far more than they do the works of writers before or since. Charlotte's compelling novel *Jane Eyre* and her three lesser yet strong narratives—*The Professor, Shirley, Villette*—form the most extensive achievement of the sisters, but critics and common readers alike set even higher the one novel of Emily Jane's, *Wuthering Heights,* and a handful of her lyrical poems. Anne's two novels—*Agnes Grey* and *The Tenant of Wildfell Hall*—remain highly readable, although dwarfed by *Jane Eyre* and the authentically sublime *Wuthering Heights.*

Between them, the Brontës can be said to have invented a relatively new genre, a kind of northern romance, deeply influenced both by Byron's poetry and by his myth and personality, but going back also, more remotely yet as definitely, to the Gothic novel and to the Elizabethan drama. In a definite, if difficult to establish sense, the heirs of the Brontës include Thomas Hardy and D. H. Lawrence. There is a harsh vitalism in the Brontës that finds its match in the Lawrence of *The Rainbow* and *Women in Love,* though the comparison is rendered problematic by Lawrence's moral zeal, enchantingly absent from the Brontës' literary cosmos.

The aesthetic puzzle of the Brontës has less to do with the mature transformations of their vision of Byron into Rochester and Heathcliff, than with their earlier fantasy-life and its literature, and the relation of that life and literature to its hero and precursor, George Gordon, Lord Byron. At his rare worst and silliest, Byron has nothing like this scene from Charlotte Brontë's "Caroline Vernon," where Caroline confronts the Byronic Duke of Zamorna:

> The Duke spoke again in a single blunt and almost coarse sentence, compressing what remained to be said, "If I were a bearded Turk, Caroline, I would take you to my harem." His deep voice as he uttered

this, his high featured face, and dark, large eye burning bright with a spark from the depths of Gehenna, struck Caroline Vernon with a thrill of nameless dread. Here he was, the man Montmorency had described to her. All at once she knew him. Her guardian was gone, something terrible sat in his place.

Byron died his more-or-less heroic death at Missolonghi in Greece on April 19, 1824, aged thirty-six years and three months, after having set an impossible paradigm for authors that has become what the late Nelson Algren called "Hemingway all the way," in a mode still being exploited by Norman Mailer, Gore Vidal, and some of their younger peers. Charlotte was eight, Emily Jane six, and Anne four when the Noble Lord died and when his cult gorgeously flowered, dominating their girlhood and their young womanhood. Byron's passive-aggressive sexuality—at once sadomasochistic, homoerotic, incestuous, and ambivalently narcissistic—clearly sets the pattern for the ambiguously erotic universes of *Jane Eyre* and *Wuthering Heights*. What Schopenhauer named (and deplored) as the Will to Live, and Freud subsequently posited as the domain of the drives, is the cosmos of the Brontës, as it would come to be of Hardy and Lawrence. Byron rather than Schopenhauer is the source of the Brontës' vision of the Will to Live, but the Brontës add to Byron what his inverted Calvinism only partly accepted, the Protestant will proper, a heroic zest to assert one's own election, one's place in the hierarchy of souls.

Jane Eyre and Catherine Earnshaw do not fit into the grand array of heroines of the Protestant will that commences with Richardson's Clarissa Harlowe and goes through Austen's Emma Woodhouse and Fanny Price to triumph in George Eliot's Dorothea Brooke and Henry James's Isabel Archer. They are simply too wild and Byronic, too High Romantic, to keep such company. But we can see them with Hardy's Tess, and even more, his Eustacia Vye, and with Lawrence's Gudrun and Ursula. Their version of the Protestant will stems from the Romantic reading of Milton, but largely in its Byronic dramatization, rather than its more dialectical and subtle analyses in Blake and Shelley, and its more normative condemnation in Coleridge and in the Wordsworth of *The Borderers*.

II

The Byronism of Rochester in *Jane Eyre* is enhanced because the narrative is related in the first person by Jane Eyre herself, who is very much an overt surrogate for Charlotte Brontë. As Rochester remarks, Jane is indomitable; as Jane says, she is altogether "a free human being with an independent will." That will is fiercest in its passion for Rochester, undoubtedly because the passion for her crucial precursor is doubly ambivalent; Byron is both the literary father to a strong daughter, and the idealized object of her erotic drive. To Jane, Rochester's first appearance is associated not only with the animal intensities of his horse and dog, but with the first of his maimings. When Jane reclaims him at the novel's conclusion, he is left partly blinded and partly crippled. I do not think that we are to apply the Freudian reduction that Rochester has been somehow castrated, even symbolically, nor need we think of him as a sacrificed Samson figure, despite the author's allusions to Milton's *Samson Agonistes*. But certainly he has been rendered dependent upon Jane, and he has been tamed into domestic virtue and pious sentiment, in what I am afraid must be regarded as Charlotte Brontë's vengeance upon Byron. Even as Jane Eyre cannot countenance a sense of being in any way inferior to anyone whatsoever, Charlotte Brontë could not allow Byron to be forever beyond her. She could acknowledge, with fine generosity, that "I regard Mr. Thackeray as the first of modern masters, and as the legitimate high priest of Truth; I study him accordingly with reverence." But *Vanity Fair* is hardly the seedbed of *Jane Eyre*, and the amiable and urbane Thackeray was not exactly a prototype for Rochester.

Charlotte Brontë, having properly disciplined Rochester, forgave him his Byronic past, as in some comments upon him in one of her letters (to W. S. Williams, August 14, 1848):

> Mr. Rochester has a thoughtful nature and a very feeling heart; he is neither selfish nor self-indulgent; he is ill-educated, misguided; errs, when he does err, through rashness and inexperience: he lives for a time as too many other men live, but being radically better than most men, he does not like that degraded life, and is never happy in it. He is taught the severe lessons of experience and has sense to learn wisdom from them. Years improve him; the effervescence of youth foamed away, what is really good in him still remains. His nature is like wine of a good vintage, time cannot sour, but only mellows him. Such at least was the character I meant to portray.

Poor Rochester! If that constituted an accurate critical summary, then who would want to read the novel? It will hardly endear me to feminist critics if I observe that much of the literary power of *Jane Eyre* results from its authentic sadism in representing the very masculine Rochester as a victim of Charlotte Brontë's will-to-power over the beautiful Lord Byron. I partly dissent, with respect, from the judgment in this regard of our best feminist critics, Sandra M. Gilbert and Susan Gubar:

> It seems not to have been primarily the coarseness and sexuality of *Jane Eyre* which shocked Victorian reviewers . . . but . . . its "anti-Christian" refusal to accept the forms, customs, and standards of

society—in short, its rebellious feminism. They were disturbed not
so much by the proud Byronic sexual energy of Rochester as by the
Byronic pride and passion of Jane herself.

Byronic passion, being an ambiguous entity, is legitimately present in Jane
herself as a psychosexual aggressivity turned both against the self and against
others. Charlotte Brontë, in a mode between those of Schopenhauer and Freud,
knows implicitly that Jane Eyre's drive to acknowledge no superior to herself is
precisely on the frontier between the psychical and the physical. Rochester is the
outward realm that must be internalized, and Jane's introjection of him does not
leave him wholly intact. Gilbert and Gubar shrewdly observe that Rochester's
extensive sexual experience is almost the final respect in which Jane is not his
equal, but they doubtless would agree that Jane's sexual imagination overmatches
his, at least implicitly. After all, she has every advantage, because she tells the
story, and very aggressively indeed. Few novels match this one in the author's
will-to-power over her reader. "Reader!" Jane keeps crying out, and then she
exuberantly cudgels that reader into the way things are, as far as she is concerned.
Is that battered reader a man or a woman?

I tend to agree with Sylvère Monod's judgment that "Charlotte Brontë is
thus led to bully her reader because she distrusts him . . . he is a vapid, conventional creature, clearly deserving no more than he is given." Certainly he is less
deserving than the charmingly wicked and Byronic Rochester, who is given a lot
more punishment than he deserves. I verge upon saying that Charlotte Brontë
exploits the masochism of her male readers, and I may as well say it, because
much of *Jane Eyre*'s rather nasty power as a novel depends upon its author's
attitude towards men, which is nobly sadistic as befits a disciple of Byron.

"But what about female readers?" someone might object, and they might
add: "What about Rochester's own rather nasty power? Surely he could not have
gotten away with his behavior had he not been a man and well-financed to
boot?" But is Rochester a man? Does he not share in the full ambiguity of Byron's multivalent sexual identities? And is Jane Eyre a woman? Is Byron's Don
Juan a man? The nuances of gender, *within literary representation*, are more
bewildering even than they are in the bedroom. If Freud was right when he reminded us that there are never two in a bed, but a motley crowd of forebears as
well, how much truer this becomes in literary romance than in family romance.

Jane Eyre, like *Wuthering Heights*, is after all a romance, however northern,
and not a novel, properly speaking. Its standards of representation have more to
do with Jacobean melodrama and Gothic fiction than with George Eliot and
Thackeray, and more even with Byron's *Lara* and *Manfred* than with any other
works. Rochester is no Heathcliff; he lives in a social reality in which Heathcliff

would be an intruder even if Heathcliff cared for social realities except as fields in which to take revenge. Yet there is a daemon in Rochester. Heathcliff is almost nothing but daemonic, and Rochester has enough of the daemonic to call into question any current feminist reading of *Jane Eyre*. Consider the pragmatic close of the book, which is Jane's extraordinary account of her wedded bliss:

> I have now been married ten years. I know what it is to live entirely for and with what I love best on earth. I hold myself supremely blest —blest beyond what language can express; because I am my husband's life as fully as he is mine. No woman was ever nearer to her mate than I am; ever more absolutely bone of his bone and flesh of his flesh.
>
> I know no weariness of my Edward's society: he knows none of mine, any more than we each do of the pulsation of the heart that beats in our separate bosoms; consequently, we are ever together. To be together is for us to be at once as free as in solitude, as gay as in company. We talk, I believe, all day long: to talk to each other is but a more animated and an audible thinking. All my confidence is bestowed on him, all his confidence is devoted to me; we are precisely suited in character—perfect concord is the result.
>
> Mr. Rochester continued blind the first two years of our union: perhaps it was that circumstance that drew us so very near—that knit us so very close! for I was then his vision, as I am still his right hand. Literally, I was (what he often called me) the apple of his eye. He saw nature—he saw books through me; and never did I weary of gazing for his behalf, and of putting into words the effect of field, tree, town, river, cloud, sunbeam—of the landscape before us; of the weather round us—and impressing by sound on his ear what light could no longer stamp on his eye. Never did I weary of reading to him: never did I weary of conducting him where he wished to go: of doing for him what he wished to be done. And there was a pleasure in my services, most full, most exquisite, even though sad— because he claimed these services without painful shame or damping humiliation. He loved me so truly that he knew no reluctance in profiting by my attendance: he felt I loved him so fondly that to yield that attendance was to indulge my sweetest wishes.

What are we to make of Charlotte Brontë's strenuous literalization of Genesis 2:23, her astonishing "ever more absolutely bone of his bone and flesh of his flesh"? Is *that* feminism? And what precisely is that "pleasure in my services, most full, most exquisite, even though sad"? In her "Farewell to Angria" (the world of her early fantasies), Charlotte Brontë asserted that "the mind would cease from excitement and turn now to a cooler region." Perhaps that cooler region was found in *Shirley* or in *Villette*, but fortunately it was not discovered in *Jane Eyre*. In the romance of Jane and Rochester, or of Charlotte Brontë and George Gordon, Lord Byron, we are still in Angria, "that burning clime where we have sojourned too long—its skies flame—the glow of sunset is always upon it—."

III

Wuthering Heights is as unique and idiosyncratic a narrative as *Moby-Dick*, and like Melville's masterwork breaks all the confines of genre. Its sources, like the writings of the other Brontës, are in the fantasy literature of a very young woman, in the poems that made up Emily Brontë's Gondal saga or cycle. Many of those poems, while deeply felt, simply string together Byronic commonplaces. A few of them are extraordinarily strong and match *Wuthering Heights* in sublimity, as in the famous lyric dated January 2, 1846:

> No coward soul is mine
> No trembler in the world's storm-troubled sphere
> I see Heaven's glories shine
> And Faith shines equal arming me from Fear
>
> O God within my breast
> Almighty ever-present Deity
> Life, that in me hast rest
> As I Undying Life, have power in Thee
>
> Vain are the thousand creeds
> That move men's hearts, unutterably vain,
> Worthless as withered weeds
> Or idlest froth amid the boundless main
>
> To waken doubt in one
> Holding so fast by thy infinity
> So surely anchored on
> The steadfast rock of Immortality
>
> With wide-embracing love
> Thy spirit animates eternal years
> Pervades and broods above,
> Changes, sustains, dissolves, creates and rears

Though Earth and moon were gone
And suns and universes ceased to be
And thou wert left alone
Every Existence would exist in thee

There is not room for Death
Nor atom that his might could render void
Since thou art Being and Breath
And what thou art may never be destroyed.

We could hardly envision Catherine Earnshaw, let alone Heathcliff, chanting these stanzas. The voice is that of Emily Jane Brontë addressing the God within her own breast, a God who certainly has nothing in common with the one worshipped by the Reverend Patrick Brontë. I do not hear in this poem, despite all its Protestant resonances, any nuance of Byron's inverted Miltonisms. *Wuthering Heights* seems to me a triumphant revision of Byron's *Manfred*, with the revisionary swerve taking Emily Brontë into what I would call an original gnosis, a kind of poetic faith, like Blake's or Emerson's, that resembles some aspects (but not others) of ancient Gnosticism without in any way actually deriving from Gnostic texts. "No coward soul is mine" also emerges from an original gnosis, from the poet's knowing that her *pneuma* or breath-soul, as compared to her less ontological psyche, is no part of the created world, since that world fell even as it was created. Indeed the creation, whether heights or valley, appears in *Wuthering Heights* as what the ancient Gnostics called the *kenoma*, a cosmological emptiness into which *we have been thrown*, a trope that Catherine Earnshaw originates for herself. A more overt Victorian Gnostic, Dante Gabriel Rossetti, made the best (if anti-feminist) observation on the setting of *Wuthering Heights*, a book whose "power and sound style" he greatly admired:

It is a fiend of a book, an incredible monster, combining all the stronger female tendencies from Mrs. Browning to Mrs. Brownrigg. The action is laid in Hell,—only it seems places and people have English names there.

Mrs. Brownrigg was a notorious eighteenth-century sadistic and murderous midwife, and Rossetti rather nastily imputed to *Wuthering Heights* a considerable female sadism. The book's violence is astonishing but appropriate, and appealed darkly both to Rossetti and to his close friend, the even more sadomasochistic Swinburne. Certainly the psychodynamics of the relationship between Heathcliff and Catherine go well beyond the domain of the pleasure principle. Gilbert and Gubar may stress too much that Heathcliff is Catherine's whip, the answer to her most profound fantasies, but the suggestion was Emily Brontë's before it became so fully developed by her best feminist critics.

Walter Pater remarked that the precise use of the term *romantic* did not apply to Sir Walter Scott, but rather:

> Much later, in a Yorkshire village, the spirit of romanticism bore a more really characteristic fruit in the work of a young girl, Emily Brontë, the romance of *Wuthering Heights*; the figures of Hareton Earnshaw, of Catherine Linton, and of Heathcliff—tearing open Catherine's grave, removing one side of her coffin, that he may really lie beside her in death—figures so passionate, yet woven on a background of delicately beautiful, moorland scenery, being typical examples of that spirit.

I always have wondered why Pater found the Romantic spirit more in Hareton and the younger Catherine than in Catherine Earnshaw, but I think now that Pater's implicit judgment was characteristically shrewd. The elder Catherine is the problematical figure in the book; she alone belongs to both orders of representation, that of social reality and that of otherness, of the Romantic Sublime. After she and the Lintons, Edgar and Isabella, are dead, then we are wholly in Heathcliff's world for the last half-year of his life, and it is in that world that Hareton and the younger Catherine are portrayed for us. They are—as Heathcliff obscurely senses—the true heirs to whatever societally possible relationship Heathcliff and the first Catherine could have had.

Emily Brontë died less than half a year after her thirtieth birthday, having finished *Wuthering Heights* when she was twenty-eight. Even Charlotte, the family survivor, died before she turned thirty-nine, and the world of *Wuthering Heights* reflects the Brontë reality: the first Catherine dies at eighteen, Hindley at twenty-seven, Heathcliff's son Linton at seventeen, Isabella at thirty-one, Edgar at thirty-nine, and Heathcliff at thirty-seven or thirty-eight. It is a world where you marry early, because you will not live long. Hindley is twenty when he marries Frances, while Catherine Earnshaw is seventeen when she marries the twenty-one-year-old Edgar Linton. Heathcliff is nineteen when he makes his hellish marriage to poor Isabella, who is eighteen at the time. The only happy lovers, Hareton and the second Catherine, are twenty-four and eighteen, respectively, when they marry. Both patterns—early marriage and early death—are thoroughly High Romantic, and emerge from the legacy of Shelley, dead at twenty-nine, and of Byron, martyred to the cause of Greek independence at thirty-six.

The passions of Gondal are scarcely moderated in *Wuthering Heights*, nor could they be; Emily Brontë's religion is essentially erotic, and her vision of triumphant sexuality is so mingled with death that we can imagine no consummation for the love of Heathcliff and Catherine Earnshaw except death. I find it difficult therefore to accept Gilbert and Gubar's reading in which *Wuthering Heights* becomes a Romantic feminist critique of *Paradise Lost*, akin to Mary Shelley's *Frankenstein*. Emily Brontë is no more interested in refuting Milton than in sustaining him. What Gilbert and Gubar uncover in *Wuthering Heights* that is antithetical to *Paradise Lost* comes directly from Byron's *Manfred*, which certainly *is* a Romantic critique of *Paradise Lost*. *Wuthering Heights* is *Manfred* converted to prose romance, and Heathcliff is more like Manfred, Lara, and Byron himself than is Charlotte Brontë's Rochester.

Byronic incest—the crime of Manfred and Astarte—is no crime for Emily Brontë, since Heathcliff and Catherine Earnshaw are more truly brother and sister than are Hindley and Catherine. Whatever inverted morality—a curious blend of Catholicism and Calvinism—Byron enjoyed, Emily Brontë herself repudiates, so that *Wuthering Heights* becomes a critique of *Manfred*, though hardly from a conventional feminist perspective. The furious energy that is loosed in *Wuthering Heights* is precisely Gnostic; its aim is to get back to the original Abyss, before the creation-fall. Like Blake, Emily Brontë identifies her imagination with the Abyss, and her *pneuma* or breath-soul with the Alien God, who is antithetical to the God of the creeds. The heroic rhetoric of Catherine Earnshaw is beyond every ideology, every merely social formulation, beyond even the dream of justice or of a better life, because it is beyond this cosmos, "this shattered prison":

> "Oh, you see, Nelly! he would not relent a moment, to keep me out of the grave! *That* is how I'm loved! Well, never mind! That is not *my* Heathcliff. I shall love mine yet; and take him with me—he's in my soul. And," added she, musingly, "the thing that irks me most is this shattered prison, after all. I'm tired, tired of being enclosed here. I'm wearying to escape into that glorious world, and to be always there; not seeing it dimly through tears, and yearning for it through the walls of an aching heart; but really with it, and in it. Nelly, you think you are better and more fortunate than I; in full health and strength. You are sorry for me—very soon that will be altered. I shall be sorry for *you*. I shall be incomparably beyond and above you all. I *wonder* he won't be near me!" She went on to herself. "I thought he wished it. Heathcliff, dear! you should not be sullen now. Do come to me, Heathcliff."

Whatever we are to call the mutual passion of Catherine and Heathcliff, it has no societal aspect and neither seeks nor needs societal sanction. Romantic love has no fiercer representation in all of literature. But "love" seems an inadequate term for the connection between Catherine and Heathcliff. There are no elements of transference in that relation, nor can we call the attachment involved either narcissistic or anaclitic. If Freud is not applicable, then neither is Plato. These extraordinary vitalists, Catherine and Heathcliff, do not desire in one another that which each does not possess, do not lean themselves against one another, and do not even find and thus augment their own selves. They *are* one another, which is neither sane nor possible, and which does not support any doctrine of liberation whatsoever. Only that most extreme of visions, Gnosticism, could accommodate them, for, like the Gnostic adepts, Catherine and Heathcliff can only enter the *pleroma* or fullness together, as presumably they have done after Heathcliff's self-induced death by starvation.

Blake may have promised us the Bible of Hell; Emily Brontë seems to have disdained Heaven and Hell alike. Her finest poem (for which we have no manuscript, but it is inconceivable that it could have been written by Charlotte) rejects every feeling save her own inborn "first feelings" and every world except a vision of earth consonant with those inaugural emotions:

> Often rebuked, yet always back returning
>> To those first feelings that were born with me,
> And leaving busy chase of wealth and learning
>> For idle dreams of things which cannot be:
>
> To-day, I will seek not the shadowy region;
>> Its unsustaining vastness waxes drear;
> And visions rising, legion after legion,
>> Bring the unreal world too strangely near.
>
> I'll walk, but not in old heroic traces,
>> And not in paths of high morality,
> And not among the half-distinguished faces,
>> The clouded forms of long-past history.
>
> I'll walk where my own nature would be leading:
>> It vexes me to choose another guide:
> Where the gray flocks in ferny glens are feeding;
>> Where the wild wind blows on the mountain side.
>
> What have those lonely mountains worth revealing?
>> More glory and more grief than I can tell:
> The earth that wakes *one* human heart to feeling
>> Can centre both the worlds of Heaven and Hell.

Whatever that centering is, it is purely individual, and as beyond gender as it is beyond creed or "high morality." It is the voice of Catherine Earnshaw, celebrating her awakening from the dream of heaven:

> "I was only going to say that heaven did not seem to be my home; and I broke my heart with weeping to come back to earth; and the angels were so angry that they flung me out, into the middle of the heath on the top of Wuthering Heights; where I woke sobbing for joy."

INGA-STINA EWBANK

Artistic Truth in the Novels
of Charlotte Brontë

I intend, then, to examine Charlotte Brontë's novels by trying to see how her principle of artistic "truth" operates in them: how she achieves truth in her two senses of lifelikeness and of personal experience imaginatively transmuted. As far as such a division is possible, I intend to deal first with the more external features of narrative technique, plot, and structure, secondly with language, and thirdly with the emotional and intellectual contents of the novels. But, needless to say, all these elements are inextricably interrelated, so that no strict separation can be made.

All through her four novels, Charlotte Brontë stresses the lifelikeness of her material, from the programme-declaration at the beginning of chapter 19 in *The Professor*: "Novelists should never allow themselves to weary of the study of real life," to the reminder near the end of *Villette* (chap. 34): "Let us be honest, and cut, as heretofore, from the homely web of truth." She often does this, as these quotations show, by intrusive comments on the art of the novel—but not for its own sake: her claims for lifelikeness are an attempt to create a bond of agreement between her and the reader. Thus in *Shirley* she repeatedly steps out of the narrative to lecture the reader on what she is doing, often also implying a criticism of the kind of thing she is *not* doing. In the second paragraph of the novel the reader is warned not to expect anything but realism:

> If you think . . . that anything like a romance is preparing for you, reader, you never were more mistaken. Do you anticipate sentiment, and poetry, and reverie? Do you expect passion, and stimulus, and

From *Their Proper Sphere: A Study of the Brontë Sisters as Early Victorian Female Novelists.* © 1966 by I.-S. Ewbank. Edward Arnold, 1966.

melodrama? Calm your expectations; reduce them to a lowly standard. Something real, cool, and solid, lies before you; something unromantic as Monday morning.

And at the beginning of the last chapter, "The Winding-Up," satire of the curates develops into some rather heavy-handed satire on public reactions to realism:

The unvarnished truth does not answer; . . . plain facts will not digest . . . the squeal of the real pig is no more relished now than it was
in days of yore.

No doubt she is paying back some of the criticism of *Jane Eyre* when she describes how the truth tends to be received with exclamations of "impossible!"
"untrue!" "inartistic!" By similar means she urges her reader to accept her characters —

You must no think, reader, that in sketching Miss Ainley's character
I depict a figment of the imagination — no — we seek the originals of
such portraits in real life only —

or a change in narrative view-point, as in chapter 13 where we first listen to the
dialogue between Robert Moore and Shirley via the ears of Caroline, but then,
Caroline being too delicate and too overcome with jealous emotion to stay, continue listening without an intermediary, because "the reader is privileged to remain, and try what he can make of the discourse"; or as in chapter 29 where it is
necessary that we should learn the progress of the story from what Louis Moore
writes in his note-book, and therefore are invited: "Come near, by all means,
reader . . . stoop over his shoulder."

Devices of this self-conscious kind are not needed in *Jane Eyre*, where an
all-over claim to authenticity is made by the fiction of autobiography; yet the
reader is often appealed to, in order that he be drawn into closer involvement
with the story. These appeals tend to come at crucial moments in the action:
when, in the afternoon of their interrupted wedding, Rochester asks Jane to forgive him ("Reader! — I forgave him"), or when the happy ending approaches
("Reader, I married him"), or, most insistent of all, when Jane runs away from
Rochester:

Gentle reader, may you never feel what I then felt! May your eyes
never shed such stormy, scalding, heart-wrung tears as poured from
mine. May you never appeal to Heaven in prayers so hopeless and so
agonized as in that hour left my lips: for never may you, like me,
dread to be the instrument of evil to what you wholly love.

In *Villette* the buttonholing of the reader is often simply used at the beginning of a new chapter or a new section, to gather up the threads of the narrative. ("Has the reader forgot Miss Ginevra Fanshaw?," or "The reader will, perhaps, remember . . . ," or "The reader is advised not to be in any hurry with his kindly conclusions.") Yet at times we are close to the *Shirley* type of appeal to our taste for realism:

> My reader, I know, is one who would not thank me for an elaborate
> reproduction of poetic first impressions;

and at least once the appeal to us from out of the autobiographical framework creates an unhappy anticlimax. In the superbly realised moment when Lucy Snowe has been led, almost against her will but desperately needing to talk to *someone*, to go into the confessional, our involvement is suddenly destroyed by an anti-Catholic diatribe:

> Did I, do you suppose, reader, contemplate venturing again within
> that worthy priest's reach? As soon should I have thought of walking
> into a Babylonish furnace.

But in the main we are asked to assent to the psychological realism of the novel:

> Reader, if in the course of this work, you find that my opinion of
> Dr. John undergoes modification, excuse the seeming inconsistency. I
> give the feeling as at the time I felt it; I describe the view of character
> as it appeared when discovered—

the appeal here, in keeping with the whole character of the novel, referring us back to the emotions of Lucy Snowe; for it is here that "truth" in the novel rests.

The fact that the direct appeals to the reader increase rather than decrease in frequency in her later novels, suggests that Charlotte Brontë used them as a very deliberate device. in *The Professor* they are not frequent, and they are chiefly used to cheer the reader on, to involve him with the story—as at the opening of chapter 7: "Reader, perhaps you were never in Belgium? . . . This is Belgium, reader! Look, don't call the picture a flat or a dull one"—or with the hero, explaining his attitudes: "Know, O incredulous reader! that a master stands in a somewhat different relationship towards a pretty, light-headed, probably ignorant girl, to that occupied by a partner at a ball, or a gallant on the promenade." The reader need not have the lifelikeness of individual characters or situations pointed out to him, for the plot and structure of the novel as a whole are entirely shaped so as to be true to life. "I said to myself," wrote Charlotte Brontë in the Preface she prepared when, after the appearance of *Jane Eyre* and *Shirley*, she again hoped to get her first novel accepted for publication,

> that my hero should work his way through life as I had seen real
> living men work theirs—that he should never get a shilling he had
> not earned—that no sudden turns should lift him in a moment to
> wealth and high station; that whatever small competency he might
> gain, should be won by the sweat of his brow . . . that he should not
> even marry a beautiful girl or a lady of rank.

This is a very adequate description of both plot and structure in this uneventful
story of a young man, an orphan, who leaves school, has a short spell as a clerk
under his unpleasant industrial magnate of a brother, then goes to Brussels and
becomes a teacher, sharing his duties between a boys' school and a "Pensionnat
de Demoiselles." In the latter he gets to know its owner, Mlle. Reuter, whose
amorous advances he soon sees through, and also a young girl, Frances Evans
Henri, of half-English descent. She is a poor and persecuted teacher of sewing in
the school but also comes to his English lessons. Without too many vagaries of
fate, he marries Frances, and through their joint industry in teaching, they in ten
years accumulate enough money to retire with their one son, at a surprisingly
early age, to an idyllic house in the English countryside (from which they intend
to send the boy, like his father before him, to Eton!). The novel closes quietly
with a family tea on the lawn.

As in *Agnes Grey*, the desire to portray realistically a life that is tough and
often dreary has led to art that is drab and dull. But where *Agnes Grey* is saved
by the utter simplicity of its design, *The Professor* sometimes irritates us by its
narrative and structural features. The narrative technique is awkward. The first
chapter is a letter from the hero to an old school acquaintance; it takes us up to
his arrival at Crimsworth Hall, his brother's residence, and there, for no particular reason, it ends, and we are simply told that "to this letter I never got an
answer." From then on the absent friend disappears altogether from the novel,
and William decides to dedicate the rest of his life story to "the public at large."
Accordingly, the rest of the novel is a straightforward first-person narration—
which, of course, it would have been better to stick to in the first place. Inexperience, of the kind that got Anne Brontë involved in a laborious narrative structure in *The Tenant of Wildfell Hall*, is obviously reflected here. It is as though
Charlotte Brontë, having determined on a male hero, had found it difficult to
come to terms with him; and she herself later thought the beginning of the novel
"very feeble." Again, unlike the completeness which Anne Brontë achieves in
Agnes Grey by carefully selecting her details, Charlotte Brontë introduces some
situations and characters which the story cannot allow to be developed. The
sadistic elder brother (in whom Miss Ratchford justifiably sees a survival of an
Angrian motif), occupies a central position in the first few chapters, but is then
dropped, except for a brief reference to his bankruptcy and an even more per-

functory reference to his successful railway speculations in the final paragraph. On the other hand, Frances, the heroine, is introduced only well over a third of the way through the book. The structure is organised and held together purely by the character of the hero, and rather than being a bildungsroman where the character is shaped by his contacts and conflicts with society, it becomes a kind of bourgeois pilgrimage, in which the hero's rectitude and will-power remain static and society around him learns to recognise and reward his virtues. William Crimsworth is very clear and explicit about being better than most of the people he meets. Charlotte Brontë tries to avoid priggishness in her hero by having the cynic Hunsden place him, but the total effect is much more of William Crimsworth placing Hunsden. It is significant that Charlotte Brontë later saw the value of *The Professor* as being that it gives "a new view of a grade, an occupation, and a class of characters," for it is a very socially conscious novel. Through Hunsden, who is an aristocrat and something of a snob, the question of "caste" is explicitly raised: Crimsworth is an inverted snob in that he glories in introducing his chosen bride to Hunsden as a lace-mender. Thematically the novel establishes a meritocracy consisting of people who are intelligent and work hard (William and Frances), and it thus looks forward to the later Victorian preoccupation with the sanctity of work—to a novel like *Great Expectations*, in which the hero is saved from his corruption and snobbery when he learns to make his own way and earn his own money. The appeal of *The Professor* is economic as much as, or more than, aesthetic: the pleasure of seeing a good man getting on in the world, from a poor and humble start, by his own efforts. It is the appeal of much mid-Victorian fiction, just as it was the appeal of much of the didactic fiction of the early nineteenth century. *The Professor* is a link between the tales of Mrs. Hofland and Mrs. Craik's *John Halifax, Gentleman*, a novel which appeared in 1856, the year before *The Professor* finally got into print. But even in the homely and bourgeois world of John Halifax there are some spectacular events—a flood, an approach to a Luddite riot, an election—and, albeit seen at a disapproving distance, there is high life, including debauchery and a fallen woman. Nothing so colourful lights up the pale world of *The Professor*, the merits of which Charlotte Brontë—rereading her first work while casting around for a successor to *Jane Eyre*—saw entirely in terms of "reality":

> The middle and latter portion of the work, all that relates to Brussels, the Belgian school, etc., is as good as I can write: it contains more pith, more substance, more reality, in my judgment, than much of *Jane Eyre*.

As she was writing this, only she could have been aware of the self-abnegation through which this kind of realism had been achieved. From what

we now know of her own stay in Brussels and the letters she wrote after her
return, there is no doubt that the most decisive emotional experience in her life
was her love for Constantin Héger, her teacher and the husband of Madame
Héger to whose *pensionnat* she and Emily went to learn French and German in
1842, and where Charlotte returned alone in 1843 for a further year, after the
death of Aunt Branwell had brought them home to Haworth. Enough has been
written on this love, so one-sided and so truly begotten by despair upon impossibility; and I do not want to overemphasise the autobiographical elements in her
novels. But nor do I think it can be denied that this was the experience most
formative for her art: that when she speaks of "truth" as actual experience transmuted by the imagination, this was the experience which she most intensely
worked on; that, in one way or another, each of her novels is a different version
of the same "truth." Therefore we cannot rightly understand the art of *The Professor* without appreciating the extent to which in it personal experience has
been hammered into objectivity.

The declaration of love between William and Frances in *The Professor* is
brought about via a technically awkward device: listening outside her door he
hears her recite part of a poem (in French, but we are given William's translation)
which she has obviously written herself; entering he reads the rest for himself. It
is a poem about a pupil who loves her master—her name, Jane, looks forward
to Charlotte Brontë's next novel—and it makes the state of Frances's feelings
sufficiently clear to William. The poem is in fact one of which the original draft
is in an exercise-book used by Charlotte Brontë in Brussels in 1843. It has little
value as art, but in terms of the Brussels experience, it is a sad little piece of
wishful thinking; in its stilted way it also suggests the tension in one who had
come seeking the knowledge necessary to realise her ambition to start a school
but had also discovered other needs:

> The strong pulse of Ambition struck
> In every vein I owned;
> At the same instant, bleeding broke
> A secret, inward wound.

Charlotte Brontë's share in the *Poems, by Currer, Ellis and Acton Bell* in
1846 suggests that her gift is not lyrical. She does not have the quiet sense of
form that Anne has, nor the structural and verbal power of Emily. Though often
in song form, most of her poems are dramatic monologues, and sometimes enough
of character and situation is implied to make them into miniature novels. Most frequently the situation is one of love and passion, ill-fated, spurned or ill-rewarded.
To describe the creative process behind them, one could use the very words in
which William Crimsworth speaks of Frances's poem: it is not exactly, he says,

the writer's own experience, but a composition by portions of that experience suggested. Thus while egotism was avoided, the fancy was exercised, and the heart satisfied.

Or, one could use T. S. Eliot's term and speak of the search for an objective correlative. Two of Charlotte Brontë's poems—not, of course, published in her lifetime—speak directly of an unhappy and frustrated love, "Unloved I love, unwept I weep" (the first stanza of which is worked into the 1846 poem "Frances") and "He saw my heart's woe, discovered my soul's anguish"; and, as in the two personal poems on the deaths of her sisters, occasional lines in them have a poignancy of their own:

> In dark remorse I rose; I rose in darker shame;
> Self-condemned I withdrew to an exile from my kind.

But in the main it is not inherent poetical qualities but biographical pathos which forms their appeal:

> Unloved I love, unwept I weep,
> Grief I restrain, hope I repress;
> Vain is this anguish, fixed and deep,
> Vainer desires or dreams of bliss.
>
> My life is cold, love's fire being dead;
> That fire self-kindled, self-consumed;
> What living warmth erewhile it shed,
> Now to how drear extinction doomed!
>
> Devoid of charm how could I dream
> My unasked love would e'er return?
> What fate, what influence lit the flame
> I still feel inly, deeply burn?
>
> Alas! there are those who should not love;
> I to this dreary band belong.

The poems suggest that Charlotte Brontë sorely needed to put some objectifying distance between her and her experience in order to make art of it. *The Professor* shows her to us caught in the dilemma of being too anxious to draw on her own experience and at the same time too anxious to objectify. Her first novel is an example of truth to life gained deliberately at the expense of imaginative truth.

I have spent some time on Charlotte Brontë's least successful novel, because, of all her works, it shows most clearly the artistic problems facing her when she tries to find her proper sphere as a novelist. The novels that follow can be dealt with more briefly because in them—at least in *Jane Eyre* and *Villette*—she has found the form that suits her and that allows for realism as well as imagination. The decisive move from *The Professor* to *Jane Eyre* lies, I think, in her turning to a female narrator. Both *Jane Eyre* and *Villette* are autobiographies, as was *The Professor*, but in both the problem of being a woman stands at the centre and gives life, form and shape to the whole narrative, in a way impossible in *The Professor*.

The plot of *Jane Eyre* is too well known to need repeating. Clearly Charlotte Brontë had decided to take the publishers' advice to supply the reading public with something more exciting than the rejected first novel; clearly, on the other hand, writing with an audience in mind did not lead to a piece of book-making: the attempt at a greater imaginative scope touched off the fuse to a new kind of "truth." Thus, as Robert B. Heilman has shown in an interesting article on "Charlotte Brontë's 'New' Gothic," the Gothic plot elements—Rochester's mad wife in the attic, the spectacular burning of Thornfield Hall, the weird, premonitory dreams—are used by Charlotte to achieve psychological realism of a kind previously unknown to the English novel. The events around Jane are there to test her, and to give the author the opportunity to probe into her mind: above all to explore love as it affects a woman's mind in all its aspects. Again, because of the nature of the narrator, as an orphan and a governess with a strong will and mind of her own, refusing to put up with social injustice, all the themes of the novel can be focused on the one character: Jane embodies in herself the woman problem, the governess problem and the class-question. I shall deal more with Charlotte Brontë's handling of these themes, and of love in the novel [elsewhere]; here we need only note the structural unification which is achieved through Jane.

To Charlotte, as we have already seen, realism in *Jane Eyre* lay above all in the Lowood chapters because, built on her experience at Cowan Bridge school, they faithfully reflected life as she had known it. To us the realism of the novel as a whole lies in its acute psychological observation, and the school section is realistic because it shows us, unmistakably, the mind of the child that was going to grow into Jane Eyre, the woman. They belong, structurally, in a novel which otherwise is largely about the Jane–Rochester relationship, because they are part of the logic that governs the book. That logic is one in which events appear only in so far as they affect Jane's mind: there is no sense of narrative material being brought in for its own sake; every incident and every character has a bearing on the growth of Jane into a woman of passion and absolute moral integrity.

Much of the same narrative technique and structural pattern recur in *Villette*, Charlotte Brontë's last novel, after she had made a detour (which we shall follow presently) in *Shirley*. *Villette* is again a governess story: orphaned and poor Lucy Snowe goes to Belgium where, in Villette (Brussels) she finds employment, first as a nurse for the children of Madame Beck, the owner of a *pensionnat*, but very soon as a teacher of English in the school itself. In Villette are also living the Brettons, mother and son (Graham, or as he is known in the *pensionnat*, Dr. John), with whom Lucy had spent some time in her early adolescence. Lucy falls in love with Graham who, far from returning this love, first has an infatuation for a flighty English schoolgirl in the *pensionnat*, and thereafter falls seriously in love with Paulina, another Villette inhabitant from Lucy's past. But by this time a second love has come into Lucy's life in the shape of M. Paul Emanuel, a teacher in the school, and the novel ends with Lucy established—by Paul Emanuel—in a school of her own, while he goes off for three years to look after some family properties in the West Indies, and is shipwrecked (or so the end hints) on the way home. So much for the plot, which, as Charlotte Brontë's publishers complained, on the surface lacks concentration, moving longitudinally through two sets of characters, with Lucy as the only link. Charlotte Brontë, as we have seen, defended this structure by a reference to its true-to-lifeness; and in this case, what she defended as realism is also the source of the deeper truth of psychological realism. For the story is Lucy's, and Lucy is the focus, even more so than is Jane Eyre in her novel. The story certainly lacks a neat structural pattern—it does not even fall into those natural divisions which are created in *Jane Eyre* by Jane's movements to and from Thornfield Hall—but its unique power lies in that very lack.

In its stubborn concentration on Lucy, *Villette* becomes a novel about loneliness, lovelessness, about a woman with a sense that "fate was my permanent foe, never to be conciliated." Lucy's emotions, rather than any external events, create the real structure of the novel: a series of crises, in which utter depression threatens Lucy, and, between them, stretches of the empty life of an unloved being. The first major crisis comes in the chapter called "The Long Vacation" (chap. 15) where Lucy is left alone, apart from a cretinous child, in the school, while all the others are off to visit their friends and relations. Physical illness, fever—matched by the equinoctial gales outside, as Lucy's states of mind always reflect her "dreary fellowship with the winds and their changes"—and sleepless suffering are powerfully realised; they are gathered up into one nightmare which touches the depths of human depression: a nightmare

> sufficing to wring my whole frame with unknown anguish; to confer
> a nameless experience that had the hue, the mien, the terror, the very
> tone of a visitation from eternity. Between twelve and one that night
> a cup was forced to my lips, black, strong, strange, drawn from no
> well, but filled up seething from a bottomless and boundless sea.

One evening Lucy goes out, ill but not delirious, and is driven by "a pressure of affliction on my mind of which it would hardly any longer endure the weight" into the confessional of a Catholic church. Relieved by having spoken to a human being, she leaves the church, struggles against the wind, and faints. The intensity with which the situation is rendered is such that we are forced towards a symbolical reading: Lucy is found by Graham and taken back to his mother; and the temporary companionship they offer Lucy gets all the meaning of a rebirth into hope after the death of utter despair. The next movement of the novel is governed by Lucy's agonies of waiting for Graham's letters, the only thing that gives hope to her emotional life; and it ends in the unwitting cruelty of Graham telling Lucy about his love for Paulina. By this time, however, the rising movement of Lucy's relationship with Paul Emanuel is being prepared for; it grows stronger, and eventually culminates in another feverish nocturnal climax: a fête-night in Villette when Lucy wanders around and sees the love and friendship of others (including, as she believes, Paul Emanuel with a girl who is to be his wife), herself an outsider. The *peripeteia* of the novel is Lucy's irrepressible cry of despair when it looks as though she is to be separated from Paul Emanuel for ever:

> Pierced deeper than I could endure, made now to feel what defied suppression, I cried—"My heart will break!"

Lucy's heart does not break; instead it finds a briefly granted solace in Paul Emanuel's love. But it is the probings into the deprivations of that heart and into the neuroses of its owner which make the novel into what must be one of the greatest psychological novels in English in the nineteenth century. If we compare it to *The Professor*, of which it is obviously another, artistically maturer, version, we can see that it is the product of a woman who had now realised that her proper sphere lay in drawing on her own experience for imaginative truth.

Shirley is another matter altogether, and is in many ways the odd one out among Charlotte Brontë's novels. Both *Jane Eyre* and *Villette* take one woman through a long period of time; in *Shirley* she tries to give a cross-section of a piece of Yorkshire society over a shorter period. To do so, she abandons her usual method of first-person narration and becomes, as we have already seen, a somewhat self-conscious omniscient observer, who repeatedly lectures the reader on what she is doing, and why. The effect is, almost inevitably, a lack of focus, and this is strengthened by the fact that, to cover her larger canvas, she introduces several, not always interdependent, themes and several modes of writing. The love-interest is split, as in Miss Martineau's *Deerbrook*, between two couples: Caroline Helstone, orphan niece of the vicar of the parish, and Robert Moore, half-Flemish mill-owner; Shirley Keeldar, orphan heiress and owner of Fieldhead Manor, and Louis Moore, poor tutor brother of Robert. The social interest is divided between Luddite troubles, culminating in an attack on Robert Moore's mill, and the troubles of governesses, as represented by Shirley's companion, Mrs. Pryor (who, in one of the few melodramatic devices of the novel, turns out to be Caroline's mother); but there is also a great deal of social satire, especially of the three unfortunate curates who, as far as the plot of the novel goes, are completely superfluous. And all around the major characters, there is a set of secondary ones —like the radical Yorke family—who, one feels, have each been developed for their own sake, rather than for any central purpose.

Shirley shows that Charlotte Brontë had taken G. H. Lewes's advice to heart and was deliberately working at observational realism, after the flights of (apparent) fantasy in *Jane Eyre*. (It is ironical that Lewes should have criticised *Shirley* so strongly on the grounds that the author had tried to step out of her own experience.) Together with the fragment of a novel left on her death and published in *The Cornhill Magazine* as "Emma," it is the nearest Charlotte Brontë ever got to the mode of Jane Austen. Social manners are very nicely observed: the vicarage tea-party, the "Jew-basket," the small domestic concerns of a country parish. Where her wider social satire is often heavy—such as the disquisition on Selfishness and the British Merchant—on this ground she can create social comedy with a sure touch: one remembers the mock-heroic battle when the Church of England Sunday school procession meets, in a narrow lane, the "Dissenting and Methodist schools, the Baptists, Independents, and Wesleyans, joined in unholy alliance" and puts its opponents to the rout by singing "Rule, Britannia" to the tune of their brass band.

Perhaps her deliberate effort at realism is best seen from the point of view of *Shirley* as a novel dealing with the problems of industrialism. "Details, situations which I do not understand and cannot personally inspect, I would not for the world meddle with . . . my observation cannot penetrate where the very deepest political and social truths are to be learnt," she wrote to W. S. Williams; and this attitude informs her treatment of the Luddite situation. We know that, apart from memories of stories she had heard during her school days at Roe Head, she went to some trouble to find out about the conditions in the West Riding heavy woollen district during the time of the Orders in Council; and clearly she tried to make her story as authentic as possible. At the same time she refuses to turn into a social critic:

> Child-torturers, slave masters and drivers, I consign to the hands of jailers; the novelist may be excused from sullying his page with the record of their deeds.
>
> (chap. 5)

There is implied in this comment the same distaste at seeing the novel used for illegitimate—because ill-informed—social criticism as we find in her reference to the "ridiculous mess" of Mrs. Trollope's *Michael Armstrong*. By moving her action back a generation, to Luddite rather than Chartist times, she is excused from handling "topics of the day"; her handling of the theme of child-labour reminds us of her confessed inability to write for a philanthropic purpose:

> The little children came running in, in too great a hurry, let us hope, to feel very much nipped by the inclement air. . . . The signal was given for breakfast; the children, released for half an hour from toil, betook themselves to the little tin cans which held their coffee, and to the small baskets which contained their allowance of bread. Let us hope they have enough to eat; it would be a pity were it otherwise.
>
> (chap. 5)

If we compare this with what Disraeli makes of a similar situation in *Sybil* (book 3, chap. 1) —

> See, too, these emerge from the bowels of the earth! Infants of four and five years of age, many of them girls, pretty and still soft and timid. . . . They endure that punishment which philosophical philanthropy has invented for the direst criminals. . . . Hour after hour elapses, and all that reminds the infant trappers of the world they have quitted and that which they have joined, is the passage of the coal-wagons for which they open the air-doors of the galleries—

we see the difference between a novel-with-a-purpose and one which uses a situation without sermonising about it. Yet it would be wrong to think that Charlotte Brontë was as unconcerned about social injustice as the above quotation might suggest. She will not preach theoretically, but, when it comes down to the individual character, she can realise poverty and misery in moving terms: we see this in her treatment of William Farren and his family, who have had to sell

> "t'chest o'drawers, and t'clock, and t'bit of a mahogany stand, and t'wife's bonny tea-tray and set o'cheeney 'at she brought for a portion when we were wed."

From passages like this, we can understand why Charlotte, on reading *Mary Barton*, should have thought herself "in some measure anticipated both in subject and incident." She has certainly achieved social realism here; but in *Shirley* as a whole, this kind of realism has been gained at the expense of the psychological depth of *Jane Eyre* and *Villette*, and one cannot help feeling that in *Shirley* she betrays her own best gifts.

The language of Charlotte Brontë's novels, like their form and structure, shows her working towards her two kinds of truth, realism and poetry; and again she achieves her best results when the two fuse: when psychological realism is arrived at by imaginative means.

Compared to its contemporaries, *Agnes Grey* and *Wuthering Heights*, *The Professor* suggests that Charlotte Brontë had not yet arrived at a style of her own, nor one which was in keeping with what she was trying to do in the novel. There is none of the effortlessness of the dialogue in *Agnes Grey*, or of the absolute rightness of both dialogue and narration in *Wuthering Heights*; the dialogue is stiff and awkward (quite apart from the intrusive habit of quoting snatches of speech in French—one which is still retained in *Villette*), and the narrative and descriptive passages have a self-consciously "literary" ring about them. The style, in other words, is at war with the other elements of the novel. The promise of strength to come lies mainly in the imagery, which occasionally is vigorous and suggestive, as when a life wasted in vice is seen as "a rag eaten through and through with disease, wrung together with pain, stamped into the churchyard sod by the inexorable heel of despair." But the image just quoted is part of a general contemplation on life (from which the hero extracts himself rather clumsily by a "Well—and what suggested all this? and what is the inference to be drawn therefrom?"); rather than being informed by, and illuminating, plot or character, it is a piece of added decoration. Much the same holds true for Charlotte Brontë's handling, at this stage, of one of her favourite stylistic devices, the personified abstract. Mental conflicts in *The Professor* are depicted as a debate between Reason and Passion or Prudence and Conscience, often in such a way as to make them only mock-serious. At one point the hero, though he has to make a living, has given up his teaching post, as keeping it would have meant an involvement with Mlle. Reuter. His action is imprudent, but right. This is how its effects on him are described:

> I walked a quarter of an hour from the wall to the window; and at the window, self-reproach seemed to face me; at the wall, self-disdain: all at once out spoke Conscience:—
>
> "Down, stupid tormentors!" cried she; "the man has done his duty; you shall not bait him thus by thoughts of what might have been; he relinquished a temporary and contingent good to avoid a permanent and certain evil; he did well."

Instead of helping to realise a mental struggle, the personifications here put a bar of rhetoric between us and it. This tendency is even more apparent when personifications are used, as it were, as a shorthand device for handing over mental states—as if a concept or feeling became more vivid as soon as it is spelled with a capital letter. Thus the Professor on Mlle. Reuter:

> I knew her former feeling was unchanged. Decorum now repressed, and Policy masked it, but Opportunity would be too strong for either of these—Temptation would shiver their restraints.

The effect sometimes touches on the ridiculous, as when the Professor finds Frances after a four weeks' search for her:

> Amazement had hardly opened her eyes and raised them to mine, ere Recognition informed their irids with most speaking brightness;

and sometimes it is one of sentimentality, as when Frances in her room is described thus:

> Twilight only was with her, and tranquil, ruddy Firelight; to these sisters, the Bright and the Dark, she had been speaking, ere I entered.

It is the language of an author steeped in eighteenth-century descriptive poetry (as is the case with many novels of the first half of the nineteenth century); and Hunsden's description of the state of the English countryside—

> "Just put your head in at English cottage doors; get a glimpse of Famine crouched torpid on black hearth-stones; of Disease lying bare on beds without coverlets, of Infamy wantoning viciously with Ignorance, though indeed Luxury is her favourite paramour, and princely halls are dearer to her than thatched hovels"—

sounds like a not very good prose paraphrase of some of Goldsmith's *The Deserted Village*.

Altogether, then, the language in *The Professor* intervenes between us and the characters: another indication that Charlotte Brontë was deliberately holding them away from her, distancing herself, and therefore us, from them. In *Jane Eyre* the relationship is the reverse: the descriptive passages draw us into the action, the dialogue realises the interplay of minds, and the imagery carries over to us emotion proved on the pulses.

The dialogue between Jane and Rochester—from the stichomythia of their first meeting as strangers on the road and their later interview at Thornfield Hall, via the declarations of love and the banter of affianced lovers, to the agonised battle of their parting—all this is not only "true" in both Charlotte Brontë's senses, but also new to the English novel. Particularly so are the interchanges between lovers—a form of dialogue which Jane Austen had carefully avoided, cutting short the problem in a way of which the engagement of Edmund and Elinor in *Sense and Sensibility* is typical:

> How soon he had walked himself into the proper resolution, how-ever, how soon an opportunity of exercising it occurred, in what manner he expressed himself, and how he was received, need not be particularly told. This only need be said;—that when they all sat down to table at four o'clock, about three hours after his arrival, he had secured his lady.
>
> (chap. 49)

Bulwer Lytton similarly refuses to cope, though, unlike Jane Austen, hinting at oceans of sensibility:

> We will not tax the patience of the reader, who seldom enters with keen interest into the mere dialogue of love, with the blushing Made-line's reply, or with the soft vows and tender confessions which the rich poetry of Aram's mind made yet more delicious to the ear of his dreaming and devoted mistress.
>
> (*Eugene Aram*, chap. 10)

The lady novelists of the '40s liked to have a try, but the result is often like Lady Fullerton's, in *Ellen Middleton*, both hysterical and hyperbolical, over-strained and over-patterned, in more than one sense unspeakable. In the following pas-sage, the heroine relates how sometimes in her lover's embrace she would murmur "in a tone of thrilling and passionate emotion, 'Let me die *here*'," and how, not unnaturally, he would ask why:

> "Ask not," I would then reply. "Ask not why some flowers shut their leaves beneath the full blaze of the sun. Ask not why the walls of the Abbey Church tremble, as the full peal of the organ vibrates through the aisles. Ask not why the majesty of a starry night makes me weep, or why the intensity of bliss makes me shudder."
>
> "But I love you, my Ellen," Edward would answer, "I, too, love you with all the powers of my soul. My happiness is as intense as yours; and yet, in the very excess of both, there is trust and peace."

We need only put beside this a piece of the dialogue between Jane and Rochester after their abortive wedding to see what has been gained in directness of expres-sion, and therefore in depths of genuine feeling: Rochester asks Jane,

> "If you were mad, do you think I should hate you?"
> "I do indeed, sir."

> "Then you are mistaken, and you know nothing about me, and
> nothing about the sort of love of which I am capable. Every atom of
> your flesh is as dear to me as my own: in pain and sickness it would
> still be dear. Your mind is my treasure, and if it were broken, it
> would be my treasure still."

But dialogue alone gives little sense of the power with which emotion is
realised in *Jane Eyre*—this no doubt is one reason why dramatisations of the
novel tend to fall so miserably short of the impact of the original. The core of
the book lies in Jane's description of what goes on in her own mind, and it is
here that not only the most striking but also the most functional imagery in the
novel is to be found. In chapter 26, after the tumult that follows upon the interrupted wedding, Jane is finally left alone, to think and to receive in her consciousness the full impact of the blow. To begin with, she can still see herself from the
outside, in the third person, as "Jane Eyre, who had been an ardent, expectant
woman" but is now "a cold, solitary girl again"; she sees her prospects blasted as
by a frost at mid-summer, her hopes, in characteristic Biblical imagery, "struck
with a subtle doom, such as, in one night, fell on all the first-born in the land of
Egypt." And as Macbeth could see pity, "like a naked new-born babe," so she
sees her love, "like a suffering child in a cold cradle." Through this progression of
images, observer and observed, subject and object, merge; and the mental crisis
naturally culminates in the caving-in of consciousness which is the total surrender
to despair:

> My eyes were covered and closed: eddying darkness seemed to swim
> round me, and reflection came in as black and confused a flow. Self-
> abandoned, relaxed, and effortless, I seemed to have laid me down in
> the dried-up bed of a great river; I heard a flood loosened in remote
> mountains, and felt the torrent come: to rise I had no will, to flee I
> had no strength. . . .
>
> It was near . . . it came: in full, heavy swing the torrent poured
> over me. The whole consciousness of my life lorn, my love lost, my
> hope quenched, my faith death-struck, swayed full and mighty above
> me in one sullen mass. That bitter hour cannot be described: in truth,
> "the waters came into my soul; I sank in deep mire: I felt no stand-
> ing; I came into deep waters; the floors overflowed me."

Character, situation, and image are absolutely fused here, into a single rhythm,
by a language which has become a superb tool of psychological analysis. One
can well see how, after writing passages like this, Charlotte Brontë found that
Jane Austen's style suggested unfamiliarity with "the stormy sisterhood" of the

deeper feelings. Her images are not always so fully developed as here; sometimes a brief metaphor will embody a whole situation. "A hand of fiery iron grasped my vitals," is how Jane expresses the tension between her desire to be Rochester's and her moral knowledge that she must leave him. Nor, of course, is the imagery always so inextricably knit into the context: at one extreme it stops the internal action and grows into self-contained allegory which draws attention to itself rather than to any psychological development. Thus, for example, when Jane returns to Thornfield Hall after hearing Rochester's mysterious call, and finds it gutted by fire, Charlotte Brontë arrests the flow of the narrative with a "Hear an illustration, reader," and then proceeds to elaborate on an analogous situation — that of a lover who finds his mistress asleep on a mossy bank and, when he bends over to kiss her, discovers that she is dead. This could, I suppose, be defended on functional grounds — there is a valid parallelism — but the effect of the image remains a dilution, rather than a concentration, of the impact on us of Jane's shock. It suggests what other parts of the novel confirm, that Charlotte's language only becomes truly imaginative when she is working on a mind in an agony of passion. In such cases even the half-allegorically developed situation becomes an intimate and revealing part of Jane's mind: we can see this in the two haunting dreams of the little child which Jane tells Rochester on the eve of their wedding and which look forward to the impending disaster, the "suffering child in a cold cradle"; and we can see it in the descriptions of Jane's paintings in chapter 13, which again both define her mind and anticipate her fate.

The fullness and consistency with which she has realised the Jane-Rochester relationship is seen in her use of iterative imagery to accompany it. For example, Rochester keeps likening Jane, thinking both of her physical and her mental qualities, to an eager little bird, and in the early stages of their relationship, Jane sees herself as one of the "stray and stranger birds" to which Rochester throws his crumbs. When she has run away from Rochester, her heart becomes "impotent as a bird" which, "with both wings broken . . . still quivered its shattered pinions in vain attempts to seek him"; but when she returns, to find a struck and mutilated Rochester, the bird image is transferred to him: her first impression of him is that of a "fettered wild beast or bird, dangerous to approach in his sullen woe," and their final relationship, in which he is dependent on her, is that of "a royal eagle, chained to a perch" which is "forced to entreat a sparrow to become its purveyor." Events and objects in the novel, too, become iterative images: most notably the horse-chestnut at the bottom of the orchard, which is struck and split into two on the night when Jane and Rochester declare their love for each other, which Jane sees as an ominous allegory on the eve of her wedding, and to which Rochester compares himself when he proposes to Jane a second time, near the end. Whether reading *Wuthering Heights* had taught Charlotte Brontë something about the use of iterative imagery to cement the inner structure of a novel, or whether the intense realisation of her subject produced this spontaneously, we cannot say; but it is certain that none of this quality is foreshadowed in *The Professor*.

As in *The Professor* so in *Jane Eyre* Charlotte Brontë's language tends to turn, in moments of crisis, to personifications; but in the second novel personifications draw strength from their context and so give strength back to it. This is Jane, rousing herself from her stupor of despair, and saying to herself,

> "that I must leave him decidedly, instantly, entirely, is intolerable. I cannot do it."
>
> But, then, a voice within me averred that I could do it; and foretold that I should do it. I wrestled with my own resolution: I wanted to be weak that I might avoid the awful passage of further suffering I saw laid out for me; and conscience, turned tyrant, held passion by the throat, told her tauntingly, she had yet but dipped her dainty foot in the slough, and swore that with that arm of iron, he would thrust her down to unsounded depths of agony.
>
> "Let me be torn away, then!" I cried. "Let another help me!"
>
> "No; you shall tear yourself away, none shall help you: you shall, yourself, pluck out your right eye: yourself cut off your right hand: your heart shall be the victim; and you, the priest, to transfix it."

Meaning—individual, emotionally comprehended meaning—is given here by the context of the plot and character to words like "conscience" and "passion"; and these concepts then engage in a drama, a morality play whose climax is the cruel irony of morally inevitable self-mutilation. They form, as it were, an inner action which the language superimposes on the outer action, so that we perceive as one Jane's agony and its emotional and spiritual implications. What was merely a set of counters in *The Professor*, distancing us from the characters and suggesting the distance between them and their creator, has here become a vital bond between author, character and reader.

It is interesting to notice how much rarer personified abstracts are in *Shirley*: no character in this novel is trying to analyse his or her feelings or states of mind to the same extent as Jane Eyre. Caroline Helstone is the character who most feels the pangs and tensions of love, but in her there is no struggle because no strength; she just suffers the traditional Victorian heroine's "decline." Around her there is sometimes an inane, even bathetic, use of personifications, as when she hopes to pass her evening "with Happiness and Robert"; or when, on the same page, False Hope whispers to her that Robert might come and see her. In the novel as a whole, personifications cluster around the Louis–Shirley relationship. One of Charlotte Brontë's most elaborate allegories is Louis's heraldic-emblematic vision of his position in regard to Shirley:

> Her Gold and her Station are two griffins, that guard her on each side. Love looks and longs, and dares not: Passion hovers round and is kept at bay: Truth and Devotion are scared. There is nothing to lose in winning her—no sacrifice to make—it is all clear gain and therefore unimaginably difficult.

The imagery does not define or suggest anything; the abstracts remain abstract; the whole relationship remains as theoretical as, one feels, it must have been to Charlotte Brontë's mind. Louis Moore is as much of a male governess heroine as was William Crimsworth, and one feels that he must have been the most difficult character in the novel for Charlotte Brontë to realise. He was needed for the plot and the thematic pattern, but he never seems to spring alive from those abstractions with which he is surrounded whenever he appears, musing at great length on Solitude or soliloquising on his previous contacts with Shirley, "when Confusion and Submission seemed about to crush me with their soft tyranny." Louis, though an extreme case, is an indication of some of the overall quality of the style in *Shirley*. Instead of abstracts being turned into emotional realities by the heroine-narrator in *Jane Eyre*, we have here the generalisations of an omniscient (and, inevitably, less emotionally involved) narrator, such as the discourse on Youth, Death, Reality, Hope, Love and Experience at the beginning of chapter 7. They suggest how anxious Charlotte Brontë was in this novel to place the love-stories in an objectified context, and how, accordingly, her style becomes in some respects a throw-back to *The Professor*.

Where *Shirley* presents us with a new kind of writing, and where in particular the personifications are subsumed in a new kind of stylistic "truth," is in those sections of the novel that deal with social and economic problems. Having got the introduction of her curates safely out of the way, Charlotte Brontë in the second chapter of the novel turns to map out the political and social situation of the country:

> A bad harvest supervened. Distress reached its climax. Endurance, over-goaded, stretched the hand of fraternity to sedition. The throes of a sort of moral earthquake were felt heaving under the hills of the northern counties. But, as usual in such cases, nobody took much notice.

Before this, her typical sentence had been a period one, often with interlinked clauses forming a cumulative pattern. Here her subject needs authority and lucidity, and she achieves both, through short sentences so arranged that the pause

after each implies the causal connection between it and the next. Too vivid personifications would distract—and indeed the third of the quoted sentences is the
least successful one, threatening to destroy the tone she is establishing—whereas
the brief metaphor of the "moral earthquake" is an economic way of making the
situation both concrete and ominous; it also forms an effective contrast to the
flat comment in the last sentence, and helps to make this into a pointed anticlimax. The same qualities inform the paragraph where she puts the Luddite
situation into a nutshell and at the same time relates it to her own material:

> Misery generates hate: these sufferers hated the machines which they
> believed took their bread from them: they hated the buildings which
> contained those machines; they hated the manufacturers who owned
> those buildings. In the parish of Briarfield, with which we have
> at present to do, Hollow's-mill was the place held most abomi-
> nable; Gérard Moore, in his double character of semi-foreigner and
> thorough-going progressist, the man most abominated.

Here, too, her fondness for a rhetorical pattern built on the repetition of a crucial
word is put to a functional use. The first clause gives the premise (and Professor
Asa Briggs has shown how its social truth has made it into a catch-phrase), the
others follow with inevitability, so that objectivity of attitude and economy of
style are equally achieved. Unfortunately, she does not maintain this tone consistently; in the excitement of the attack by Luddite rioters on Hollow's-mill she
resorts to personified abstracts which weaken the effect where they were meant
to strengthen it:

> Wrath wakens to the cry of Hate: the Lion shakes his main, and rises
> to the howl of the Hyena: Caste stands up, ireful, against Caste; and
> the indignant, wronged spirit of the Middle Rank bears down in
> zeal and scorn on the famished and furious mass of the Operative
> Class.

Such a passage seems over-written, especially when compared with the way she
handles differences of "caste" in the dialogue, as in William Farren's conversation
with Shirley and Caroline in the chapter "Which the Genteel Reader Is Recom-
mended to Skip, Low Persons Being Here Introduced." The dialogue in *Shirley*
is often excellent—whether it serves the comedy-of-manners by letting us listen
in to a vicarage tea-party, or shows up Shirley's spirit as she gives the wrong
answers to her snobbish uncle's catechism, or brings alive the children of the
Yorke family, whose slightly mannered and infinitely knowing way of speech
makes them sound as if they had come out of an Ivy Compton-Burnett novel.
But there is also often a wrench from natural dialogue to stiff generalising com-

ment, which suggests that Charlotte Brontë is not altogether happy with her role as omniscient narrator, and that the novel lacks a narrative focus.

In *Villette* we are back with the single focus, the autobiographical narrator, and with the style which is at its best when it probes the mind of that narrator. At the end of chapter 23 in *The Professor* there is a passage in which "hypochondria" is personified: William Crimsworth's mind is invaded by "a horror of great darkness" and this makes him remember how in his boyhood he was visited by this demon, "taking me entirely to her death-cold bosom, and holding me with arms of bone." Powerful in itself, this passage has no justification in plot or character; there is nothing either before or after to suggest such nervous sensibilities in the very sensible hero. His breakdown here is introduced, it would seem, only to give an excuse for what is a welling-up from the suppressed ego of the author. We know that in Brussels and after her final return from there Charlotte Brontë had experienced such hypochondria; and in that sense there is truth to life here, but this truth clashes with the truth of the novel as a whole. In *Villette*, on the other hand, Charlotte Brontë has, in Lucy Snowe, found an adequate objective correlative; and personal truth is transmuted into the true agonies of Lucy's mind. To analyse that mind Charlotte Brontë again uses highly metaphorical language. Lucy, having set out on her pilgrimage to Villette, feels

> the secret but ceaseless consciousness of anxiety lying in wait on enjoyment, like a tiger crouched in a jungle. The breathing of that beast of prey was in my ear always; his fierce heart panted close against mine; he never stirred in his lair but I felt him: I knew he waited only for sun-down to bound ravenous from his ambush.

This piece is typical of much of the writing in *Villette*: to convey the tensions and neuroses of Lucy's mind a brief image is not enough; it has to be fully developed, as a tool of exploration. As in *Jane Eyre*, Charlotte Brontë often draws on Biblical analogies, and here they tend to grow into miniature dramas or *tableaux*, as at the beginning of chapter 17, when Lucy sees her own emotional needs like the physical needs of the cripples lying around the pool and waiting for a miracle. The key to Lucy's character lies in what she says about herself in chapter 8: "I seemed to hold two lives—the life of thought and that of reality"; and Charlotte Brontë manages to give us the sense of a character with a cold and composed exterior (it is worth remembering that Charlotte changed her heroine's name from Snowe to Frost and back to Snowe again and insisted that Lucy *should* be a repellent character) and a passionate and troubled inner life. It is because of the persistence with which the inner life, "the life of thought," of Lucy Snowe is explored that a basically uneventful story, with a central character superficially just as plain and narrow as is William Crimsworth, gets scope and depth.

Time and time again, as Lucy's inner needs are thwarted by her outer circumstances, her state of mind is rendered to us in terms of a *psychomachia*, a dialogue in her soul between Reason and Imagination (or Hope, or Feeling, the three being almost synonymous for Lucy). There is a particularly full example of this in the chapter called "Reaction" (chap. 21), where Lucy returns from her stay with the Brettons to her usual loveless existence in the *pensionnat*, with only the doubtful promise of letters from Graham to live on. As soon as she is alone, Reason, here as always surrounded by images of cold and pain, appears, like an old hag, "laying on my shoulder a withered hand, and frostily touching my ear with the chill blue lips of eld"; and the bitter struggle which ensues makes Lucy remember all her other struggles:

> Often has Reason turned me out by night, in midwinter, on cold snow, flinging for sustenance the gnawed bone dogs had forsaken: sternly has she vowed her stores held nothing more for me—harshly denied my right to ask better things . . . Then, looking up, have I seen in the sky a head amidst circling stars, of which the midmost and the brightest lent a ray sympathetic and attent. A spirit, softer and better than Human Reason, has descended with quiet flight to the waste—bringing all round her a sphere of air borrowed of eternal summer.

As in this example, the personifications produced by Lucy's emotional crises tend to lengthen out into whole allegories; these do not arrest the action of *Villette*, for in a sense they *are* the action: even more than in *Jane Eyre* the imagery in *Villette* tends to act out an inner drama which superimposes itself on, or even substitutes for external action. It is therefore unfortunate that Charlotte Brontë sometimes, with a kind of Byronic irony, undercuts her own technique, as when after a vivid elaboration of the moods of a night spent longing for "something to fetch me out of my present existence, and lead me upwards and onwards," she interrupts herself:

> By which words I mean that the cool peace and dewy sweetness of the night filled me with a mood of hope;

or when the personifications are so handled as to mock the self they usually express:

> Must I, ere I close, render some account of that Freedom and Renovation which I won on the fête-night? Must I tell how I and the two stalwart companions I brought home from the illuminated park bore the test of intimate acquaintance? . . . Freedom excused himself, as

for the present, impoverished and disabled to assist; and Renovation
never spoke; he had died in the night suddenly.

Maybe these are meant to be seen as examples of Lucy's Reason at work; but in
effect they point to an uncertainty of tone in the author.

But in the great emotional crises of the novel, there is no such uncertainty;
there is a unique and sustained tone. In that nightmarish, hallucinatory night of
the fête Lucy Snowe sees Paul Emanuel with his ward and believes (quite unjus-
tifiably) that he is going to marry her. The way Lucy's reaction is presented
makes it something quite other than the frequent misunderstandings and pangs
of jealousy which conventionally prevent the course of true love from running
smooth in the Victorian novel. Lucy rushes at what she thinks is the truth and
works herself up to a kind of orgasm of self-abnegation:

> I gathered it [the truth] to me with a sort of rage of haste, and folded it
> round me, as the soldier struck on the field folds his colours about his
> breast. I invoked Conviction to nail upon me the certainty abhorred
> while embraced, to fix it with the strongest spikes her strongest
> strokes could drive; and when the iron had entered well my soul, I
> stood up, as I thought, renovated.
>
> In my infatuation, I said, "Truth, you are a good mistress to your
> faithful servants! . . . and here I stand—free!"

The narrative technique here makes possible both the immediacy of Lucy's emotions and the placing of them by the later Lucy, the one who tells the story in
retrospect ("as I thought," "in my infatuation") and therefore knows how illu-
sory that achievement of "freedom" is. Only in creating St. John Rivers had
Charlotte Brontë previously got anywhere near this image of masochism, but
St. John is cold almost right through, where Lucy's coldness is self-enforced.
In this passage the frenzy of rhythm and imagery—as the simile of the mortally
wounded soldier develops into a metaphor virtually of crucifixion—contradicts
the direction which Lucy *wants* her feelings to take; and the total effect is one of
a mind shattered and utterly disordered. Here, as in all the greatest passages of
Villette, Charlotte Brontë has by poetic means reached the truth of psychological
realism.

W. A. CRAIK

The Tenant of Wildfell Hall

*"Consult your own understanding, your own sense of the probable, your
own observation of what is passing around you—Does our education
prepare us for such atrocities? Do our laws connive at them? Could they be
perpetrated without being known, in a country like this, where social and
literary intercourse is on such a footing; where every man is surrounded by
a neighbourhood of voluntary spies, and where roads and newspapers lay
everything open?"*

—JANE AUSTEN, *Northanger Abbey*

Anne Brontë, whose temperament inclines her to agree with Henry Tilney and
his creator about the answer to these rhetorical questions, undertakes in *The
Tenant of Wildfell Hall* to reveal what happens when the answer to all but the
first of them is not the expected "no," but "yes." Her second novel is necessarily
very unlike *Agnes Grey*. A rake's progress is certainly no usual topic for a domestic novel. *The Tenant of Wildfell Hall* contains much that is unusual, uncongenial to readers in 1848, and unpleasant by any standards. It is Anne Brontë's
business to be unusual, uncongenial, and unpleasant. She never shrinks from it
by euphemisms of expression or presentation, by contriving her characters, or
even by following acknowledged conventions of the novel. She is like her sister
Emily in being apparently unaware that she is often shocking, when she takes as
a matter of course things usually arousing strong reaction. While knowing that
the subject of her novel is dreadful, she never considers that she herself may be
thought shocking for undertaking it; her attitude is thus much less self-aware
than Charlotte's. She sees for instance only one thing to prevent Helen from
leaving her husband—even though he controls all her fortune, and though she
has no right to a divorce: that she cannot legally take, or hope to be given the
care of, the son for whose sake she wants to go. Nor, on an earlier occasion, does
Anne Brontë find it at all remarkable for Helen to refuse her husband his marital
rights (chap. 33).

From *The Brontë Novels.* © 1968 by W. A. Craik. Methuen, 1968.

Despite material so much more lurid than *Agnes Grey*'s, Anne Brontë keeps resolutely to the normal as far as she can. She keeps melodrama from her methods and hysteria from her voice. Her purpose is a didactic one, again not so much to instruct, as to lay bare candidly that by which the reader may instruct himself. Though the story is fiction, it is told like fact, and documented wherever possible by what the reader may recognize as fact.

The author's intention is thus much clearer than in most novels: Anne Brontë is determined that it shall be plain, and there is no suggestion of preoccupations other than what the writer wittingly devises. Self-effacing as Anne Brontë is, we have no sense that she is hiding herself from her reader. She is the most candid of writers, despite her first-person narrative. Though both the impulse and the foundation of *The Tenant of Wildfell Hall* are Anne's own experiences with her brother Branwell, she never uses any of her personalities, or their sufferings, to reveal herself and her own. One never feels that Helen is Anne, or that Anne uses her for emotional release. The narrators in *The Tenant of Wildfell Hall* do not expose their author like Jane Eyre or Lucy Snowe, nor, conversely, blot out the author from our perceptions like those of *Wuthering Heights*. Gilbert Markham and Helen Huntingdon, the narrators here, are devised in the first place to ensure conviction and a first-hand accuracy. Even though Helen Huntingdon is most deeply involved in the main story, it is always clear that Anne Brontë does not let her harrow up the reader's soul except to good purpose outside herself. Anne Brontë is dissecting, not the agonies of her heroine, but the horrors of drink and debauchery in all their possible private and domestic manifestations. The novel is not solely or mainly the progress of Helen's soul as it suffers retribution for the misguided vanity which made her marry Huntingdon —against all advice—to reform him. The retribution she suffers is far too gross to be thus acceptable. Helen's fate and the other elements together demonstrate her author's purpose to expose the natural consequences of self-indulgence—notably here drink, drugs, and lust—in themselves, on the self-indulgent man, on those nearest to him, and, through them, on domestic life as a whole. Hence the assembly of characters such as Hattersley or Lord Lowborough whose fates are not directly connected with Helen's own. The centre of the novel—the structural pivot of the main story, the moving power of the plot, the embodiment of Anne Brontë's purpose —is Arthur Huntingdon, who, the nadir of self-indulgence, decrees the rest of the characters and events. The story follows him inexorably to his end, from which Anne Brontë does not allow herself to be distracted by even quite legitimate interests. She does not dismiss her narrators to happiness until, as she says of Huntingdon's punishment in after-life, she "has paid the uttermost farthing" (chap. 20).

Anne Brontë clears from under her a great many difficulties that find their way into the fabric of her sisters' work, leaving herself free to handle more simply what is nearest her heart. She is wise to do so, as she is always an unsophisticated writer, a primitive in the art of the novel, gaining her results by very simple methods, which owe little to the techniques she might have learned from others. She assumes from the beginning that the reader acknowledges and agrees with her standards of right and wrong, and her view of man's duty to society, without having to share the emotional position of the narrator. Just as the reader, to judge rightly, did not have to identify himself with Agnes Grey, still less does he have to with Helen Huntingdon.

There are two narrators, who between them unfold the story and give a perspective: Gilbert Markham, the young farmer who, having met Helen when she is hiding with her son, becomes eventually her second husband; and Helen herself, whose journal of her married life forms the bulk of the novel (thirty out of fifty-three chapters). As far as Anne Brontë's main purpose goes, Gilbert Markham seems superfluous, even though the first fifteen chapters are his. The story began, chronologically, when Helen met and married Huntingdon, and ends when he is dead, Anne Brontë having therein faced all the personal, social, and moral situations that can be perceptible from the standpoint and method she has chosen. One must consider, however, whether the time spent at the beginning and end on Helen's second courtship and happy marriage may also reveal Anne Brontë's purpose, whether it is anything more worthy than submitting to the popular liking for a happy ending. *The Tenant of Wildfell Hall* demonstrates, like *Agnes Grey*, that the writer is conscientiously and earnestly unsentimental. Just as in *Agnes Grey* she clearsightedly traces the disastrous consequences of Rosalie's disastrous marriage, so here she equally clearsightedly recognizes that a handsome, strong-minded young widow of twenty-five does not spend the rest of her days mourning a worthless husband, in retreat from the domestic happiness of which it had been one of his crimes to deprive her. To have her *not* marry again would be the sentimental, conventional ending so uncongenial to Anne Brontë. That there is much in common in Anne Brontë's attitude to her two narrators also reveals her purpose. She allows a young man, clearly no hero, to expose ironically his own small follies and vanities; but when her heroine begins her story she exposes herself in the same way, the method becoming less reserved, but no less detached, as the events become more serious. Furthermore, to make Gilbert's commonplace, credible story form the introduction renders Helen's sensational one more credible also. While wishing to hide nothing of the horrors she is committed to revealing, the author has no intention of overplaying her hand, by seeming beyond the bounds of probability, and so losing the game.

The shape and the plot of *The Tenant of Wildfell Hall*, that of the tale within a tale, resemble those of *Wuthering Heights*. The narrative is begun by

Gilbert Markham, who in the first fifteen chapters tells of his growing acquaintance with the mysterious supposed widow of Helen Graham. It continues with her narrative in journal form of the five previous years of her life. It ends with a return to Gilbert's story, interspersed with Helen's letters, of her husband's death and her own remarriage. The plot is essentially a single one, as simple as that of *Agnes Grey*, taking Helen from her meeting with her first husband to her marriage with her second. Such a résumé (like that of *Agnes Grey*) does not accurately suggest the content of the novel, still less its purpose or flavour. Just as that novel was more essentially Rosalie's fate than Agnes's, so this is more concerned with Huntingdon's than Helen's. While there are a few subordinate interests—the married life of the drunkard Hattersley and his gentle wife Milicent, or the struggles of Milicent's younger sister Esther to resist an uncongenial match—there is no subplot. It is tempting to say that there is indeed no plot, only a graded series of events.

Nevertheless the story is the most important single element in the novel, because the moral is inherent in the events forming Huntingdon's career, and their consequences to all those around him. The events dictate the characters who participate in them, rather than the characters seeming to cause the events, as is usually the case in any novel worthy of serious consideration.

The material from which Anne Brontë builds up her story and documents it is, like the story itself, of two sorts, that provided by Markham's narrative, and that by Helen's. Markham's is all domestic, rural, and unsensational. The Yorkshire farm and village life, going no higher up the social scale than the rector and the gentleman farmer and their families, is assumed to be familiar ground. The events are those of daily occurrence, or of very modest excitement, never rising above a small party for neighbours or a picnic by the sea four miles away. Such an opening section successfully enhances the more socially elevated setting and startling events of Helen's story, and at the same time, by being homely, ensures that the narrative keeps its feet on the ground when its material threatens to raise it to melodrama or fantasy.

The contrast soon established between this indigenous life and society, and the newcomer artist-recluse with no origins or known connections, is a nice use of modest materials for a character whose mystery is itself only a modest one. Anne Brontë's success may be seen by comparing Helen, as a mysterious newcomer, with Jane Eyre during her time as schoolmistress at Morton, where Charlotte Brontë creates nothing at all of the impact so mysterious an arrival must have had on village gossip.

Even this preliminary story is more elaborate than *Agnes Grey*, with more character, more varied settings—the farm, the Rectory, Wildfell Hall, and the fields and moors—and more different kinds of events—private family chats, parties, lovers' quarrels, men's disputes—showing how Anne Brontë has gained both confidence and power.

Helen's narrative (chaps. 16–45) is made as far as possible out of the same stuff of everyday country living. The social level is slightly higher: the society is that of the country house, and the gentry who can afford not to know how to farm their own land. The distresses and neglect of the earlier episodes and the horrors of Helen's later married life are firmly based in domesticity, and revealed through social gatherings of the same kind as those of Markham's story. Helen's embarrassments and distresses spring from immediately intelligible situations: such as having her portfolio rifled against her will (chap. 18) or having her writing-desk and boxes ransacked and the keys taken away (chap. 40). Huntingdon's atrocities are all domestic ones: abusing the food and his wife's household management, when his digestion is at fault (chap. 30), brawling drunkenly in the drawing-room (chap. 31), encouraging his son to swear and to get drunk after dinner (chap. 39), and committing adultery under his own roof with the wife of his friend and guest (chap. 33). The most horrifying scenes use the same elements: frightening violence is suggested when a man uses a drawing-room candle to burn the hands of the drunkard restraining him; the depths of drunken sottishness by a man who scoops out half-dissolved sugar lumps from his over-sweetened coffee, and dumps them back in the sugar bowl (chap. 31). Society at Grassdale Manor—the outside world and surrounding families—is made of the same stuff as in the opening section; but has changed to alien beings who can only exacerbate private domestic agony. The heartless but harmless fortune-seeking, represented by Jane Wilson, is seen in a new light in the Hargrave family: Mrs Hargrave, wishing for the same worldly success as Jane Wilson, thrusts her elder daughter into marriage with a brutal debauchee, and makes her younger one miserable when she refuses the same fate: her son, through irresponsible sympathy with Helen, becomes yet another torment to her as a would-be seducer. The likeness is driven home when Gilbert, miserable for Helen, is tormented by the gossip and scandal about her. Society—Henry Tilney's "neighbourhood of voluntary spies"—is rendered comic or horrific by circumstance, not by nature. Hargrave—almost the greatest of Helen's trials—sinks, when Helen's happiness is safe, into comic obscurity and marriage, not to the wealthy widow with whose "rare long purse" he had hoped to console himself, but with a woman "not quite as rich—nor as handsome either" (chap. 52); a fate of the same sort as Jane Wilson's who

> wholly unable to re-capture Mr Lawrence or obtain any partner rich and elegant enough to suit her ideas of what the husband of Jane Wilson ought to be . . . took lodgings in ——— the country town,

where she lived, and still lives, I suppose, in a kind of close fisted,
cold, uncomfortable gentility, doing no good to others and but little
to herself.

(chap. 48)

With such material and such a society, it is probably unavoidable that Anne
Brontë in *The Tenant of Wildfell Hall* should resemble Richardson, especially
when she employs the journal as method, and has a situation that also might have
suited him. In Helen's story, there are a number of very characteristic situations —
such as Helen mediating between Hattersley and his timid wife Milicent, explaining each to the other and telling both their duty (chap. 32); or Helen be-
having with magnanimity to her rival Annabella —which recall the way Sir
Charles Grandison and Harriet Byron are held up to be admired for similar feats.
Such scenes generally seem to a modern reader both ill-conceived and tasteless.
Since Richardson is almost the only novelist who could offer Anne Brontë any
assistance in her task, it is more interesting and significant to see how often she
avoids being Richardsonian. Helen, beset on all sides, usually manages to extri-
cate herself by some device that is neither heroism nor sentiment, while Anne
Brontë is always quite as concerned with chronicling Huntingdon on his downward path of depravity, as Helen's sufferings during it. He, unlike Lovelace, exists
primarily for something other than to test a noble spirit to the uttermost limits of
endurance. However extraordinary or sensational the events, Anne Brontë documents constantly and accurately with concrete, vivid, and economical detail, of
action, the physical results of action, or of setting. Huntingdon's proposal of
marriage is a powerful scene, not only for what is said, but for its accessories.
Helen, finding him unendurable "made an effort to rise, but he was kneeling on
my dress" (chap. 19), the clause vividly realizing the almost unavoidable conse-
quence of proposing to a woman in a crinoline; the language of passion leads to
practical, prosaic bodily results:

> "Then let me add, that I cannot live without you, and if you answer,
> No, to this last question, you will drive me mad — Will you bestow
> yourself on me? — You will!" he cried, nearly squeezing me to death
> in his arms.

(*ibid.*)

Scenes are carefully localized; the library, for instance, is Helen's refuge from her
husband and his rowdy friends. Hargrave's advances gain more power when he
has invaded it:

> Mr Hargrave followed me thither, under pretence of coming for a
> book; and first, turning to the shelves, he selected a volume; and

then, quietly, but by no means timidly, approaching me, he stood beside me, resting his hand on the back of my chair, and said softly, —
   "And so you consider yourself free, at last?"

(chap. 35)

The setting and gesture are as significant as the actual speech. The unpleasant is
documented in the same way, allowing the reader to build up his response from
the evidence, not from a character's own reaction. After the grotesque scene of
drunkenness in the drawing-room, Anne Brontë faces the consequences.

> At last he came, slowly and stumblingly, ascending the stairs, sup-
> ported by Grimsby and Hattersley, who neither of them walked quite
> steadily themselves, but were both laughing and joking at him, and
> making noise enough for all the servants to hear. He himself was no
> longer laughing now, but sick and stupid—I will write no more
> about *that*.

(chap. 31)

Since Anne Brontë has no wish to be either exhaustive or revolting, her handling
of the unpleasant always strikes a perfect balance between truth and decorum:
Helen's physical fortitude in nursing the dying man is perceived by the two or
three allusions she makes to the sickroom atmosphere (chap. 49):

> I did but exchange a few words with them, just outside the portico
> —inhaling the fresh, bracing air as I stood.

> I gently disengaged my hand from his, intending to steal away for a
> breath of fresh air, for I was almost ready to faint.

as well she might, in a Victorian bedroom with a patient with gangrene.

   Characterization for Anne Brontë is far from being what is seems so often
in the Victorian novel, the overriding impulse. Events, situations, and actions
take priority. As any competent novelist must, she reconciles the claims of both
plot and personality; but basically *The Tenant of Wildfell Hall* is a story of what
happens as a result of drunkenness and dissoluteness—the qualities Helen sums
up as self-indulgence. The characters are conceived as, at the centre, those who
would either create, or get into, events such as Anne Brontë is committed to depicting; and at the periphery, those who exemplify all the possible consequences.
The author's hand is very strong on her characters, who are, much more even
than Thackeray's, puppets on the strings of a superb puppet-master. There is
never any chance that one of them may win the kind of independent life that
Trollope and Thackeray both admitted theirs did, which let them alter or dictate
their fate, according to the nature they had assumed. Anne Brontë ensures that

what happens and those who make it happen shall fulfil her purposes; nor does she ever suggest that she herself can be influenced by them, or identify herself with her creations. Her characters have only the semblance of free-will that enables them to fulfil their destiny, and convince, like puppets, according to how well they do so. In *The Tenant of Wildfell Hall*, modest as it is, Anne Brontë might well claim like Milton to justify the ways of God to man; and never invite the hint that she is in the least danger of making a hero of her Satan. Like puppets again, her characters are naive (in no derogatory sense) in type and presentation. Their personalities and their behaviour—even their crimes and deceits— are straightforward. Easily intelligible causes produce natural consequences. She never deals with good intentions that produce disastrous results, or with doing the right deed for the wrong reason, or even with a simple dilemma of motives: Helen, for instance, does not ponder or hesitate long over whether to leave her husband, and has no doubts, when she does so, that it is for her son's sake rather than her own, as she explains in her letter to her aunt:

> I told her I was sensible of my error: I did not complain of its punishment, and was sorry to trouble my friends with its consequences; but in duty to my son, I must submit no longer; it was absolutely necessary that he should be delivered from his father's corrupting influence.
>
> (chap. 43)

The novel would of course become an over-complex one if such matters were entered into with secondary characters—even George Eliot has to abandon the stance of the impartial narrator to do so—but, even among the major ones, the fairly central question of whether Helen, with unimpeachable motives, may yet herself be creating evil by her effect on her husband, is not one the novel raises; while the whole complex structure of causes and impulses rooted in the individual's personality, but not his to control, such as move *Wuthering Heights*, is simply not in question; nor is Jane Eyre's dreadful dilemma when she leaves Mr Rochester, though recognizing that to do what is morally right may drive him to despair and destruction. By the time Helen leaves her husband, she has lost what little power over him she possessed, and her flight cannot alter him in any way.

Anne Brontë's achievement in making memorable such characters, obviously not deeply observed, who do so little to influence events, is an original one, closer, like *Agnes Grey*'s, to Fielding than to any before her, but also a little akin to Scott's in such a work as *Guy Mannering*. But Anne Brontë differs from them because her creations are memorable in groups, rather than separately, and because they depend on action to provoke self-revelation. Annabella Wilmot (the fortune-seeking beauty, Helen's rival, who becomes Lady Lowborough) is a fine instance, in the convincing way she reacts when Helen has found out that she is Huntingdon's mistress. At first angrily disconcerted that Helen has discovered—

> "Ah, you are suspicious!" cried she, smiling with a gleam of hope—hitherto, there had been a kind of desperation in her hardihood; now she was evidently relieved.
>
> (chap. 34)

she changes to inflated promises, nicely punctured, if Helen agrees not to tell Lord Lowborough:

> "I shall think you the most generous of mortal beings—and if there is anything in the world I can do for you—anything short of—" she hesitated.
>
> "Short of renouncing your guilty connection with my husband, I suppose you mean," said I.
>
> (chap. 34)

and changes again as her stay draws to its end and her sense of security reestablishes itself:

> She does not scruple to speak to my husband with affectionate familiarity in my presence, when no one else is by, and is particularly fond of displaying her interest in his health and welfare, or in anything that concerns him, as if for the purpose of contrasting her kind solicitude with my cold indifference.
>
> (chap. 35)

All of this rings precisely and originally true as the record of how such a person would behave in such circumstances. Anne Brontë is equally sure where a mixture of good and bad qualities in one person must be shown; Ralph Hattersley's insensitive affection for his wife is thoroughly convincing:

> "What does it amount to, Ralph? Only to this, that though you admire Annabella so much, and for qualities that I don't possess, you would still rather have me than her for your wife, which merely proves that you don't think it necessary to love your wife: you are satisfied if she can keep your house and take care of your child. But I'm not cross; I'm only sorry; for," added she, in a low, tremulous accent, withdrawing her hand from his arm, and bending her looks on the rug, "if you don't love me, you don't, and it can't be helped."
>
> "Very true; but who told you I didn't? Did I say I loved Annabella?"

"You said you adored her."

"True, but adoration isn't love. I adore Annabella, but I don't love her; and I love thee, Milicent, but I don't adore thee!" In proof of his affection, he clutched a handful of her light brown ringlets, and appeared to twist them unmercifully.

(chap. 32)

In the novel's two narratives—Gilbert's and Helen's—characters, though of the same kind, are used to different ends. Those in Gilbert's narrative are essentially examples and instances of what is to be encountered in such a place and situation as Gilbert's, who do little or nothing towards advancing the story. The village-dwellers are instances of the "neighbourhood of voluntary spies" of Henry Tilney's opening paragraph, the purpose of them all being to show how irresponsible and random behaviour can, in unusual circumstances, become unjust and even cruel. These characters are closer than Helen's to *Agnes Grey*, but they show Anne Brontë more assured and more competent than in that novel: there are more individuals kept in the action, from several contrasting families (the farmer Wilsons, the rector Millwoods, Gilbert's own); there are men, of all ages, from the boy Fergus to the middle-aged rector; and there are middle-aged women, like Mrs Markham and Mrs Wilson; as well as the young girls on whom Anne Brontë concentrated in *Agnes Grey*. The personalities in themselves are more varied. They are—as Rosalie Murray is said to be—"artful," or they are not faulty, but limited: of the first kind are the two young ladies Jane Wilson and Eliza Millwood, who begins as "a pretty, playful kitten" (chap. 1) and concludes as a cat; of the second are Gilbert's sister Rose and his mother, who wisely advises Gilbert not to engage himself to Eliza, who scorns Helen for teaching her son to hate alcohol, and whose idea of marriage is sadly low:

"He always said I was a good wife, and did my duty; and he always did his—bless him!—he was steady and punctual, seldom found fault without a reason, always did justice to my good dinners, and hardly ever spoiled my cookery by delay—and that's as much as any woman can expect of any man."

(chap. 6)

On such straightforward persons Anne Brontë does well; but her chosen topic compels her to tackle what is beyond her, her least adequate character being Mr Lawrence, the landlord of Wildfell Hall and Helen's brother, the essential link between Gilbert's world and Helen's, and the person on whom Gilbert depends for all that concerns him and Helen in the last six chapters covering Huntingdon's death and the year following. The "morbid feeling of delicacy, and a peculiar diffidence, that he was sensible of, but wanted energy to over-come" (chap. 4) diagnosed by Gilbert, is too complicated a state for Ann Brontë's simple methods, since they always employ speech and action, the two things in which Lawrence is deficient.

In Helen's narrative the characters justify their existence by their bearing on the moral purpose. All are examples or victims of the varying degrees of self-indulgence. Huntingdon is the utterly corrupt and corrupting, attended by Grimsby who lacks Huntingdon's gusto but not his will, Hattersley who is weak-willed but capable of eventual reform through feeling for his wife and family, and Lowborough who reforms himself through deluded love of a worthless wife. The women are equally exemplary. Helen is the incorruptible and completely desolate, Milicent Hattersley the completely subdued, Annabella the wholly sel-fish and corrupt, Esther Hargrave the prospective victim. Less neatly classifiable is the third Hargrave, Milicent's brother, who consorts with Huntingdon in order to pay court to Helen. Anne Brontë suggests that he is not wholly vicious—his actions show the self-control the others lack—but here, as with Lawrence, the methods at her disposal are inadequate to reveal the man who can spend four years laying siege to a married woman.

Where characters can be explicit, Anne Brontë rarely fails, even in situations so unlikely as never to have been faced in fiction before. A fine instance is the dialogue (in chap. 38) between Helen and Lord Lowborough, when he has dis-covered that his wife is Huntingdon's mistress, and that he is the last to find out. He reproaches Helen for not telling him when she herself found out two years before; the whole conversation is astonishing, the climax excellent:

> "It was wrong—it was wrong!" he muttered, at length. "Nothing can excuse it—nothing can atone for it,—for nothing can recall those years of cursed credulity—nothing obliterate them!—nothing, nothing!" he repeated in a whisper whose despairing bitterness pre-cluded all resentment.
>
> "When I put the case to myself, I own it *was* wrong," I answered; "but I can only now regret that I did not see it in this light before, and that, as you say, nothing can recall the past."
>
> Something in my voice or in the spirit of this answer seemed to al-ter his mood. Turning towards me, and attentively surveying my face by the dim light, he said in a milder tone than he had yet employed—
>
> "You too have suffered, I suppose."
>
> "I suffered much, at first."
>
> "When was that?"
>
> "Two years ago; and two years hence you will be as calm as I am

now,—and far, far happier, I trust, for you are a man, and free to
act as you please."

Something like a smile, but a *very* bitter one, crossed his face for a
moment.

"You have not been happy lately?" he said, with a kind of effort
to regain composure, and a determination to waive the further discussion of his own calamity.

"Happy!" I repeated, almost provoked at such a question—
"Could I be so, with such a husband?"

"I have noticed a change in your appearance since the first years of
your marriage," pursued he: "I observed it to—to that infernal demon," he muttered between his teeth—"and he said it was your own
sour temper that was eating away your bloom: it was making you old
and ugly before your time, and had already made his fireside as com-
fortless as a convent cell—You smile, Mrs Huntingdon—nothing
moves you. I wish my nature were as calm as yours!"

The exchange covers all views of the situation—the wronged husband fiercely
hating his ignorance, the wronged wife's cold bitterness, their gradual acknowl-
edgement of the other's plight and its dues; and it precisely notes the changes of
tone and mood possible to Helen at this time of dreadful emotion recollected in
an appalling tranquillity. At their best Anne Brontë's characters are like these
two, impressive and surprising for the variety, not only between them but within
them, and for the quite complicated responses she can produce by such simple
means.

The three characters who demand individual attention are the two narrators, Gilbert Markham and Helen Huntingdon, and the evil genius himself, Arthur Huntingdon. Gilbert Markham fails, as a personality, even more obviously
than Charlotte Brontë's Crimsworth, because Anne Brontë has nothing to do with
idiosyncrasy, but keeps close to life as seen by ordinary people, against which
Gilbert's deficiencies are obvious. Yet he proves that she is a conscious, sensitive,
and conscientious writer, refusing to repeat the safe success of *Agnes Grey*, working still with the stuff of life, and having no literary model available for the mixture that she creates of sound farmer, spoilt son, and aspirant to the artistic and
literary. He is both a more complicated nature than Agnes Grey, and in a more
complicated situation. Whereas Agnes's family are not part of the novel's business, Gilbert's are a considerable element in his dealings with Helen. Helen causes
him moral problems—by the evidence, as it seems of her bad character—and
emotional ones. Anne Brontë here keeps a balance between a character no longer,
like Agnes, morally unimpeachable and generally detached, and the reader's need

for a dependable witness. In her treatment of him she shows herself aware of the likely deficiencies of a woman's male hero. She wisely keeps him mainly in the society of women: his family comprises a widowed mother, a sister, and a brother who is as yet a boy; and she makes him an eligible bachelor, of interest to the young women around him. In his role as commentator she provides him with more women than men to work upon, since, like his author, he understands them better.

Gilbert's purpose as a whole is never forgotten. His opening chapters prepare for his later ones. The good sense and uprightness that make him a dependable narrator naturally make him a proper husband for Helen; the impractical aspirations to be something better than a farmer—

> self-conceit assuring me that, in disregarding [ambition's] voice, I was burying my talent in the earth, and hiding my light under a bushel.
>
> (chap. 1)

—suggest a romantic nature, predisposed to wonder and sentimentalize over a mysterious young widow; the humorous, intelligent detachment he shows in looking at himself here, renders convincing his intelligent summaries of others, while not making him either very sympathetic, or even absorbing. It is not intended that he should be so, when Helen is to be the main concern, and any serious anxiety over his ultimate success would be intolerable when the bulk of the novel is involved with other, much graver, anxieties which concern another narrator, Helen.

Her role is in two parts, as the mysterious Mrs Graham of Gilbert's story, and as the teller of her own. The most notable points about her appearance as Mrs Graham are coolness and lack of romance. Mystery is avoided as far as possible, and pity for her difficult position, and sympathy for her as a lonely widow with a young child are never asked. Her situation is one that in novel terms may call for a sentiment which the presentation does nothing to encourage. Her first appearance is neither soft nor winning:

> there was a slight hollowness about her cheeks and eyes, and the lips, though finely formed, were a little too thin, a little too firmly compressed, and had something about them that betokened, I thought, no very soft or amiable temper.
>
> (chap. 1)

This anticipates her role as one who is to resist great suffering.

From chapter 15 onwards, when she is the narrator, Helen is the only personality who can be said to change. She is the moral barometer of Hunting-don's career. The core of her is honest resolution, able to be orthodox on moral or ethical questions, yet think and act independently, or even flout social conven-tion when this is what the action requires. She is equally the person who could choose to marry Huntingdon. Anne Brontë does not shirk the problem (as she might by beginning her story with Helen already married) but most convincingly makes the obstinacy and overconfidence, which cause the downfall of Helen at eighteen, transmute themselves into the determination and assurance that ulti-mately rescue her and her son.

She is not, as already said, the all-absorbing heroine, though she is much closer to it than Agnes Grey, since suffering as well as observation is part of her role. She is the means of presenting a dreadful example who is himself an ab-sorbing study. Helen, the person closest to Huntingdon, can best reveal him, by seeing most of him, and by experiencing his dreadful career most acutely. Anne Brontë reveals those aspects of her personality that are relevant to his: she subor-dinates, for instance, her visits to her aunt, her friendship with Esther and with Milicent, and her growing intimacy with her brother; they are taken into account only when they impinge on Huntingdon or on those, such as Hattersley, who represent his influence.

Her constant function is as the norm of good sense and right thinking, to which her journal-story is very appropriate. She writes for herself only, not for a reader, so that the reader can never suspect hypocrisy or self-consciousness, but only the necessary and desirable self-awareness that keeping a journal presup-poses. Helen is honest, feeling, just, and detached. She is most successfully al-ways right, with Huntingdon always at a moral disadvantage, yet is never sanc-timonious; always suffering, yet never self-pitying, masochistic, or feeble. One reason is that any possible objections to Helen that may occur to the reader, or improper motives for her conduct, are invariably voiced by Huntingdon himself, from whom they are *ipso facto* unacceptable.

> "Oh, I see," said he, with a bitter smile, "it's an act of Christian charity, whereby you hope to gain a higher seat in heaven for your-self, and scoop a deeper pit in hell for me."
>
> (chap. 47)

Another reason is that Helen suffers greatly, and is far from being in saintly elevation above her own trials. She convinces by being able to say, like Jane Eyre, "*I* care for myself." The reader does not wonder much that she comes to hate Huntingdon, but he receives the shock of unexpected truth when, tempted mo-mentarily to yield herself to Hargrave's advances, she bursts out:

then I hate [Huntingdon] tenfold more than ever for having brought
me to this!—God pardon me for it—and all my sinful thoughts!
Instead of being humbled and purified by my afflictions, I feel that
they are turning my nature into gall.

(chap. 35)

As purveyor of the moral lesson Helen is not spokesman but theatrical producer.
She reveals scenes, and lets the points make themselves, or she examines her
responses, and leaves the reader to draw conclusions:

I must have a bad disposition, for my misfortunes have soured and
embittered me exceedingly.

(chap. 40)

This, her own comment, leaves it to the reader to indict Huntingdon for having
brought her to such bitterness and self-doubt.

Huntingdon is the most important person in the novel—the prince of Den-
mark in this *Hamlet*. He is the awful warning on whom the moral purpose
depends, the initiator or instigator behind all the events, the most original and
vividly represented personality. Though we see only what thoughts his actions
and speech choose to reveal and Helen can guess, he is a frighteningly convincing
and original creation. Doubtless much of him must be drawn from Branwell
Brontë—whose potential brilliance and personal charm, over men at least, are
witnessed reliably by those outside his own family—from whose downward
career much of the convincing detail of the way the dipsomaniac mind works
must have been drawn. But while he is lifelike, he is so in the manner of the
documentary, not of the author's personal experience. He horrifies the reader by
what he does and is, and by the consequences of his actions upon himself and
others, not by what either the author or the other characters may be supposed to
feel about him. Indeed we abhor and detest him much more strongly than Helen,
and feel his charm much less.

He functions uncompromisingly and consistently as the example, not only
of what indulgence does to the man himself, but of the—to Anne Brontë quite
as serious—evil it creates around him. The latter is the first point made about
him, and probably the most damning, when he tells his affianced Helen, as a
joke, how he has been the means of preventing Lord Lowborough from reform
(chap. 22). From this point he is clearly very much more than merely the victim
of his own weakness, who renders his wife and family miserable. While in fact
he cannot alter, only degenerate, Anne Brontë manages to create a sense of development, achieved by letting his character and conduct be more fully seen and

known as the novel progresses. From seeming one of a group of roisterers (by whom he may seem to be influenced) he comes to be seen as the leader, and himself the main source of corruption, without whom Lowborough would have reformed sooner and would have kept a chaste wife, and Hattersley would have more readily recognized his duty as a landowner and head of a family. The growing sense of his power counterpoints increasing degeneracy, adding interest to what would otherwise be a straightforward downhill path.

The variety of his misdeeds also preserves interest in him. After he has sickened his wife (and the reader) with the drunken disorder of chapter 31, he commits a sin in seducing Lady Lowborough, which seems, conversely, to demonstrate his powers of attraction. This skilful presentation of him never flags: we are never permitted to have a surfeit of him, or to sup too full of horrors. The crime for which Helen leaves him is rightly one repellent in idea only, not in representation: there are no revolting scenes between him and his resident mistress, the governess. Thus the way is properly prepared for his dreadful end, which disgusts in all the possible ways open to Anne Brontë to use.

His death is a fine example to add to the Brontë collection of unforgettable death scenes, devoid of sentimentality, conventional responses, or cant. The toughness in the face of artistic truth that makes Charlotte Brontë's Mrs Reed hate Jane Eyre right to the end, and die with only Jane's

> grating anguish for *her* woes—not *my* loss—and a sombre tearless dismay at the fearfulness of death in such a form.
>
> > (*Jane Eyre*, chap. 21)

for epitaph; makes Anne Brontë's Helen face like truths:

> "I know you cannot love me as you once did—and I should be very sorry if you were to, for I could not pretend to return it."
>
> > (chap. 48)

She will have nothing to do with deathbed repentance—even a maudlin one—and uncompromisingly goes on depicting Huntingdon's habit of misconstruing Helen's motives:

> "I would give my life to serve you, if I might."
> "Would you *indeed*?—No!"
> "Most willingly, I would."
> "Ah! that's because you think yourself more fit to die!"
>
> > (chap. 49)

Arthur Huntingdon exemplifies another of Anne Brontë's unobtrusive powers as a novelist: he always exists physically. His attraction for Helen is in physical terms—he is her "flesh and blood lover" (chap. 21), his "luxuriant chestnut locks" are frequently noted (*ibid.*), and his phrenology is significant

> "But look here, Helen—what can a man do with such a head as this?"
> The head looked right enough, but when he placed my hand on top of it, it sunk in a bed of curls, rather alarmingly low, especially in the middle.
> "You see I was not made to be a saint," said he, laughing.
>
> (chap. 23)

and he dies emphatically in the body as well as the spirit, of gangrene:

> His body will be consigned on Thursday to that dark grave he so much dreaded; but the coffin must be closed as soon as possible.
>
> (chap. 49)

As a creation of character in the medium of the novel, he must stand high as one of the few delineations of powerful evil, of the vicious man who is also socially popular, who indulges in the more attractive vices—those of drink, food, and love—and has to his credit a handsome person, a vigorous nature, and for a time a loving wife, yet who is never felt by the reader to be for one moment enjoyable or sympathetic.

Anne Brontë's ways of constructing and presenting what she has to say, use, like her characterization, very simple and unobtrusive means, for results that are effective and original, and more elaborate than they seem. She continues to rely, as in *Agnes Grey*, on a candid literal narrative, without any but the very simplest and commonplace imagery, and still relies also on dialogue to produce an effect of reality, distinguishing her speakers by the content of what they say, rather than by idiom. *The Tenant of Wildfell Hall* represents an advance on *Agnes Grey* however, by its very much more complicated structure.

Like *Wuthering Heights*, *The Tenant of Wildfell Hall* makes vital use of its very precise time-scheme and its narrators to explore the complexities inherent in a very simple story, by using narrative within narrative, and different degrees of retrospect. It begins, like *Wuthering Heights*, about a year before its end, with a narrator who is more observer than actor, who has no part in the central happenings of the story, which are told to him in his turn by a teller who, much more involved in what she tells, reaches back into the past. For the first fifteen chapters Gilbert Markham narrates the events of the last months of 1827; Helen's journal—the next thirty-nine chapters—covers the earlier years from the summer of 1821; the novel concludes with eight chapters which are again Gilbert's account of the events of 1828, supplemented by Helen's letters. Gilbert purports to be retelling the whole novel from twenty years later, from the position of the contented middle-aged family man surrounded by his own and Helen's "promising young scions," in the author's "present" of 1847. The result is a movement which resembles *Wuthering Heights*, where the most vital and moving sections are at the centre of the novel; the beginning being startling, and mysterious, by arousing curiosity rather than inviting participation; and the end being the necessary resolution of what has gone before. Like *Wuthering Heights*, the end is rapidly brought about, with two short chapters to comprehend Gilbert's courtship and marriage. Yet it would not be safe to say that Anne Brontë has imitated *Wuthering Heights*. Her structure seems the natural and proper outcome of her intentions, not something imposed. The resemblance between the two novels shows a similar way of seeing life and human experience—one that involves seeing life as a whole that is formed by the concept of "paying the uttermost farthing"—rather than a similar idea of how to construct a novel.

There are considerable differences between the methods and effects of Anne Brontë's two narrators. The first, Gilbert Markham, though not completely realized as a person, is more successful as a structural device; though, since his personality actually influences the story, he cannot, like Lockwood in *Wuthering Heights*, be judged to succeed merely because he fulfils his structural purpose. One of his functions is a means of creating the mystery. Anne Brontë shows the influence of *Jane Eyre* in the movement of the first fifteen chapters, through an unconventional courtship to a proposal of marriage to one who is married already, with the whole accompanied by hints of mystery and concealment. The mysterious circumstances in *The Tenant of Wildfell Hall* are far more commonplace—a widow with no connections who supports herself, who never lets her son out of her sight, who puts false titles on her paintings of local scenes, and possesses portraits of a strange man she refuses to identify—but even so, mystery was a method not hinted at in *Agnes Grey*, which was written before *Jane Eyre*.

The result of Gilbert's narrative, moving steadily through its short time-span (the autumn of 1827) and looking back at it from a point twenty years on, is to rob Helen's sensational story of much of its sensationalism before it begins, and to present mystery with the minimum of suspense. Both effects are necessary, when Anne Brontë is so intent on making her horrors not sensational, but real, and when the solution to her mystery cannot be the rapid one suspense would demand (and *Jane Eyre* supplies), but the whole story of Helen's married life. Gilbert's narrative forms a solid convincing reality against which later outrageous events may be assessed; it gives the chance to see the heroine Helen from the observer's point of view before becoming absorbed in her own history; and to see her for the first time when most of her troubles are over. The reader is, therefore, when hearing Helen's story, free enough from anxiety over the outcome to concentrate on the significance of the events.

Helen's journal brings the reader into much closer proximity to the events it relates. There is no sense of retrospect and proportion as there is in Gilbert's account, or as there was in Agnes Grey's story, written by a happy woman years after the unhappy events. Anne Brontë makes sure that the reader shall perceive the brutalizing effects of debauchery, on the debauchee and all his associates, at close range; otherwise the reader, were he not led like Helen to accept one enormity after another, would not credit Huntingdon's final brutalities. Anne Brontë has all the advantages of Richardson's epistolary method and the claustrophobic closeness it produces, while evading most of the improbabilities it entails. Being literal-minded and realistic she tries very successfully to create something like a genuine journal, without depending on literary convention to extenuate improbabilities. She makes Helen's outpourings in her journal her one relief; her journal is her confidante, and telling her troubles helps her to withstand them:

> I have found relief in describing the very circumstances that have destroyed my peace, as well as the little trivial details attendant upon their discovery. No sleep I could have got this night would have done so much towards composing my mind, and preparing me to meet the trials of the day—I fancy so, at least;—and yet, when I cease writing, I find my head aches terribly; and when I look into the glass I am startled at my haggard, worn appearance.
>
> (chap. 33)

Helen's feats of memory in reporting conversation are not past belief, when compared with what Boswell, for instance, can do; while Anne Brontë's own neutral style, which makes little use of personal idiom for different speakers, makes Helen's reporting even more lifelike.

The journal narrative offers a greater number of different perspectives than either the epistolary mode it resembles—of the letter written just after the event —or the autobiography written some time after the events it narrates, like *Agnes Grey*. At moments of climax such as chapter 34, in which Helen faces Annabella, the journal entry, of events of the morning, is written the same evening; but when a longer view is needed, such as Helen's assessment of her second year of married life (in chaps. 28–30), the entry that comprises them looks back from almost a year later.

That Anne Brontë knows that this diary-structure is not literary structure is proved by the other scheme she imposes on her novel: the customary one of dividing into the normal chapters of the three-volume novel. The journal entries vary from a few lines to over twenty pages, and often run across the divisions of the chapters. A chapter may contain several short journal entries (chaps. 14–15), or may not contain the whole of a single one. Clearly the journal-division is decided by what the author wishes to do through her narrator, whereas the division into chapters is one of the few direct evidences of the author herself. The chapters mark the passage of time in the normal way, without the change of view of a new journal entry, or mark a sudden complete change of topic as at chapter 39 where, from a Huntingdon relieved that Annabella has left —

> "She was so deuced imperious and exacting," said he: "now I shall be my own man again, and feel rather more at my ease."

—Helen moves on abruptly to fears for her son:

> My greatest source of uneasiness, in this time of trial, was my son, whom his father and his father's friends delighted to encourage in all the embryo vices a little child can show.

Anne Brontë is like her sisters in being unique, in being apparently very little influenced by any writer before her, and in writing for ends which the novel had not previously been made to serve. While she is not as great as either of them, she is never a bad or second-rate artist. She seems to do all that is possible by taking pains, by being fully conscious of the end to which she is working, and by directing all her powers towards it. She is not a great novelist, because she has no passion to express, nor any new or original view of human nature to expound. But she is never meretricious or showy, having always a purpose in writing worthy in itself, and fit for a novel. Her two novels are original, because both use new material to illuminate old truths about man in his society, and because both work out their own personal methods. She is not derivative—although she does not hesitate to admit influences where an earlier novelist's effects are similar to her own—since no novelist offers her a model in a similar field; and she has no successors, partly because her achievement is so modest (despite the popular success of *The Tenant of Wildfell Hall*), and partly because her effects are so closely the result of her purpose that they cannot be used for any other. The contemporary who comes closest to *The Tenant of Wildfell Hall* —as Mark Rutherford to *Agnes Grey*—is not a novelist, but a writer, Harriet Martineau, who also found that fiction was at some points the fit and proper medium for a theory, even though the theories of Harriet Martineau were more coherent, philosophical, and practical. Both women write robustly and plainly, with the startling truth that comes from the apparently self-evident and unremarkable; though neither can make the claim to the single masterpiece that Emily Brontë makes with *Wuthering Heights*, or the claim to be a major novelist with a corpus of professional writing that Charlotte Brontë's four novels make for her. Few people now dispute Emily's claim. Charlotte's, admitted in her lifetime, later suspect and disallowed, is vindicated by close critical scrutiny. Anne has rarely been thought worth the trial, but yet sustains it with a success that, though modest, is complete.

RAYMOND WILLIAMS

Charlotte and Emily Brontë

It is some indication of the originality of those twenty months in 1847 and 1848 that two novels should come out as different from Dickens and from each other as *Jane Eyre* and *Wuthering Heights*. Since Charlotte and Emily were sisters the novels have always been linked in a general way, and there is something else, more specific, that links them: an emphasis on intense feeling, a commitment to what we must directly call passion, that is in itself very new in the English novel. In the end the critical interest is how different the novels are, what a radical difference of method each shows and sustains. But as a first emphasis the intensity of the feeling is decisive.

And this belongs, I think, in the moving earth, the unprecedented disturbance of those English years. Later, much later, by a process we shall trace, it was possible to set what was called social criticism against what was called psychology, or a response to poverty and oppression against a response to the intensities and difficulties of love and growth. On that later projection the interests of the Brontë sisters and the interests of Dickens and Elizabeth Gaskell are in different continents, the East and West of society and personality. But in experience and in these novels it is not like that. The world we need to remember if we are to see these connections of the 1840s is the world of Blake: a world of desire and hunger, of rebellion and of pallid convention: the terms of desire and fulfilment and the terms of oppression and deprivation profoundly connected in a single dimension of experience.

Nobody later achieves Blake's kind of unity; he could only barely maintain it himself. But I think we need to start from the feeling, the central feeling, that

From *The English Novel: From Dickens to Lawrence*. © 1970 by Raymond Williams. Chatto & Windus, 1970.

an intensity of desire is as much a response, a deciding response, to the human crisis of that time as the more obviously recognisable political radicalism. Indeed, to give that kind of value to human longing and need, to that absolute emphasis on commitment to another, the absolute love of the being of another, is to clash as sharply with the emerging system, the emerging priorities, as in any assault on material poverty. What was at issue really was relationship itself: a dimension of relationship made problematic and dangerous by the increasing pressure, the external and internal and continuing pressure, to reshape, to deform—it is how Blake saw it—this most human, most absolute experience.

An affirming emphasis had been powerfully there in the greatest Romantic poems. And the significance of this emphasis is that it connects, structurally, what seems very different feelings: an intense affirmation of love and desire and an intense often desperate apprehension of isolation and loss. For a number of reasons this was slow to enter the novel. A certain worldliness, readily understandable in earlier periods (though never, I think, as persuasive as is made out), made for the qualification of love; found its value as social exchange and respect, as most coolly in Jane Austen; or its value as a factor, an isolable factor, in orthodox romance. What was directly expressed in Blake and in Keats and in different ways in Shelley and Byron seems to have gone underground, before the 1840s, in fiction and even in drama; indeed is literally underground in the dark images of the Gothic and in the produced straining extravagances of melodrama. The achievement of the Brontë sisters, before we say anything else, is that in different ways they remade the novel so that this kind of passion could be directly communicated.

There are precedents certainly: precedents as elements of these new forms. The fire and madness of romance; the apparitions and dreams of the Gothic: these isolable elements can of course be picked up, are still often picked up to push *Jane Eyre* or *Wuthering Heights* into a familiar tradition. But then we have also to ask what the achieved social mode, social tone, in itself excluded. Especially if we remember that in a more evidently powered society it was a masculine mode. I don't mean universally or generically masculine, but what manly was coming to mean. It's a difficult point now, in public, but it has always seemed to me significant that through this mid-nineteenth century, through a process of alteration of feeling, of acknowledgeable feeling, which especially in the new public schools found its confident training institutions, men learned not to cry, I mean not to show themselves crying (even the word, this late, has a defensive laugh near it, standing guard). Within two generations not only the convention but perhaps the impulse had changed. What was taught and learned was a new and rigid control, "self-control"—even weak men not crying and being very stiff and proud of it where much stronger men before them had quite openly wept when the feeling, the impulse was there. It's only one point among many: the new rigidity, public soberness of dress—men and women—is I think related. And in this tightening world it's then significant, surely, how much was kept alive, how much was newly affirmed, by a group of women novelists—by Elizabeth Gaskell, by Charlotte and Emily and Anne Brontë, and by—but see how the convention bore down—by Currer and Ellis and Acton Bell, by Marian Evans becoming George Eliot. That tension, I think, can never at all be forgotten. And it isn't only, to use the terms of the change, keeping a woman's world going. On the contrary: in certain vital ways simply a human world.

But that they were also women had another effect. People still have to fight past the governess to get to the Brontë sisters. I mean fight past the image, the depressing image, that is still taken for granted. Before women could be educated, in anything like equal ways, it was there girls went if they had the start of an education but not enough private income: the women teachers, the woman intellectuals, and I don't doubt others, of later and different periods. Seen from the middle-class way round, and especially from the male middle-class way, the governess as a figure is repressive, unfeminine, dowdy. But I'd follow those girls through, pushed out as they were into one of the only available jobs, follow Jane Eyre and Lucy Snowe to Sue Bridehead in Hardy or Ursula Brangwen in Lawrence; or beyond them, even more, to Tess and to Miriam. I don't know how much I now need to insist on breaking the image: that deforming image which obscures—and is meant to obscure—a particular and a general repression. But at least we must say that the Brontë sisters knew directly a whole structure of repression in their time; knew it and in their own ways broke it with a strength and a courage that puts us all in their debt.

In their own ways broke it: that's where we must concentrate. The power and intensity of *Wuthering Heights* needs no additional emphasis. The recognition has been given. The control of *Wuthering Heights*, the equally remarkable control, is now also quite generally acknowledged. And the power of *Jane Eyre* and of *Villette* needs no further adjectives. Readers still respond to the novels and critics follow them; sometimes critic following reader a bit uneasily in the same personality. What I mainly want to say is concerned with the differences between the novelists: differences that are profoundly important in the subsequent history. And then take *Wuthering Heights* first, for there it might seem is a novel without a history: a novel without precedents or descendants.

Its structure indeed is unique, though in spirit it is in no way isolated; it belongs in an English tradition with Blake and Lawrence and very specifically with Hardy. What is most remarkable about it, though, as a form is its exceptional fusion of intensity and control. No novel in English contains more intense and passionate feeling, but contains, then, is a word to consider. What we most remember from the novel, the passion of Cathy and Heathcliff, is in its actual creation very precisely, very consciously inset, qualified, modulated. The multiple narrative through secondary characters, the complications of the time-scheme, the precision of the complicated plot of inheritance and generations are so deliberate, so measured, and the staple of their language so consciously formal—in so many different ways formal, among the roughness, the plainness, of so much of the speech and the life—that we know in reading an extraordinary and intricate tension; and even when we know it are surprised, looking back, to find how large a proportion of the novel—in quantity and emphasis—is this measuring, qualifying, consequential narrative. Only an abstracted version of the single intense theme could support the still common description of extravagance, whether approved or disapproved. Yet this theme itself is so profoundly insistent that the novel refuses to be reduced to the sum of its other parts. Its interaction, its extraordinary intricacy of opposed and moderated but still absolute feelings, is an active, dynamic process: not balance but dialectic: contraries.

Seeing part of this, some critics have turned the discussion, rightly turned it, from the ordinary terms of romance—or from the more extreme emphases of the mystical and the melodramatic—and located *Wuthering Heights* in a social history. And it is certainly true that the Brontës lived in a border country, on the empty moors near a new and disturbed industrial area. Charlotte used this experience directly in *Shirley*, though backdating its events to the Luddites. And it has been argued that this same disturbance—the new industrial dislocation, the birth of an outcast class, dark, unprecedented and exposed—is at the root of *Wuthering Heights*; even, as has been said, that Heathcliff is the proletariat. But social experience, just because it is social, does not have to appear in any way exclusively in these overt public forms. In its very quality as social reality it penetrates, is already at the roots of, relationships of every kind. We need not look only, in a transforming history, for direct or public historical event and response. When there is real dislocation it does not have to appear in a strike or in machine-breaking. It can appear as radically and as authentically in what is apparently, what is actually personal or family experience. Any direct reference of *Wuthering Heights* to that transforming social crisis seems to me then displaced, for this exact reason: that its real social experience is then explicitly reduced.

The same is true, I would say, of that closer reading, not symbolic displacement but a kind of naturalist extension. Thus it is certainly clear that the contrast between the Heights and the Grange *is* a conscious contrast between two kinds of life: an exposed unaccommodated wrenching of living from the heath, and a sheltered refined civilised and *rentier* settlement in the valley. We don't have to force this: it is directly rendered when Heathcliff and Cathy look in on the Lintons and at many other points in the complicated journeys—the connected personal and social moves—between the two houses. But this social experience is the condition within which a more precise and more searching action occurs and is measured, and there is no convincing way in which the context—the real social description—can be made to override the direct and preoccupying relations between persons. What we have again to say is that social experience is a whole experience. Its descriptive or analytic features have no priority over its direct realisation in quite physical and specific personal feelings and actions. Without the central relationships, the physical and social landscape of *Wuthering Heights* would be a country waiting to be entered, waiting to be understood, for all its careful detail. What makes it a human landscape is that specific people with specific desires live and relate there.

We cannot then draw back from that immediate and intricate experience, as either the symbolist or the naturalist mode would involve. Yet the central experience is at first sight so strange that there is some obvious anxiety, from conventional positions.

> If all else perished, and *he* remained, *I* should still continue to be; and if all else remained, and he were annihilated, the universe would turn to a mighty stranger: I should not seem a part of it. My love for Linton is like the foliage in the woods: time will change it, I'm well aware, as winter changes the trees. My love for Heathcliff resembles the eternal rocks beneath: a source of little visible delight, but necessary.

These words of Cathy have been called mystical, or a romantic extravagance. But I don't know how that can be said if we listen and follow the action. The kind of bond, that sense of absolute presence, absolute existence in another, in one another, is indeed an ordinary though of course always a transforming experience. In many lives, again and again, it is the central reality of everything else that happens, and indeed quite often doesn't need to be emphasised: the reality of the relationship is simply there and unbreakable.

In *Wuthering Heights* what has most to be said is that Cathy's affirmation is a matter of reality but that in her very statement of it, at that point in the action, something is being denied as well as affirmed. What happens really is that this central affirmation—not desire *for* another but desire *in* another; a depth of relationship around which an idea of oneself and literally then of the universe forms—is both stated and taken for granted: and the taking for granted is the profound, the dislocating error. "A source of little visible delight, but necessary": but if it is necessary it can't be assumed or taken for granted, however deep it may lie. It has to be lived. Everything, literally everything, has to be lived in its light. It is a reciprocated feeling, literally a relationship: that kind of relationship which is truly given rather than taken, which is there and absolute before anything else can be said. In its quality as given—here in a childhood, a shared childhood in a place—it is where social and personal, one's self and others, grow from a single root.

And it is then a terrible blasphemy but also a real process—a social and historical process in a life and in a time—when the necessary is seen so deep that under pressure, under pressure from other people, other ways, it is taken for granted; when on other bearings or in a different light it is in effect set aside so that another sort of reality—indeed an apparently desirable reality—can be attempted and made.

Cathy, specifically, marries Linton for what Heathcliff does not have: money, position, ease: the visible elements of society. She thinks she can retain a double identity: the indestructible identity, the profound and the necessary, but also the contingent identity, the temporary the superficial and the pleasing. There is nothing unusual in this kind of betrayal, this characteristic error, and it can be interpreted from outside in a number of ways, given our alternative terms for the necessary and the permanent and for the kinds of denial, of detachment, which can then be described. But the action is specific. She takes Heathcliff for granted and she marries Linton, and the real dislocation—the disruption, the savagery, the storm—then inevitably follows. So great a breach is made in all necessary relationships that only in another generation, and then through time, is any effective fabric restored. But just because it was necessary the affirmative persists; indeed it goes beyond life, because it is in the life of another and in the shared reality of a place. Denied where it ought to have existed, it persists in an experienced transcendence: in what others see. Heathcliff, near the end, is still trying to live where the reality had been, but now in a terrible isolation because of the denial:

> In every cloud, in every tree—filling the air and night, and caught by glimpses in every object by day—I am surrounded with her image. The most ordinary faces of men and women—my own features— mock me with a resemblance. The entire world is a dreadful collection of memoranda that she did exist, and that I have lost her.

"Image," "resemblance": that is the displacement, the mourned loss. What he feels is so ordinary that we need no special terms for it. It is that finding of reality in the being of another which is the necessary human identity: the identity of the human beyond the creature; the identity of relationship out of which all life comes. Deprived of this reality there is indeed only image and resemblance, and it is exactly right that even physical life then stops or must be willed:

> I have to remind myself to breathe—almost to remind my heart to beat.

Between the given and the willed, between the necessary and that plausible world which can appear to be separable, the action drives to its conclusion. A necessary experience of what it is to be human—of that life-desire, that relationship which is given—is frustrated, displaced, lost in those specific difficulties; but is then in a profoundly convincing way—just because it is necessary—echoed, reflected back, from where it now exists only in spirit: the image of the necessary, seen moving beyond that composed, that rearranged life; the reality of need, of the human need, haunting, appearing to, a limit scaled-down world.

When I say that *Wuthering Heights* is quite central to its time I don't mean its documentary element or what can be called its symbolism; the experience is so direct it doesn't have to be translated. It is the positive experience which has elsewhere been given a negative translation—a negative term—as alienation, and the process beyond that catchword is undoubtedly real. And because this is so, the organising experience of the novel is a more than personal desire, a more than personal longing. Indeed the intensity of persons has to be seen being displaced and then qualified, observed, interpreted; there and yet seen at a distance, seen in other modes; convincing and yet in necessary opposition with other persuasive versions of reality. And this is its critical difference from the ordinarily related fiction of intense and personal feeling.

Jane Eyre, for example, is in the world of *Wuthering Heights*, much more than we now usually admit. It is a structured presentation of some of the same urgent themes, with one critical difference: that its organising principle, its specific gravity, is quite directly personal. And this is of course much more than technique, though in that it shows clearly enough. *Jane Eyre* is first-person in a quite radical way where *Wuthering Heights* is multipersonal: an effect of experience before ever it is a method. The connecting power of Charlotte Brontë's fiction is in just this first-person capacity to compose an intimate relationship with the reader: from the easy friendly beginning—"I was glad of it, I never liked long walks"—to the final and secret sharing—"I kept these things then, and pondered them in my heart": things the reader knows but the others—the other characters, the outside world—do not.

"Reader, I married him." But that address to the reader, that capital public address, is a late pulling-away as the story fades into retrospect, into the given account. While the experience lasts, the "I" of the novel and the subjective position—the only available position—of the reader are on a much closer bearing. What matters throughout is this private confidence, this mode of confession: the account given as if in a private letter, in private talk; the account given to a journal, a private journal, and then the act of writing includes—as it were involuntarily, yet it is very deliberate and conscious art—the awareness of the friend, the close one, the unknown but in this way intimate reader: the reader *as* the writer, while the urgent voice lasts.

Given the action of *Jane Eyre*, which is in every sense dramatic, there is a pull, all the same, between action and consciousness: a tension and a power which relate it to *Wuthering Heights*. To see the full difference between the mode of *Wuthering Heights* and this persuasive personal mode of Charlotte Brontë's main fiction, we need to turn to *Villette*. Multipersonal and varied in consciousness: these decisive elements of *Wuthering Heights* have to do, I suggested, with *relationship*, with intense relationship and with its experienced alternatives. And then of course you can say that the directing impulse of all Charlotte's novels is also relationship: a desired relationship, actually more overtly desired and more apparently achieved in *Jane Eyre* or in *Villette* than at all in *Wuthering Heights*. The desire, I mean, gets through; the relationships seem to arrange themselves. But what I'm trying to say is that it *isn't* the same desire, the same kind of desire. This is very difficult because the word, the feeling, bears strongly both ways. But I've tried to distinguish between desire *for* another and desire *in* another: that distinction that is made, very closely made, in *Wuthering Heights* itself. Desire *for* another can be very intense and of course it is subject to all the accidents of the world: death, loss, disturbance, misunderstanding—those are continually important; but also those harder experiences—he is tied to another, involved with another; convention, law, property stand between; or still harder again— and it is not uncommon—the desire for another which is not returned, not responded to; yet the desire *for* is still intensely, painfully there. But desire *in* another: I don't say it's better, that doesn't arise, since it happens too deep, too early, for that kind of comment. I say only it's different because it's a relationship: I mean an achieved relationship, before anything else. A necessary relationship, in which a self, a world, is at once found and confirmed; and which of course— it's always happening, it's how the violence is done—can be broken, disastrously broken. And this is different, radically different, from the failure to find another, the failure to find a desired object, or the loss of a possession or what is desired to be possessed. These failures and losses are so breaking that we can easily run them together, but the essential process is always different; it is a question of how far, how necessarily, the life-connections are made.

> Shall I yet see him before he goes? Will he bear me in mind? Does he purpose to come? Will this day—will the next hour bring him? or must I again assay that corroding pain of long attent—that rude agony of rupture at the close, that mute, mortal wrench, which, in at once uprooting hope and doubt, shakes life, while the hand that does the violence cannot be caressed to pity because absence interposes her barrier?

In passages like this from *Villette* Charlotte seizes a kind of experience— of frustration and waiting—which connects very closely with what I called the

secret sharing: not the public process, though it can be generalised towards that—
"that mute, mortal wrench which shakes life"—but the particular immediate
experience. And this is indeed her strength. The prose is very different from anything in *Wuthering Heights* because the essential composition—the structure of
the narrative—is quite other: is not multipersonal and varied, qualified and ob-
scured in time, but subjective single and immediate:

> *What* should I do; oh! *what* should I do; when all my life's hope was
> thus torn by the roots out of my outraged heart?

That is the exact movement: the recreated question to oneself that is specifically the question, the involving question, to the reader, the sharer; and then the
rhetorical extension that tries to name the common emotion:

> The hopes which are dear to youth, which bear it up and lead it on,
> I knew not and dared not know. If they knocked at my heart some-
> times, an inhospitable bar to admission must be inwardly drawn.
> When they turned away thus rejected, tears sad enough sometimes
> flowed; but it could not be helped; I dared not give such guests lodg-
> ing. So mortally did I fear the sin and weakness of presumption.
> Religious reader, you will preach to me a long sermon about what I
> have just written, and so will you, moralist; and you, stern sage: you,
> stoic, will frown; you cynic, sneer; you, epicure, laugh. Well each
> and all, take it your own way. I accept the sermon, frown, sneer, and
> laugh; perhaps you are all right: and perhaps, circumstanced like me,
> you would have been, like me, wrong.

I repeat, this is conscious art. The actual reader, feeling these other responses
forming, is distanced, named; or to put it another way, those observing questioning criticising responses are distanced, so that the effective relation with the
reader—and this is the only reader really in mind—can come powerfully through:
"circumstanced like me, you would have been . . . " and the "perhaps" falls back
into a forgotten distance; "you would have been, like me." "Wrong?" But that
doesn't arise, in the terms of the moralist or the sage. This is "wrong" inside
confession, inside intimate confession: a fault, if at all, within a wholly revealed,
wholly accepted experience.

Seen in this early example, there is remarkable skill in the process of sympathy. The questions I quoted—"*What* should I do; oh! *what* should I do?"—
are present and suspended, with almost a pause for response, before the narrative
moves, including many possibilities, to

> what I *should* have done, I know not, when a little child—the least
> child in the school—broke with its simplicity and unconsciousness
> into the raging yet silent centre of that inward conflict.

"The raging yet silent centre": this is what, in *Villette*, is heard. It is lonely un-expressed feeling, that has now found a voice. As in waiting desperately for a letter; finding somewhere quiet to read it, through all the noise of the classes:

> "Will it be long—will it be short?" . . . It was long.
> "Will it be cool—will it be kind?" It was kind.

The process is instantaneous, with no author ahead of it; and like the letter itself is meant for reading alone, somewhere quiet, where the relation, the sharing, is direct. I've noticed again and again—you've all probably noticed—how difficult it is reading *Villette* out, reading it out in public. For that isn't its world.

> The poor English teacher in the frosty garret, reading by a dim can-dle guttering in the wintry air. . . . To my longing and famished thought . . .

It's that kind of closeness, that kind of recognition: like the mark in the margin of the book in the library—the secret sharing, the assent. And it's easy to destroy; dangerously easy; just as it's easy not to feel what went into that mark, that sharing, that silent recognition and reference.

I only wanted to define it and to show its difference from *Wuthering Heights*, where the light falls from so many directions, in so many accents, on an intensity that is worked, open and in that sense public: an intensity of stated relationship which is examined and lasts, persists, through the intricacies of observation and of time.

And I'd then say, finally, that Charlotte stands very obviously at the head of a tradition, in a way that her sister does not; and I think that is history, a significant history, when we come to reflect. For the method of *Villette* is what I called once, coldly, the fiction of special pleading. I mean that fiction in which the only major emotion, and then the relation with the reader, is that exact stress, that first-person stress: "circumstanced like me." The stress is this really: the world will judge me in certain ways if it sees what I do, but if it knew how I felt it would see me quite differently. And then the particular weakness of this form has become very obvious. Its persons outside this shaping longing demanding consciousness have reality only as they contribute to the landscape, the emotional landscape, of the special, the pleading, the recommending character. That is all we know of them, all we really know of her, and some extraordinary things have been done in its name: use of others, abuse of others; a breakdown of discourse —and with discourse so much else, so many other needs and realities—as the all-including voice, the voice pleading for this experience, for understanding of it, for the exclusion of alternatives—alternative voices, alternative viewpoints—

comes through and creates its own world. I think that makes us now look back at *Villette* with a certain awe, a certain wariness. Certainly *Wuthering Heights* beside it is fresh and open air. But the power is there, the original power: the immediate personal and creative form: the inclusive sharing of what had been an unspoken voice, as opposed to that other extending, dislocating, affirming world.

ROSALIND MILES

A Baby God: The Creative Dynamism of Emily Brontë's Poetry

It is never easy to say anything worthwhile about a great writer; and among poets Emily Brontë was perhaps the most heedless of her future critics and biographers, pitilessly suppressing the raw materials needed for the task of describing and assessing her. The hopeful commentator finds himself handicapped by the existence of two central puzzles or mysteries in her life, which have a direct bearing upon her work. The necessity of coming to terms with these forms the first imperative in any approach to Emily Brontë's poetry.

First, despite the wealth of primary and secondary material, Emily Brontë remains extraordinarily remote from us. Not for nothing does the comparison with Shakespeare so readily and repeatedly present itself, from the earliest recorded comment upon "the Bells." Like Shakespeare's her work stands alone and challenges us, forces us, to do without the authorial gloss or "personal touch" which academic and general readers alike so love to have upon or read into a work. Mrs Humphry Ward summed this up in her perceptive preface to the Haworth edition of *Wuthering Heights*:

> The artist remains hidden and self-contained; the work . . . has always that distinction which belongs to a high talent working solely for its own joy and satisfaction, with no thought of a spectator, or any aim but that of an ideal and imaginative whole. . . . She has that highest power . . . the power which gives life, intensest life, to the creatures of the imagination, and, in doing so, endows them with an independence behind which the maker is forgotten.

From *The Art of Emily Brontë*, edited by Anne Smith. © 1976 by Vision Press.

Emily Brontë was, of course, a determinedly private individual, both as an artist and as a person; so much so that she succeeded in intimidating even her sisters from any intrusion upon her inner self. She was, simply, without that urge to communicate, to explain, defend, elaborate and describe the ups and downs of her mental, emotional, and creative life which has brought Charlotte so endearingly close to us; and thus, as with Shakespeare, we know so little about the writer's process of creation that we are but tenuously justified in drawing personal inferences from the result. We may *feel* that a certain poem "must" be autobiographical, but we can never know, as we can, for instance, with Keats.

Keats indeed expressed, on Emily Brontë's behalf, as it were, the artistic attitudes which we know from her behaviour to have been hers. She too could well have declared, as he did in a letter to Reynolds of April 9, 1818, "I never wrote one single Line of Poetry with the least Shadow of public thought"; or again, "my imagination is a monastery, and I am its monk" (letter to Shelley, August 1820). Who more than Emily Brontë felt able to "refuse the poisonous suffrage of a public" in the knowledge that "the soul is a world of itself, and has enough to do in its own home" (Keats's letter to Reynolds, August 25, 1819)? By the adoption of such attitudes, implicit though unarticulated, Emily Brontë repels rather than invites critical attention, discouraging any casual or trivial approaches to her work.

The second source of Emily Brontë's enigmatic quality lies in the importance of the Gondal saga in her life and poetry. Emily Brontë herself distinguished between "Gondal Poems" and others, to which she gave no group title (Hatfield's A and B manuscripts). But all her work does not fall conveniently within these two volumes and categories. There are many poems which we could not definitely say belong either in the "personal" or in the Gondal group; this tantalising fragment, for instance (Hatfield 161):

> Had there been falsehood in my breast
> No thorns had marred my road,
> This spirit had not lost its rest,
> These tears had never flowed.

Clearly there is a very real sense in which the distinction ceases to be relevant. To borrow her own unforgettable dream image from chapter 9 of *Wuthering Heights*, from its length and centrality in her life, the Gondal saga must have gone through Emily Brontë like wine through water, and altered the colour of her mind.

This fusion is very evident from any scrutiny of the poems with definite Gondal attributions. Gondal experiences, despite their lurid, often quite ghastly trappings, are often in essence plainly borrowed from and blended with those of Emily Brontë herself. The Gondal saga, what we know of it, was melodramatic, but then so was some of Emily Brontë's own life. Are we to take it, for instance, that given the narrowness of her daily round, and the rule of her well-intentioned but hardly imaginative aunt and the domestics, she would not know at first hand the sense of being constrained, the denial of her "wild will," even "the agony of still repining" (chap. 15), however she disguises these emotional events, masks them as Gondal characters, Gondal voices, Gondal plights and disasters? Why should we doubt that the young woman who spent so many nights gazing at the moon and stars should, when she slept, have dreamed as often and as vividly as her creatures do?

> "Dreams have encircled me," I said,
> "From careless childhood's sunny time;
> Visions by ardent fancy fed
> Since life was in its morning prime."
> (H. 27)

Similarly it seems clear that the memories, fantasies, and experiences of the past remained alive to her, and rose up to revitalize a newly contrived Gondal situation with a reservoir of emotional truth from a previous occasion; see H. 102, for instance, where she makes a character say, "Old feelings gather fast upon me / Like vultures round their prey." Inevitably, too, the weight of her emotional experiences, both real and vicarious, increased as the years went by, so that she was, by and in herself, carrying a growing burden of the knowledge of "torment and madness, tears and sin"; she was able to relieve this pressure by voicing through her characters attitudes which progress from a rather downhearted pragmatism (H. 118 and 119), through an occasionally hysterical cynicism—"the poison-tainted air / From this world's plague-fen" (H. 143)—to a generalized disillusion and despair (H. 157, 174). Again, though, to borrow from one of her characters, we know that Emily Brontë herself could "journey onward, not elate, / But *never* broken-hearted" (H. 122; Emily Brontë's italics).

This blending of personal and Gondal material is well illustrated in H. 97, "By R. Gleneden." This poem, written on April 17, 1839, a week after Anne left home to go as a governess, repeatedly laments the absence of "one" for whose loss "cheerless, chill is our hearthstone." How could Emily not grieve for the loss of Anne, whom both Charlotte and Ellen Nussey tell us was as a twin to her? And yet, with her obsessive reticence, how could she treat the subject except under the Gondal cover, from behind the mask, on this occasion, of Gleneden? Even in the poem's theme of noble self-sacrifice for the general good there is an echo of the motive underlying Anne's departure—for none of the Brontës ever went into the joyless servitude of tutoring except to make their contribution towards relieving the common economic burden.

Again, in H. 99 and 100, in the theme of degeneration and the hardening of a young heart, we see behind the fictional portrait the shadow of Branwell's condition. Nine years were to pass before his eventual death, but it was by now abundantly plain that he would not fulfil the great destiny that he had once seemed to flourish, and that he could not even make his living as a portrait painter. In the lament for the "ardent boy" (is there a punning reference here to Branwell's distinctive flaming red hair?) we see a version or incarnation of one whom, temporarily at least, Emily dismissed as "a hopeless being," having seen him from adolescence depending upon increasingly strong doses of merry company, drink, and opium, to relieve him from cynicism and despair. Yet this personal element is informed, transformed, strengthened and distanced by its interweaving with the threads of the Gondal narrative into a cloak which allowed her in another poem, "Well, some may hate, and some may scorn" (H. 123), to anticipate not only Branwell's distressing and ignominious death, but also the wrestling of her own proud nature against feelings of contempt for those who could not match up to her exacting standards of behaviour.

What would we not give to have more knowledge of the lost Gondal stories? Of all the "might-have-beens" of English Literature—the poems of Keats's full maturity, the novels of Jane Austen's middle age, the ending of *Edwin Drood*—the survival of the Gondal material is among those which Emily Brontë's admirers are bound to wish could have occurred. It is highly possible that some of the poems now rather loftily dismissed as weak and pretentious would gain in strength if we knew, as Emily Brontë did, the supportive context in which they were conceived and written. The posturing strain, the vein of melodramatic extremism, the thrill of what can strike the reader as a false excitement, may have proved legitimate in their original surroundings.

It is almost as if Homer had left us only snatches of the *Iliad*; as if we had, for instance, Andromache's lament for Hector without understanding the implications of his fall for her, for Astyanax, for his aged parents and all his people. Again, imagine what we should make of *Njal's Saga* if we possessed only Hrut's first enigmatic response to Hallgerd, his distrust of her beauty and her "thief's eyes," without knowing what sinister use she was to make of these attributes. The devout may still continue to make it their morn prayer that, like *Love's Labour's Wonne*, the *Life of Emperor Julius* or even Anne's *Solala Vernon's Life* will somehow, somewhere, surface. But since it is not possible to recapture Gondal in the present state of our knowledge, any more than it is to make Emily Brontë herself "abide our question," we must, simply, come to terms with what we have.

This, in fact, like so much else in life, is easier said than done. Emily Brontë's strangeness, her remoteness, have meant that even her keenest commentators may mislead, pointing the way confidently up blind alleys or side tracks.

The magnitude of her achievement, taken with her reticence and the private, teasing, enclosed nature of the Gondal world, make her techniques and processes difficult to analyse and pin down. Some critics fall back on the assumption that this body of work just happened, by itself, and treat it as some tremendous awe-inspiring natural phenomenon, like Niagara falls or the Grand Canyon. Even her admirers may play down the idea of her work as something *made*, the product of a controlling intelligence of acute creative ability.

For, from the beginning, the stress has been on Emily Brontë's "unconscious felicities," "instinctive art," side by side with her lyrical power. These remarks were made by an early reviewer, who, while praising *Wuthering Heights* honestly and perceptively, pronounced it "the unformed writing of a giant's hand; the 'large utterance' of a baby god." Another reviewer says, "she has not to do with intellect, but emotion . . . the passion she has chosen is love," later identifying in her work "that *original* cadence, that power of melody" as the sign of "the born poet."

Praise of the art, which yet gives insufficient credit to the artist, is no praise at all. In this way Emily Brontë has been done something of a disservice, even by those who have felt most strongly for her. Charlotte Brontë, in her love for one who must have been a most awkward person to love, mourned her sister in strange ways, recreating an idealized Emily in Shirley, and trying to obtain from the world a posthumous pardon for the "rude and savage" *Wuthering Heights*. Charlotte Brontë in fact contributed to notions of Emily Brontë as an untutored genius piping her native woodnotes wild, with her stress upon the physical limitations of Emily Brontë's life (her rarely going out, or talking to people, and so on), and also with placing so much emphasis upon the mysterious and uncontrollable power of genius as "something that strangely wills and works for itself." Notice too Charlotte Brontë's concentration upon the "wild," and, paradoxically, the "homely" in Emily Brontë—but the whole line of thought posits a truly classical belief in the need and efficacy of training for genius—something that to our way of thinking has been amply disproved, for example by Emily Brontë herself.

It seems curiously difficult, with Emily Brontë, to accept what is there; to begin with and from the authority of the text itself. Red herrings abound, and we are too readily drawn into such irrelevancies as poor loving Charlotte Brontë's talk of Emily Brontë as she would have been "in health and prosperity," had she been in contact with "other intellects," or even the unwittingly comical "Ellis will not be seen in his full strength till he is seen as an essayist." Needless to say, Emily Brontë's French *devoirs* have since been given to the world without dislodging *Wuthering Heights* and the poems from their supremacy in our estimation.

Another potentially misleading area of discussion, and one which needs to be approached with caution and precision, is the question of the dramatic in Emily Brontë's poetry. It is true that she shows herself capable of using the dramatic technique of direct address in an enormous variety of different situations and *personae*. Among these we may isolate the simple approach of H. 14, "I saw thee, child, one summer's day," or that of H. 80, "Geraldine, the moon is shining"; the Blakean H. 3, "Tell me, tell me, smiling child"; or the differing moods of exclamation and apostrophe, as in A.G.A.'s paean, "There shines the moon" (H. 9), and "How still, how happy!" (H. 93). Few poets are so free with the vocative; she is mistress too of the tone of effortless command—"Come, sit down on this sunny stone" (H. 93) and "Light up thy halls!" (H. 85)—although in the nature of things Gondal other characters may question or reject the demands made upon them, and her direct address technique often modifies to a question and answer structure; or even, more typically perhaps, a wild questioning which, as in H. 82, "Where were ye all? and where wert thou?," perfectly conjures up for us the silent faithless ones around the speaker. Not uncommonly, too, she uses a question to end a poem: "Geraldine, wilt thou delay?" (H. 80). Variations of this are the voices of cursing, exhortation and lamentation, which may modify into self-address or self-question: "Forget them—O forget them all" and "Why return / O'er such a past to brood and mourn?" (H. 15). Without in any way undervaluing her more reflective mood, it remains a remarkable feature of her work just how many of her poems plunge in in this direct and startling way, with a direct address—and how central is this technique for stimulating and involving readers, not relaxing the poetic hold upon them even at the end.

A unique and arresting feature of Emily Brontë's poetic world is the number of speaking parts it contains, the wide-ranging *dramatis personae* with exotic names, desires and capacities. Browning indeed seems her poetic inheritor here, with his well-peopled monologues and scenes. We may readily conceive of his handling the recurrent figures of the outcast boy, the tyrant queen and the betrayed lover; or indeed the common soldier of H. 28, and dying maiden of H. 42, the minstrel apostrophizing his harp in H. 59, or the soothing maternal voice of the lullaby in H. 62. Nor, with Browning's interest in morbid psychology, would we feel that the spirit who haunts the doomed "child of dust" in H. 14, or the other weird manifestations of Emily Brontë's haunted and guilt-ridden characters, who carry their past about them continually, would be outside his range.

Yet the comparison with Browning can take us farther into the heart of Emily Brontë's mystery. While she may, with him, cover a range of character-types and situations, we could never say that she achieves the delineation of personality, the sound of the individual voice with all the notes of anger, weariness, or resignation so intensely peculiar to each well-observed human being, as Browning was to do. "How long will you remain?" (H. 114) illustrates this. It is couched in the form of a dramatic monologue; but the reader's ear is perplexed by the alternation of question and answer, since both voices sound the same. Ultimately here, as in much of her work, the effect is not *dramatic* as we understand the term (though doubtless so in the original vivid conception).

This is not to underestimate the gripping quality of the poetry, which links with the riveting power of *Wuthering Heights*; it is very rare to have a volume of poems which it is, in the standard phrase, "impossible to put down." Incontestably she possessed the ability to speak with a strange magic, dark fascination and mesmerizing intensity; see, for instance, "I am the only being whose doom" (H. 11), with the unexpected and shocking turn in the last couplet:

> 'Twas grief enough to think mankind
> All hollow, servile, insincere;
> But worse to trust to my own mind
> And find the same corruption there.

Yet with all this, her gift is not that of the creator of characters as people, who move and talk in imitation of human action. Hers is not that "one touch of nature" that "makes the whole world kin." Like Shakespeare she did not need to be king, queen, despot or victim in order to delineate the condition; but unlike him she never penetrated it. She deployed her characters with a powerful flourish, but the conviction with which they move and speak is Emily Brontë's, rather than their own; she dons the robes, the crowns, the fetters, the boots and spurs at will, and her creations are truly hers, they speak in her voice, in her accents of defiance, rage, and love. Truly she played the "baby god" with the inhabitants of her created world; and a tyrannical one, too.

This is her peculiar gift, and the source of her fascination. We long to be admitted to share her megalomaniac fantasy. But the essentially Shakespearean facility of so entering a character as to *become* it, the greatness so to diminish oneself as to dwindle into nothing but the other, the ability to allow the character to speak not in his creator's voice but in his own—this is not Emily Brontë's, and the comparison with Shakespeare, helpful as a way in, at this point becomes misleading. Whatever the requirements of the ability to make us feel that we are hearing the words and thoughts of one person, and that one only, Emily Brontë did not have them. Hers is a ventriloquial gift, not a dramatic one, and this is a paradox indeed, in view of the dramatic nature of much of what she writes, the dramatic basis of the original Gondal "play" itself, and the intensity and energy of her mind which naturally caused her to project outward, in the more public form of drama, what she thought and felt. One final example in summing up. Her poem, "If grief for grief can touch thee" (H. 138), is a perfect illustration of her Gondal manner. A brilliant, haunting lament of betrayal, whose pain, but that the "worn heart" of the poet "throbs" rather more "wildly," recalls that of Shakespeare in the *Sonnets*—yet it is plainly not personal in the way that Shakespeare's poems are, nor could we say with any conviction which of Emily Brontë's *dramatis personae* it properly belongs to. It is, inescapably, a cry from the soul— but whose?

If, as Keats said, we hate poetry that has a palpable design on us, then that is why we love Emily Brontë. But, even in our admiration of her effects, we should not therefore confuse her masterful confidence with effortless ease and unconscious facility. Hers is the art that conceals art; the result, at its best, is truly that of "carefullest carelessness." Far from being the product of an untutored genius, her work everywhere conveys an overwhelming impression of conscious artistry. Charlotte knew this; in a letter of November 16, 1848 to W. S. Williams she declared her belief that "Ellis" possessed "the very finish and *labor limae*" which she herself lacked.

We must, though, distinguish between the dynamic of creativity, the self-generated and astonishing momentum of the poems, and the helpless headlong flow which Charlotte elsewhere describes. While we should probably all agree that poets are born, not made, poetry itself certainly isn't. It has to be generated, delivered, shaped and assisted into life. Poetry should, and rightly, come as naturally as leaves to a tree; but it will not write itself. "The road lies through application study and thought" (Keats's letter to Taylor, April 24, 1818)—any examination however cursory, of Emily Brontë's poetry, will show how carefully she attended to the techniques of creation, how painstakingly she sought the appropriate expression for her provocative vision. The success, the excitement of the result, should not blind us to the difficulties she needed to overcome in achieving it, in finding the variations of form, rhyme and rhythm to meet the challenge of the content. We can only marvel at how hard she must have worked, at the energy of her endeavour.

This energy, expressed as honesty and directness, is the source of her impact and attraction. Her hold upon her readers (and most of her admirers would agree that this hold is little short of mesmeric in its intensity) is rooted in two elements. Both are equally compelling, both are manifestations of her extraordinary drive; the one is of content, the other, style.

What is exciting about Emily Brontë's style is its astonishing confidence. Her sureness of touch would be impressive in a much older practitioner of the demanding art of versification; but in an inexperienced girl, who had hardly begun upon her mature life before she was torn out of it, it is little short of miraculous. There are, of course, the moments when her flowers are just fragrant, her grass green, and her skies blue; there are some attention-seeking archaisms like "yesternight" and "verdant"; there is perhaps an over-reliance upon certain favourite words, "drear," "dazzle," "wild," "ghastly" and "gloom" (though it could be argued that this kind of insistence is a contributory cause of her hypnotic effect). On the whole, however, we may rather wonder that her poetry is so free of youthful weaknesses and self-indulgences than waste time picking up the errors she does commit. So to do is to close our eyes to the great and good things which lie scattered about throughout her work.

One of these is certainly the gift for the memorable phrase. Who would not be haunted by "the sea of death's eternity," the "child of dust," the "portals of futurity," the "moonlight wild," "sweet as amber," or "that wide heaven where every star / Stared like a dying memory?" This facility in evocation is part of a wider gift, that of creating a variety of impressive visual images; we remember the Emily Brontë landscape in a series of photographic represents —the arch of heaven, the moor at night with one solitary inhabitant, the full moon and the lone star. Later, these natural images are interwoven with those of startling fantasy, expressing surreal moments of perception like that of the little twittering glittering spirits, sparks of fire, evoking subliminal memories of Stoic theories of reincarnation in H. 170; in this context we think too of the vision of "The Philosopher" in H. 181:

> "A Golden stream, and one like blood,
> And one like Sapphire, seemed to be,
> But where they joined their triple flood
> It tumbled in an inky sea."

Many of Emily Brontë's images are built upon the ancient principle of contrasts; not, in her case, the gradations of tone or subtle shades of meaning, but that of stark opposition. Extremes lent themselves readily to the presentation of her own intense and strongly-varied apprehension; extremes were her natural mode. Hence, for instance, the importance of one of her favourite images, that of the grave, which in itself catches up much of what she wishes to say about living *and* dying. It implies the same apposition between the stillness of death and the busyness of life which is the stuff of much of her imagery; we see constantly in her poems a recurrence of all the physical images associated with being free, and with its opposite; birds, animals, adventurers male and female, are set against tyrants, their victims, and their paraphernalia of dungeons, fetters and coercion, their reluctant prey. This simplification may appear to convey a reduction of her associative power; the grave, in her work, stands too for the paradox of life in death among the mourners beside it, for the strength of the spirit after death, for the walking ghost, the memory that is the ghost, so strong that it lives on, and for the dead, who, Banquo-like, refuse to keep their graves or take their eternal rest—as against the living death of being confined, constrained, tormented.

Extremes characterize too her remarkable use of colour; remarkable for its evocation of all the brilliant effects of nature and art without much overt employment of the epithets of colour in themselves. That is to say, while she does use for example "blue," usually in conjunction with "clear," or green, red, brown and so on, her colour effects are most frequently accomplished by the introduction of phenomena of nature which suggest ideas of colour without actually declaring them; dawn, sunset, frost, mist, the robin, blood, snow.

Among this group, and probably the most memorable of them, are all the terms of light and dark. Although predominantly a night person, Emily Brontë did not neglect the effects of day, but throughout her poetry is revealed as a "watcher of the skies" in all their phases and moods. "Darkness and glory" are everywhere opposed and contrasted through the use of such terms as "sparkling," "cloudless," "dazzling," "bright," "cloudy grey," "dim," "gloomy"; colour is defined in Emily Brontë's work as much by its absence as by its presence. Indeed, any colour pattern of her world as a whole must present itself to our imagination as a blackness shot through here and there with brilliant or vivid contrasts; "midnight and moonlight and bright shining stars." As we see from this, no one word is particularly fresh or powerful in itself; but, as with Keats's "Ode to Autumn," the effect is cumulative. "There shines the moon" (H. 9) is an early example of this method. Even in this poem of her eighteenth year we note, too, another characteristic feature of her use of colour, and one which was to increase in importance; that is, the way in which adjectives are supplemented by verbs of colour in such a way as to add weight and vigour, and to make her poems, in her own verbs, "gleam," "glow" and "flame":

> And bursting through the leafy shade
> A gush of golden sunshine played,
> Bathing the walls in amber light
> And sparkling in the water clear
> That stretched below—reflected bright
> The whole wide world of cloudless air

With maturity, too, Emily Brontë perfected even more striking and sophisticated colour effects. Even as early as "Will the day be bright or cloudy?" (H. 2), her "golden flowers" are partly literal (the next line has them "sparkling in sunshine and dew") but mainly they suggest an other-worldly vision of the promised glorious future. Later we have the fascinating and complex pattern of contrasts between the "golden suns," the blackness of night and death, the prophetic "rose-red smile" of dawn, and the shining brightness of morning achieved in stanza seven of "The busy day has hurried by" (H. 104). Equally exciting is the colour pattern in "On the Fall of Zalona" (H. 156); the Gondal adventures, naturally perhaps, stimulated the formation of gaudy scenes, painted in arresting primary colours—blue, bright, light, white, gold and emerald assault our visual sense in the first two stanzas alone.

Another striking element of Emily Brontë's verse, and one which is perhaps the most expressive of the energy of her mind and style, is her use of verbs of movement. From her earliest ventures into poetry-making she displayed a grasp that older hands might envy on one of its fundamental laws; that the force of a piece of writing lies in its verbs, not in its decorative adjectives and adverbs. So we have, in "High waving heather," for example, a torrent of verbs, bending, blending, descending, bursting, breaking, rending, extending, shining, lowering, swelling, dying, roaring, flying and flashing—in this piece (H. 5) Emily Brontë celebrates, with all the vigour of her eighteen years, a delirious frenzy of movement. She is not always to be so active again, but like Cathy's heaven in *Wuthering Heights*, hers is a busy universe; even over Elbe's quiet grave the ferns toss in the breeze. Later, in "Lines by Claudia" (H. 102), the verbs "burning," "bending" and "brooding" in three successive lines of the first four-line stanza add power and intensity to what could otherwise be a conventional pastoral scene, while in stanza two the "mellow hum of bees / And singing birds and sighing trees" again recall the young Catherine's "perfect idea of heaven's happiness" in chapter 24 of *Wuthering Heights*. It is through her verbs, too, that Emily Brontë achieves her much-admired effects of balladic simplicity and fervour; "for which we fought and bled and died" (H. 102). This use of verbs to lend authenticity and muscularity to verse lines was a skill which Emily Brontë was still perfecting at the end of her life; its culmination lies in the almost intimidatingly magnificent "No coward soul is mine" (H. 191), where of the nineteen words in the fifth stanza, nine are verbs:

> With wide-embracing love
> Thy spirit animates eternal years
> Pervades and broods above,
> Changes, sustains, dissolves, creates and rears.

Movement and colour, then, are vital elements of this work; and, of the other senses which Emily Brontë sought to stir through her poetry, well to the fore was that of hearing. A main source of the satisfaction and delight which we derive from Emily Brontë's poems lies in her creation of rich and varied sound patterns. Her lines are full of memorable resonances—that of "thunder . . . a mournful story" (H. 2), of wind (*passim*), of "inspiring music's thrilling sound" (H. 4), of stormy blasts, of the robin's "wildly tender" song (H. 7). Then, too, her lines in themselves make agreeable sounds, fall into patterns which strike very acceptably upon the ear. Her use of rhyme, for instance, simple, bold and strong, never disappoints with feebleness or evasion; she will not cheat for the sake of rhyme, working in a redundant "deceiving elf" or "little fay" as Keats and Hardy do. Occasionally she attempts feminine rhymes: forever/never, falling/ palling, weeping/sweeping, are some examples; sometimes too acceptable near-rhymes (heaven/even, laid/head, return/mourn) give way to near-misses like showered/adored, or hard/sward. But in general the overwhelming reliance upon monosyllables ensures success; her rhymes chime with an astonishing accuracy upon the mind's ear. Her manipulative skill is well illustrated in "Lines by Claudia" (H. 102), with its intricate rhyme scheme; she readily alternates four-line stanzas rhyming *abab*, with six-line stanzas rhyming *aabcbc*:

> I heard the mellow hum of bees
> And singing birds and sighing trees,
> And far away in woody dell
> The Music of the Sabbath bell.
>
> I did not dream; remembrance still
> Clasped round my heart its fetters chill;
> But I am sure the soul is free
> To leave its clay a little while,
> Or how in exile misery
> Could I have seen my country smile?

Rhyme goes hand in hand with its sister, rhythm; and the conscious artist in Emily Brontë never shrank from the often enormous technical problems implied in rhythmic variation, practising and experimenting in an impressive range of metres. Her favourite was always the brisk tetrameter, for which she showed a constant fondness over the more conventional pentameter. Yet this basically simple line—"I gazed upon the cloudless moon" (H. 110)—was constantly modified by the introduction of a trochaic inversion in the first foot, as in H. 9, "There shines the moon," where, of sixty-eight lines, twenty-three begin with the inverted foot. Notice the effect of this in line two of the third stanza of H. 113, "Mild the mist upon the hill" (which further displays her refusal to accept as a tyranny her chosen rhythm, her ability to pack a line almost to overflowing with sound and meaning):

> I watch this cloudy evening fall,
> After a day of rain:
> Blue mists, sweet mists of summer pall
> The horizon's mountain-chain.

See too "Loud without the wind was roaring" (H. 91) where the introduction is constructed upon the basis of the tetrameter, which then modulates into a running parlour-ballad rhythm which is quite different.

This ability to change gear within a poem (as also in "Alone I sat," H. 27), is only part of a general interest in different forms of stress and emphasis. Emily Brontë liked too the trimeter, an aggressive little line very demanding of the reader, and potentially hypnotic in intensity, especially when, as here, it gives way to a fuller line and then reverts again:

> And truly at my side
> I saw a shadowy thing
> Most dim, and yet its presence there
> Curdled my blood with ghastly fear
> And ghastlier wondering.
>
> (H. 12)

She always reserved to herself the freedom of adding to or subtracting from one of the regular rhythms, so that the reader is stimulated by a beat which recalls, but yet does not sound like, one that he knows well in other contexts. Interesting here is the balladic "A.G.A. to A.E." (H. 16), which is roughly based on an anapaestic measure like *Lochinvar*, and "Awake! awake!" (H. 40), which has an iambic pentameter with an intermittent feminine ending. This has the effect of making it sound like a hymn, a battle-hymn; one can readily imagine it as a sung rhythm, and also as a marching one. Some of the unfinished pieces or fragments are particularly fascinating in a consideration of Emily Brontë's use of rhythm; one manuscript sheet holds "Iernë's eyes were glazed and dim" (H. 46), where many trochaic lines unite to produce an urgent and balladic effect, and also this skilfully-wrought snippet:

> All hushed and still within the house;
> Without—all wind and driving rain;
> But something whispers to my mind,
> Through rain and through the wailing wind,
>   Never again.
> Never again? Why not again?
> Memory has power as real as thine.
>
> (H. 45)

In her handling of rhythm as much as in her presentation of her characters Emily Brontë knew how to be flowing or terse, knew how to storm or soothe. In H. 74, for instance, the long lines have a smooth and elegiac glide to them:

Old Hall of Elbë, ruined, lonely now;
House to which the voice of life shall never more return;
Chambers roofless, desolate, where weeds and ivy grow;
Windows through whose broken arches the night-winds sadly mourn;
Home of the departed, the long-departed dead.

Yet in stark contrast is the sinister manipulation of the trimeter in H. 111, "Shed
no tears o'er that tomb," were every syllable carries a doom-like beat of grief and
reproach; the same technique is used again in H. 163, "In the earth," which
contains many such heavily impressive lines charged to capacity with thought,
feeling, and stress. Even in her last years, when the bright future which had
beckoned to the members of her family in their teens had given way to a world
of doubt and despair; when Charlotte, Branwell, and Anne had all been disappointed in their ambitions, and the two girls were suffering, with an immediacy
which revitalizes a tired phrase, the pangs of unrequited love—even amid all
this, the pulse of the true artist continued to beat strongly in Emily Brontë.
Within one year, 1844, she ranged from the simplicity of her old favourite, the
ballad refrain of the tetrameter which she had by now mastered as well as any
other writer in English was ever to do, through a more complex set of six-line
stanzas in "To Imagination" (H. 174) whose metrical pattern recalls the second
part of a Shakespeare sonnet, rhyming *abab* with a final clinching couplet, *cc*,
through to the extraordinarily daring and complex "D.G.C. to J.A." (H. 175):

Come, the wind may never again
Blow as now it blows for us;
And the stars may never again shine as now they shine;
Long before October returns,
Seas of blood will have parted us;
And you must crush the love in your heart, and I the love in mine!

All this unites to form, for the reader, her quite unmistakable tone. Her
variety and skill exist to serve a rare talent, and one with some quite unique
features of perception. Her awareness of the dark side of nature, for instance, of
the underworld of human affairs, and her reliance upon the Gothic element as its
objective correlative, lend backbone to her work—it is this which can transfigure
what might otherwise be the utterances of a versifying pet lamb. The opening
couplet of H. 94, "The blue bell is the sweetest flower / That waves in summer
air," could almost come from any nineteenth-century miss's notebook of poetic
effusions. But even in stanza two we recognize a different and weightier talent—
"There is a spell in purple heath / Too wildly, sadly dear"—the intense and

unexpected adverbs here so entirely characteristic of her mode of apprehension. The poem as a whole indeed, so apparently artless in its inception, moves us on through a complex progression of aural, tactile, and emotional sensations—the remembered scent of the violet, the mouring tears and lamentation of the narrator, the silvery, sapphire and emerald of the flower, its colours artificially heightened by the passion of the moment of perception of it; until the poem builds to a climax which is inescapably Emily Brontë, in tone, form and content:

> If chilly then the light should fall
> Adown the dreary sky
> And gild the dank and darkened wall
> With transient brilliancy,
>
> How do I yearn, how do I pine
> For the time of flowers to come,
> And turn me from that fading shine
> To mourn the fields of home.

What was the aim, the drive behind Emily Brontë's poetry, the struggle of her artistry to be at all costs accurate? She put the honesty of her energy to work at one of the most unusual and difficult task of poetry, the account of her mystical experiences. If her style is, as we have seen, sinewy, personal and impressive, how much more so is the content of this theme—uniquely personal, uniquely impressive. An important preconditioning influence, here, and one we may do well to begin with, is that of nature.

Emily Brontë is, *par excellence*, our poet of nature's less benign aspects. Few writers have so consistently celebrated, or at least incorporated, the action of relentless rain, dreary winds, storms, mist, and the sunless hours of a "heaven lorn." Did any better know than Emily Brontë how to "form [her] mood to nature's mood," and vice versa? In places, of course, there is considerable degree of reliance upon the standard "props" of nature, snow, frost, summer, sun, and so on, occasionally conveyed in archaic and self-conscious poetic terminology: "Cynthia's silver morning," for example. But this type of pseudo-pastoral effect was to give way to the truly-felt and simply moving "How clear she shines! How quietly / I lie beneath her silver light" (H. 157). This in fact summarises for us the constant style of Emily Brontë's nature references. The environment is all important. The details are observed in their place, but they are rarely particularized, or presented with the startling immediacy of the freshness of first observation.

There are exceptions to this, occasions when her epithets are wonderfully apt, unpredictable, and vivid. Her "iron clouds," for instance, the "waves in their boiling bed," or "the blue ice curdling on the stream"; all these waken our own duller senses to the singularity and strange beauty of what is described. On the whole, however, nature is present rather as the essential background and preconditioning factor without which the thoughts of the poem could not have birth, rather than as a subject in itself; and consequently its contours, its peculiarities and landmarks, are not isolated and specified. In Emily Brontë's landscape we grow accustomed to seeing a wood, a lark, an aged tree; while in "I've been wandering in the greenwoods" (H. 128), with its casual catalogue of flora and fauna, there is more than a hint of the sublime Wordsworthian vagueness of "a violet by a mossy stone"—the very phrase of which occurs in Emily Brontë's "blue bell" poem (H. 94): "And that wood flower that hides so shy / Beneath its mossy stone."

Wordsworth seems at first to have more than a passing connection with Emily Brontë, as the other great nature-lover and mystic of English poetry; and Emily Brontë displayed a continuous response to the ebb and flow of the seasons, to the action and interaction of the elements of wind, sun, night and stars, and to the very sounds of nature's working, which we associate with this type of mystic, the Wordsworthian. Yet at other times she shows an infinitely calm and objective recording of nature rather than a response to it: "The deer are gathered to their rest / The wild sheep seek the fold" (H. 19)—in a mood which recalls Sappho's immortal evening piece, "O Hesper, you bring homeward . . . the sheep to the fold, the goat to the stall, the child to the mother."

This was because, like so much else, her mystical appreciation grew and developed during the course of her life. We have to trace its maturing from stage to stage as she realized and concentrated her powers. From the very first her poems are full of references to visions, tremendously clear mental images both real and imaginary; in H. 3, "Tell me, tell me," for instance, the "smiling" child "sees" in a brilliant evocation both the "green and flowery spray" with the bird poised for flight, and also the sea of glorious infinity. There is, too, the frequent representation of Gondal characters being "rapt," and "unheeding," in intensely engrossing spiritual states. What we may feel is the first declaration of this capacity finds voice in H. 12, "The night of storms had passed," although Emily Brontë still felt it necessary to present it very conventionally as "I dreamt." This however may be less of a fictional evasion for her, than a conventional excuse for us, if we are unable or unwilling to accept the implications of such visionary possession. Described here are features which we come to recognize as inextricably associated with the mystical experience; physical paralysis, the sense of space and time being different in the "dream" from that of the "real" world, the ideas of eternity and of bridging the unbridgeable void. All these strands are bound up in a sensation of horror, as if in this early version Emily Brontë had to offer it in a conventionalized Gothic treatment; also although it contains no conclusive evidence internally, it is fairly plainly a Gondal poem, and therefore a dramatic mask for Emily Brontë's personal preoccupations, from its position amid a cluster of leaves which also include "Woe for the day! Regina's pride" (H. 13).

The fragmentary H. 23, "And first an hour of mournful musing," gives us our first unmasked treatment of the onset of the mystical experience. Central here is the reference to the focusing upon one significant star. Is it the concentration upon the one bright object that induces the onset of the trance-like state (as, at a much lower level, in hypnosis)? Or is the star to be taken simply in the symbolic sense of the final line, the "star of love"? If so, whose? and for whom? It seems most likely that it is the love of and for the mysterious spirit "He," who comes, as explicitly as he ever does in this body of poetry, in H. 190, "Julian M. and A. G. Rochelle"; but there were to be various developments before this stage was accomplished.

It is of course entirely characteristic of Emily Brontë that, with this key area of her experience, we are reduced to combing the poems for clues, and piecing together the evidence. In H. 24, "Wind, sink to rest in the heather," we have the assertion of what is plain throughout, that the moon, and sometimes "dreary weather" are imperative for the right mood for the onset of the visitant. This is picked up again in "I'll come when thou art saddest" (H. 37), which Fannie Ratchford, in her Gondal notes to Hatfield's edition of the poems, describes as showing A.G.A.'s "triumph . . . clouded by loneliness and remorse." But even allowing for the fact that "A.G.A." is Emily too, this curious first-person account of the visitant as ghost is surely an effort to come to terms with these strange occurrences, and with the fact that they are not always pleasant or rewarding; H. 55, again, "It's over now," carries a reference to "the fearful vision."

With maturity Emily Brontë's capacity to fleet away an hour at a time, "with raptured eye / Absorbed in bliss so deep and dear" (H. 92) appears to have extended and become more frequent. H. 102, "Lines by Claudia," in its description of her vision specifically disclaims now any idea of daydreams—"I did not dream," is the declaration of the first line. Emily Brontë further insists as a fact that "the soul is free / To leave its clay a little while"; this type of suspense of animation is later to be described in more detail. But we need to distinguish between this type of vision of a scene, and her real visitant, her soul's partner, "that never comes with day." Also, in these visionary trips to another known place, rather than into the higher consciousness as indicated in the mystical poems, there does not seem to be the wrench of "bitter waking," the terrible return to the chains of the flesh.

Amid all the other wealth of her material, the endless explorations of

Gondal situations, Emily Brontë repeatedly returned to the attempt to catch and set down in poetry the nature and effect of this happening. At times she is emphatic in her assertion of its preeminence, as in the telling fragment of (H. 105):

> What though the stars and fair moonlight
> Are quenched in morning dull and grey?
> They are but tokens of the night,
> And *this*, my soul, is day.

At others she is more hesitant, giving expression to mixed feelings:

> It is too late to call thee now:
> I will not nurse that dream again;
> For every joy that lit my brow
> Would bring its after-storm of pain.
>
> Besides, the mist is half-withdrawn;
> The barren mountain-side lies bare;
> And sunshine and awaking morn
> Paint no more golden visions there.
>
> (H. 135)

Then again, in H. 140, "The Night-Wind," she attempts a version of her visitant in a dialogue with the night wind; there is an interesting hint of pantheism in what he breathes in her ear, that the "myriad voices" of the leaves rustling "instinct with spirit seem." From this it seems that Emily Brontë's visitant was as real as a human being to her, more real perhaps; he is endowed with the capacity for affection—"Have I not loved thee long?"—he bestows kisses, even playing the part of a seducer with "I'll win thee 'gainst thy will." There is a suggestion, too, that his appeal is to Emily Brontë's sensuous emotions, and that she resists his "power to reach [her] mind."

Between May and July of 1841 Emily Brontë seems to have made a sustained effort to pin down her mystical experiences. In H. 147 "Shall earth no more inspire thee?," an outside being addresses the poet as a "lonely dreamer." This visitant appears to reprove the dreamer for permitting useless intellectual questing in an unknown void—"regions dark to thee"—and as the poem progresses we gain renewed intimations of the poet as Pan, seducing the poet-dreamer, "I know my mountain breezes / Enchant and soothe thee still," reminding the poet of past dependency, "I've seen thy spirit bending / In fond idolatry," and demanding a return to the old allegiance, "I know my mighty sway"; finally blandishing, "Return, and dwell with me." It is as if at this stage Emily Brontë is progressing beyond an earlier uncritical rapturous surrender to sensuous natural delights, in the direction of an experience in which her considerable intellect sought to play its part, and that a dominant one.

In the even more interesting H. 148, "Aye, there it is!," Emily Brontë adopts the distancing *persona* of an outside observer. The poet describes the appearance of the effect of the visitant upon the subject; it comes in a "glorious wind," sweeps "the world aside," and kindles "feeling's fires" as vividly as in former times. The narrator continues relentlessly, as if hypnotizing the subject:

> And thou art now a spirit pouring
> Thy presence into all —
> The essence of the Tempest's roaring
> And of the Tempest's fall —

We should notice too the reference to the suspense of animation in the last line — "lost to mortality"—not least for its expression of another fascinating paradox, that of the poet of the "wild will" voicing, however transiently, a desire for a surrender of personal identity.

Is it with the "mystical" group of poems that we should place the tantalizing "My comforter" (H. 168)? The grim couplet "What my soul bore my soul alone / within its self may tell," if nothing else, indicates the iceberg nature of Emily Brontë's poetry—most of the meaning lies beneath the surface of the text. We can at least exclude such poems as H. 170, "A Day Dream," from consideration. Winifred Gérin, in *Emily Brontë* (Oxford, 1971), describes this as an account of a mystical experience. But this overlooks Emily Brontë's own way of referring to her different states. Here she tells us firmly that she sinks into "a reverie," in which she still consciously reflects upon what she sees. Her consciousness of the outside world is reflected in the awkward disclaimer, "Now whether it were really so / I never could be sure," as she introduces a Coleridgean scene of "a thousand thousand glancing fires" which "*seemed* kindling in the air" (my italics). The "little glittering spirits" of this poem are too artfully wrought, too moral, too well-drilled, like a professional choir, to convey the sublime strangeness of a mystical experience—a fact acknowledged by Emily Brontë in the last stanza—this is a "noonday dream," a "fond creation," the product of "fancy," not fervour.

"O thy bright eyes," H. 176, brings us a little nearer to understanding something of this experience which much of the time appears to defy comprehension. Here there is at least some degree of personification of her "God," when she appeals to the "bright eyes" and "sweet tongue" of her visitant to check the frown of Reason. Here, too, Emily Brontë is perhaps at her most explicit as to the nature of her visitant. It is, she seems to imply, an irrational thing (this links with earlier hints of sensuousness and emotional significance). It is a "radiant

angel," "ever-present," though "phantom"; it is "slave," "comrade," and "king."
This last is the operative noun; he is her "God of visions"; *this* is his gift to her.
It is not without its cost—she refers to her "darling pain," and the oxymoron
effectively glances at the painful tensions within her. He also offers escape by
"deadening [her] to real cares." Yet stirrings of orthodoxy cast doubt upon the
validity of her experiences, where instinct alone, faith and hope, support and
sustain her choice. Another paradox presents itself here; Emily Brontë's is a self-
seeking sufficiency—"My own *soul* can grant my prayer"—which, when pursued, leads to a total annihilation of self and selfish preoccupation with "wealth,"
"power," "glory," and "pleasure," all the things of this world.

Inevitably the more intense her visions grew, the duller in comparison lay
the world outside, robbed of its colour by the vividness of the dream world.
H. 184, "Ah! why, because the dazzling sun," shows us Emily Brontë going
more and more into her inner existence, the night life of spirit and thought. The
"glorious eyes" that watch in this poem are pretty clearly those of the stars. But
their power is not only to soothe her into peace—once her spirit is lulled into
serenity they provide too the stimulus for the free association of thought and
feeling which lifts her into the desired but unknown state of unknowing:

> Thought followed thought—star followed star
> Through boundless regions on,
> While one sweet influence, near and far,
> Thrilled through and proved us one.

This state, virtually indescribable because virtually unimaginable by others,
achieved its finest poetic rendering in the famous central section of H. 190, "Julian M. to A. G. Rochelle." This poem catches up and illuminates afresh all the
vital elements of Emily Brontë's mystical experiences as we have noticed them in
earlier references; possibly it was not until this stage that she had sufficiently
refined and clarified her own perception of what was taking place within her. We
see again, evening, wind, and stars; we have the visitant identified as "He," and
for the first time set forth as a "messenger of Hope." He brings "visions," in the
plural, which "rise and change," indicating plainly that for Emily Brontë mystical
possession was not a static state, but one which progressed in itself and also
hinted at further progression towards an even more desirable goal—"kill me with
desire." There is a brief reference to her having passed through an earlier emotional stage, of strong but confused emotion, which was unlike what she now
feels; this supports other suggestions of some sort of emotional apprenticeship
served before the full harmonious spiritual union was realized.

The mystical experience itself is described as occurring in two stages. First
comes the cessation of physical life, and especially the irritability of expectancy.

Paradox again is the natural, indeed perhaps the only, mode of expression here—
"mute music . . unuttered harmony." Then, in one brilliant movement, the inner
self ("essence") leaps to commune with a being which can only be described in
terms of negatives—the Invisible, the Unseen. Yet despite the use of these (to us)
rather chilling abstracts, this being or condition is warm and welcoming to the
poet; note Emily Brontë's use of the two supreme metaphors of safety and reas-
surance in line eighty-three, "home" and "harbour." In agonizing contrast to this
certainty, this poem gives the fullest account of what Emily Brontë elsewhere
refers to simply as her "bitter waking." It is clear that the freedom which she
elsewhere highlights as an essential of her life is more totally hers in this state of
mystical possession than in any other mode of her life. Nothing can make her
lose her faith in this; again we see the flicker of doubting orthodoxy, when she
concedes that her vision may be "robed in fires of Hell, or bright with heavenly
shine"; but she remains insistent upon its (ultimately) divine origin.

In the face of an achievement like that of Emily Brontë, the imagination
staggers, the self-esteem creeps away rebuked. The startling originality of her
experiences combines with her mastery of poetic techniques to dwarf the accom-
plishment of many poets who are yet often higher in the general esteem. It is a
final paradox that one of the most honest of our writers, who emphasized so
strongly, using such passionate and authoritative rhythms because she wanted
above all to make herself plain, has been taken so oddly at times; especially when
the treatment of her as an instinctive, unconscious creature results in a major
critic writing off *Wuthering Heights* as a "sport," as Leavis did. Yet this is the
writer who consistently, and with amazing resources of technical skill, dealt on
our behalf with all the great intolerables of life—pain, loss, and cruelty—who
put her originality to work in the service of clarifying for us all the great unorigi-
nal occurrences of human nature and daily existence.

Emily Brontë, as a poet and as a person, was quite devoid of that winning
flirtatiousness, that capacity to charm and flatter, that gratitude for guidance and
attention which is still felt in some circles, even today, to be a prerequisite of a
literary female. While her true greatness has long been acknowledged, perhaps
we can now pay her the further tribute of an ungrudging, *unsurprised* admiration
of her achievement. We should be able to accept with grace the idea that a young
female could, without faltering, create works whose only fellows in literature are
the Greek tragedies, the Norse sagas, *King Lear.* We must see the beauty of her
artistry and skill, or see her all wrong.

MARGARET HOMANS

Repression and Sublimation
of Nature in Wuthering Heights

It is a critical commonplace that *Wuthering Heights* is informed by the presence of nature: metaphors drawn from nature provide much of the book's descriptive language—as when Cathy describes Heathcliff as "an arid wilderness of furze and whinstone"—and the reader leaves the book with the sensation of having experienced a realistic portrayal of the Yorkshire landscape. There are, however, very few scenes in the novel that are actually set out-of-doors. With a few exceptions, the crucial events take place in one or the other of the two houses. Cathy and Heathcliff, the characters whose relations to nature would seem to be the strongest and the most important to the novel, are never presented on the moors, together or apart, in either of the two major narrative layers. From their formative childhood we have as evidence of their attachment to nature Cathy's diary account of their naughty escapade under the dairy maid's cloak, but she omits any direct description of what they actually did out-of-doors. In contrast to the lack of detail about Cathy and Heathcliff, the character who is most devoted to staying indoors, Linton Heathcliff, is seen in two extensive outdoor scenes during his meetings with the second Cathy. Cathy both talks about and is seen in nature, but her grand excursion to Penistone Crags, her most significant foray into nature, is left to conjecture. All that is shown of the whole adventure is the encounter inside Wuthering Heights after Nelly arrives.

It is difficult to catalog something that is not there, but surely it is peculiar that Brontë did not show us even once what her protagonists were like in their

From *PMLA* 93, no. 1 (January 1978). © 1978 by the Modern Language Association of America. This article has been substantially revised and expanded and comes to different conclusions as "The Name of the Mother in *Wuthering Heights*," chapter 3 of *Bearing the Word: Language and Female Experience in Nineteenth-Century Women's Writing* (The University of Chicago Press, 1986).

element. Heathcliff disappears into a raging storm after hearing Cathy say it
would degrade her to marry him. Why does the author not give us one moment's
observation of Heathcliff struggling against the storm? There is a brief description of Cathy going out to the road in search of him, "where, heedless of my
expostulations, and the growling thunder, and the great drops that began to plash
round her, she remained calling, at intervals, and then listening, and then crying
outright." But Brontë quickly switches the narrative from Cathy to the scene indoors, so that most of the storm is narrated in terms of how it feels and sounds
from inside: the effect of a falling tree limb is measured by the clatter of stones
and soot it knocks into the kitchen fire and by Joseph's moralizing vociferations.
The next time Cathy enters the narrative she has come back indoors, because the
narrative is itself a kind of house, which the characters leave and enter and leave
again. Brontë always seems to bend her vision away from nature.

This avoidance of direct presentation of the natural context is caused in
part by the chosen perspective of Nelly, who cannot be expected to have followed
her characters out into the wilds. She is a "domestic" and her perspective is necessarily housebound. Nelly's indoor perspective would seem to be reinforced by
Lockwood's perspective as an invalid in bed during the first part of the narrative
and by his displeasure with nature throughout, his own single contact with the
elements having been almost lethal. Yet Nelly's narrative has achieved impossi-
bilities elsewhere in the novel, and there is no reason to think that Brontë could
not have maneuvered her narrators into position for natural observation if she
had wished to do so. She must have had a purpose in choosing two such domestic characters for narrators in the first place.

In a novel whose elaborate structure of narrator-within-narrator puts in
doubt the very possibility of talking about a "real" presence of nature or of anything else, it is still necessary to designate a hierarchy of narrative layers according
to their relative degrees of realism. The implausible fiction that Nelly spoke her
highly literate and structured tale to Lockwood and that Lockwood remembered
it and wrote it down verbatim might be evidence for an argument that Brontë is
dismissing the current convention of narrative realism. Yet, in spite of this self-
proclaiming fictiveness, the novel also makes the effort to maintain the most
common attributes of realism: characters that are meant to seem and do seem
quite plausible, a cohesive geographical layout, a plot that obeys the laws of cause
and effect. The present distinction between the reader's impression of a detailed
portrait of Yorkshire life and landscape and the actual absence of such a presentation is itself part of the fine balance Brontë maintains between fictional realism
and overt fictiveness. The layering of the narrative enacts the range of degrees of
fictiveness. The reader is asked to take Lockwood's account of his own actions
and impressions as the most real, since it is the most experiential; Nelly's quoted
story would be the next most real, because Lockwood listens to it; but descending

from these relatively trustworthy accounts is the hearsay evidence of the various interpolated narratives and letters, which are increasingly further from Lockwood's own experience and liable to greater distortion.

If a narrative scheme were to account only for degrees of narrative realism, then the diary fragment in Cathy's handwriting that Lockwood discovers on a blank page of the Reverend Jabes Branderham's "Seventy Times Seven . . ." would be among the most mediated of narrative layers, distanced as it is by time and by having been accidentally read by, and not spoken to, Lockwood. Yet the descending pattern of realism outlined above is qualified by the fact that Lockwood is also the least reliable narrator, understanding the least, while the interpolated narratives, being increasingly closer to the events themselves, are the most reliable. By this token, the diary fragment is also the most authentic, as well as the most distant, of the narrative layers. It circumvents the complexity of narrative layering, leaping out uncannily to the reader's attention, in spite of the fact that the writer is long dead and her writing is contained between dusty covers. It has the same intrusive effect on the reader that the ghostly Catherine of Lockwood's dream has: it breaks the rules of the narrative scheme just as a ghost breaks the laws of nature. Within the fictive frame of the novel, that is, momentarily allowing the assumption that the events and conversations did take place and that there is somewhere a core of truth from which Lockwood's and Nelly's reports probably swerve, the diary fragment is the only unmediated record of the veritable voice and attitudes of one of the central characters. Isabella's letter to Nelly is another "proof" document, but she is not a central character and her letter is interesting more because it supplies part of the story that Nelly could not have witnessed herself than because it is a sample of a precious voice. The content of the diary fragment is not really important from the point of view of plot, since Nelly later narrates similar episodes from her own recollections. For the rest of the story, the reader must maintain a constant skepticism about the alterations Nelly must have made in the remembered speeches of her characters and also about the alterations Lockwood may have made in his transmission of Nelly's report and in his own remembrances of conversations he himself heard. Written down, and therefore less likely to have been tampered with by Lockwood, Cathy's little testimony of woe rings true, as the closest thing to hearing her speak for herself (although it is admittedly a little disturbing to hear a supposed eleven-year-old use words like "sobriety" and "asseverated"). It is also in the diary fragment that Cathy is introduced in the novel, before the reader meets her in Nelly's narrative, so it touches the reader with a special force of priority.

The fragment serves as an opening statement of the relation between nature and writing in the novel. It is justifiable to take it paradigmatically because it is a diary, as the whole form of the novel is a diary, and, as a written text within a text, it draws attention to itself as writing, in a way that Nelly's spoken story, for example, does not. Like Lockwood's own diary, in which Nelly brings her narrative up to the present time of Lockwood's visit, Cathy starts in the past and writes up to the present time of her writing. But more important than the continuity in time is the significant break in her narrative. After she is caught up to the present she and Heathcliff go for their "scamper on the moors" under the dairy woman's cloak, but this she does not describe. Lockwood leaves a space in his account and then says, "I suppose Catherine fulfilled her project, for the next sentence took up another subject." The adventure takes place in the lacuna. A synecdoche for the narrative as a whole, this little story, like the rest, averts its eyes from nature. Cathy writes nothing about the scamper itself, narrating only what happens indoors, before and after: her anticipation of the event and then, after the gap, her sorrowful reaction to the punishment they receive as a result. The scamper is clearly the preferred alternative to writing: "I have got the time on with writing for twenty minutes; but my companion is impatient and proposes that we should appropriate the dairy woman's cloak, and have a scamper on the moors, under its shelter. A pleasant suggestion." Writing is broken off in favor of action. Further, when Cathy returns to her writing, that action suffices in itself and cannot be improved on by writing it down. Writing is no more than a solace, reserved for hours of boredom, or of loneliness, or of sorrow. Cathy does not write about the scamper itself because writing is stimulated for her only by need, and she needs nothing when she is on the moors. Writing and events in nature are, to the young Cathy, incompatible.

Cathy's omission of any description of the romp on the moors is perfectly in keeping with the pattern of Brontë's own omissions, and, further, it suggests a reason for those omissions. Writing creates an order of priority. Ordinarily, a word presents itself as coming first to the reader, putting its referent in second place. The only way to preserve the priority of something is not to have it named, so that what is primary is just that which is left out of the text, and surely these omissions of descriptions of events in nature are significant holes. Everything else about the diary fragment suggests that nature is primary and that writing is intended to be made secondary. For example, as Lockwood is leafing through the book, Cathy's writing seems at first to be commentary on the printed text, filling out the margins, adding to a text already complete. The caricature of Joseph that precedes the written diary, "rudely yet powerfully sketched," suggests an alternative mode of expression for Cathy's exasperated sense of injustice, indicating in a different way that writing is not primary. She begins writing only because she is caught indoors by the rain and by the fierce sabbath discipline of Hindley and Joseph and must fill up the dreary time because there is nothing else to do. The omission of nature is consistent with this emphasis that nature is primary or original relative to a text, and all the rest of Brontë's omissions make this point too. Both Brontë and her Cathy avoid description of nature or of events in nature because there is no way to name nature without making it secondary. Primary nature neither needs to be nor can be referred to.

The reader becomes accustomed to Brontë's habitual use of the image of the house, with its windows and doors variously locked or open, as a figure for varying psychic conditions—from the locked door that Lockwood encounters on his second visit to Wuthering Heights, where Cathy, Hareton, and Heathcliff are all prisoners of some kind, to the open doors and lattices he finds on his last visit, after the barriers of hatred have broken down between the remaining protagonists. To review this pattern quickly, the closed house generally represents some sort of entrapment: the body as a trap for the soul, as when the window of Heathcliff's room swinging open and letting the rain in signals his death or the flying out of his soul; the entrapment of one character by the will of another, as when Heathcliff locks Nelly and Cathy inside in order to force the marriage with Linton; or the trap of society or convention, as when Cathy remains inside Thrushcross Grange while Heathcliff, expelled, watches from the outside and longs to shatter the great pane of glass that separates them. In view of this symbolic system, the preponderance of scenes taking place indoors and the absence or omission of directly represented natural landscape indicate that the condition of the narrative as a whole is some kind of entrapment too; the author herself feels her creative possibilities limited by an inadequacy in the house of language.

It is important to stress here that Brontë finds language inadequate only for representing nature or events in nature. The diary fragment omits nature, but its portrayal of emotional life, once it has gone indoors, is sophisticated; Cathy's ability to re-create the dramatic scene in the house is just as remarkable as her omission of the scene outdoors. In other regards besides that of representing nature, Brontë's confidence in her rhetorical power is manifest. Most first readers feel that her portrayals of the size and subtlety of the passions exceed all expectation; one senses no limitation there besides that of life itself. She is not disturbed, as writers are today, by the inherent fictiveness of all language. For example, Nelly's first-person narration casts no shadow over the events she narrates; that Brontë dares to give her narrators such specific characters and yet expects her readers to form their own interpretations freely manifests considerable confidence in the objectivity or transparency of language. The limitations of language in regard to nature, while central to the novel, is brought into relief by the lack of limitation in other regards.

Nature is absent from literal presentation, but it is present in figurative language. All language is figurative, as most critics now see it, but there are degrees of figuration just as there are degrees of narrative realism resulting from the layering of the narrative. It must be possible to use the term "figurative language" for that which is overtly figurative, as opposed to "literal language," which is only relatively literal, less self-consciously figurative than what is properly called figuration. The idea of nature would have to undergo a radical change in the transition from a posited (but absent) literal sense to a figurative use. There is no literal use of nature because, strictly speaking, to write of it at all is to deny its literalness or primariness, but there is rarely even any relatively literal use of nature, that is, any description of nature for its own sake, without reference to anything outside the immediate scene. The respect for nature's primacy, which this abstention from description implies, is completely bypassed when nature is used for figurative purposes. Nature as a figure becomes subservient to whatever it is used to describe, dropping from the primacy of the unnamed to what might be described as a tertiary status, since it is named not for its own sake but for the sake of something else. This could be called nature as adjective or pronoun, where the place of the noun in such a syntactic model is occupied by the characters who are generally the objects of such figurative descriptions.

To use nature as a figure is to make nature secondary to what it describes, and to describe someone by means of figures—or with language at all—is to impose a limitation of perspectivism or metaphor that reduces whatever is primal in that character. When Heathcliff is "like a savage beast getting goaded to death with knives and spears," both man and beast are brought together into a region of compromise, which impinges on the primacy of each. Heathcliff's agony would seem to be unspeakable, indescribable, so that to reduce that experience to speech is, in some slight way, to diminish its grandeur. The indefinite is sublime; the finite, that which can be figured, is not. Every time the reader's vision of Heathcliff is made definite by a specific comparison, Heathcliff becomes more human and less demonic, even, curiously, when he is compared to a demon. The passages that serve instead to expand the reader's sense of him are those in which the narrator says that some event has been evaded or omitted by the narrative, when a space of absence is opened up, such as his mysterious three-year sojourn or his nighttime wanderings just before his death. Those numinous absences usually take place in unseen nature, just where we have located nature's primacy as well, and have the same status of being primary or original that unseen nature has. There are, then, two radically separate versions of nature in the novel: the primal or literal, which is unseen or evaded, and the figurative, which thrives on the textual surface of the novel.

A characteristic figurative use of nature, often cited as evidence for the presence of "real" nature in the novel, is the device of employing a natural object as a metaphor for character, almost with the force of a metonymy or a symbol, in that frequently the natural object substitutes syntactically for the person described. These are among the most memorable passages in the book not because they introduce "real" nature but because they confirm the reader's sense that the novel is organized by the two opposing principles embodied in the two houses, Wuthering Heights and Thrushcross Grange; they aid the systematization of reading. A brief survey will show that these passages almost always involve a polarity between two extremes, which are implicitly unspeakable unless reduced to a system by natural figures. By taking part in this reductive action nature is similarly reduced: both nature and character serve the ends of comprehensibility. Of Cathy's choice between Linton and Heathcliff Nelly says, "The contrast resembled what you see in exchanging a bleak, hilly, coal country for a beautiful fertile valley." Quickly following this is the related complex of Cathy's own sets of metaphors for her two lovers:

> "Whatever our souls are made of, his and mine are the same, and Linton's is as different as a moonbeam from lightning, or frost from fire."

> "My love for Linton is like the foliage in the woods. Time will change it, I'm well aware, as winter changes the trees. My love for Heathcliff resembles the eternal rocks beneath—a source of little visible delight, but necessary."

Then there is Nelly's description of the relation between Cathy and her new family: "It was not the thorn bending to the honeysuckles, but the honeysuckles embracing the thorn." Culminating the sequence is Cathy's description of Heathcliff's bestiality, though notice that it too hinges on a balancing natural description of Isabella's fragility:

> "Tell her what Heathcliff is—an unreclaimed creature, without refinement, without cultivation; an arid wilderness of furze and whinstone. I'd as soon put that little canary into the park on a winter's day as recommend you to bestow your heart on him! . . . He's not a rough diamond—a pearl-containing oyster of a rustic; he's a fierce, pitiless, wolfish man. . . . He'd crush you, like a sparrow's egg, Isabella, if he found you a troublesome charge."

The disparity between the characteristics of Wuthering Heights and those of the Grange is neatly formulated in opposable natural terms, and those natural symbols center in the part of the book most involved with the tension between the two worlds. Predictably, this kind of description occurs once again and last in a passage about Hareton, in whom the alternatives of the two houses are programmatically combined: "Good things lost amid a wilderness of weeds, to be sure, whose rankness far over-topped their neglected growth; yet notwithstanding, evidence of a wealthy soil that might yield luxuriant crops, under other and favorable circumstances." Heathcliff's furze and Linton's fertile valley combine schematically in the second generation.

These figurative uses of nature, which have always seemed to most readers to bring "real" or unorganized nature into the book, actually provide a vehicle for abstract order. This strategy brings the extremes into an arena of discussion and makes possible relations that might otherwise seem unthinkable. For example, Isabella's attraction to Heathcliff seems extraneous, as "fantastic" to us as it is to Linton, until Cathy's natural metaphors align the axis of their relationship by giving it a basis in the natural law of predator and prey and make it all too logical and comprehensible. Comparisons that intend differentiation actually subvert differentiation, serving to bring two characters closer by furnishing the necessary common ground. Similarly, Cathy means to use rock and foliage, frost and fire, to show herself and Nelly why she believes that her two loves will not impinge on each other (they fulfill two different needs as they exist in two different natural realms); yet by bringing them into such a comparison she also lets the reader, if not herself, discover why such a separation of interests will certainly fail. The natural metaphor is a basis for an interaction that she misunderstands. Any kind of figure would serve as well to bring the unspeakable into the realm of the speakable, but only nature as a source of figures is big enough to act as so effective a ground of mediation.

If natural figures work as a ground for comparisons or alignments that might otherwise not be made at all, it is implied that there must be some ground or point of reference beneath these figures, some generalized sense of "nature" that unifies the individual instances. The impression that the novel gives of depicting the rough Yorkshire landscape and climate is not a wrong one and must come from some source in the novel. This assumed reference might be the same primary nature that is omitted from the diary fragment as from the rest of the narrative, but, if that nature resists naming, it would certainly be separate from any schematization taking place at the textual level. Primal nature remains submerged. Natural figures are instead grounded in another verbal version of nature, symbolic landscapes that are only slightly less figurative than the organizing figures discussed above, in that they appear to be closer to "real" nature and less subservient to the foreground of character. These are landscapes that are described as though they were or could be literally visible but that are as descriptive of the human situation as the more explicit figures are. There remains a gulf between unwritten and written nature.

In the scene just before Heathcliff's return after his long absence, the landscape between the Grange and the Heights hovers on the edge between literal and symbolic description, between degrees of figurativeness. Cathy and Edgar are gazing out at twilight, and, to Nelly, "both the room, and its occupants, and the scene they gazed on looked wondrously peaceful." Yet the action of looking out from inside, which is peaceful, clearly predicts the event to come, almost as though the characters were waiting in expectation. The main feature of the landscape is the "long line of mist," which describes the axis of the two houses but does not quite connect them. The line of mist is on the verge of symbolizing the reconnection of the two houses about to take place, but not quite, because, although the hills called Wuthering Heights rise above the vapor, the house that takes its name from them "was invisible—it rather drops down on the other side." It is a beautiful passage, but it is almost occluded by the requirements of symbolization. The passage intends a vision of repose before the onslaught of Heathcliff's arrival, yet nature is never reposeful because it is always talking, radiating significance. Cathy and Edgar think they are looking out at the unconscious beauty of nature, but they inhabit a text, and the reader knows that they are in the presence of a veritable book of instruction.

This pattern of symbolic landscape continues throughout the novel, and there is a gradual passage from equivocal to unequivocal symbolization. In a passage about nature's obliviousness to Heathcliff's grief over Cathy's death, a symbol for tears lurks in the image of "the dew that had gathered on the budded branches, and fell pattering round him." Four pages later, only hours after Cathy's burial, the spring weather turns to winter and we are back in a fully symbolic landscape. It is no coincidence that the second Cathy's "coming of age," the dreary walk she takes at about the time of her seventeenth birthday when she confronts both her father's coming death and her knowledge of Heathcliff's true evil, is the setting for her discovery of symbolism in a landscape. Thinking of the omission in the other Cathy's diary, one might say that childhood is a time when nature is perceived as itself, with no effort to transform it into a text or to give it any extranatural significance, while adulthood is partly an initiation into symbol making. Nelly points out a last bluebell remaining from summer, under the roots of a tree where Cathy used to climb and sing, "happier than words can express," and suggests that she "clamber up, and pluck it to show papa." Cathy stares at it a long time, then gives it a meaning, as grown-ups would: "No, I'll not touch it—but it looks melancholy, does it not, Ellen?" A little later Cathy and Linton disagree about their ideas of a natural heaven, more or less realizing that nature has become a symbol for character. Toward the end, when Heathcliff's approaching death dominates the narrative, the tendency to render the landscape symbolic is epitomized in his vision of Cathy's spirit in the landscape. He does considerably more than take the landscape as a representation of Cathy, because the landscape is literally replaced by her image: "I cannot look down to this floor, but her features are shaped in the flags! In every cloud, in every tree—filling the air at night, and caught by glimpses in every object, by day I am surrounded with her image!" Days before his death, walking through the house with his eyes focused on a spot a few feet in front of him, Heathcliff seems really to see her ghost and we are asked to believe in a projection, which undoes any remnant sense that the landscape might have qualities of its own. The boy who sees the two ghosts "under t' Nab" after Heathcliff's death verifies the fact that this landscape is saturated not just with the presence of an authorial consciousness but with the human "spirit" as well.

Heathcliff's vision of the world-as-Cathy and the suggestion of ghosts in the landscape are a climax of the tendency toward rendering the landscape symbolic, and they also suggest a further reason for the omissions of scenes of literal or primal nature. We have seen earlier that Brontë does not consider language to be adequate to the task of representing nature, and such representation is neither possible nor desired, but primal nature is textually shunned for another reason as well. The use of nature as a figure and the rendering of highly and increasingly symbolic landscape suggests an active flight away from attempting a (relatively) nonfigurative representation of nature. Why should there be so pronounced a turn? The first encounter with nature in the book is also the closest textual approach to literal nature that Brontë presents. The snowstorm of chapter 3, wholly adversary, all but obliterates both the path back to Thrushcross Grange and Lockwood's health. The path was previously marked by stones daubed with lime, but the storm has covered the ground so deeply that, "excepting a dirty dot pointing up, here and there, all traces of their existence had vanished." Nature is combating the human attempt to make nature legible, and the scarcity of those "dirty dots" causes Lockwood to founder in his reading of nature. After this episode, the narrative veers away from such direct contacts with nature, as if the narrative, which constantly imposes a reading on nature, would suffer as much as Lockwood does. Literal or primary nature, entering the region of consciousness or textuality, is death-dealing. Avoiding literal nature in the novel, Brontë offers instead a tertiary version of nature, which has, in contrast, the life-sustaining qualities of all figuration: figures mark a helpful path around or over rather than through nature, avoiding the dangers of snowstorms. She compares Heathcliff to a wilderness of furze in order not to show him in an actual wilderness, which would be difficult and painful to describe. Figuration lifts her from the ground.

Freud describes repression as a defense mechanism that is turned against instincts, primarily sexual ones. To gratify these instincts would bring immediate pleasure, but it would ultimately bring an even greater degree of unpleasure, because it would call up fresh causes for repression. Literary critics interpret repression to mean an action performed not on sexual instincts but on analogous threats to psychic pleasure or psychic life. In *Poetry and Repression* Harold Bloom tells us that poets must repress their awareness of their debt to literary precursors in order to keep on writing. To over-simplify vastly Bloom's complex argument, this repression occurs because, although capitulation to the greatness of the precursor would solve the immediate painful conflict, it also would bring about the greater displeasure of writing weak poetry or no poetry at all. Jacques Derrida in his article "Freud and the Scene of Writing" gives repression a similarly privileged role in making writing possible. Repression partially breaks the contact between the unconscious or memory and the conscious or perception, so that memory does not block the acquisition of new perceptions, and writing is then the relation, the single point of contact between memory and perception. It is not necessary to go so far as to point to the displacement into nature of either Brontë's libido or her precursors as the cause of her repression of nature. The common characteristic of that which is said to be repressed, whether it be instinct, precursors, or memory, is that it carries the force of literal meaning and thus has primacy, because figuration is a deviation from the literal and is therefore secondary. Instinct, precursors, and memory are involuntary residents of consciousness: that is, if they are part of psychic content it is not because the psyche wills it so. They hinder psychic health, or creativity as a literary form of psychic health, by putting everything that is a product of the will into a secondary position, the position of having deviated from an original. They dominate the claim to primacy. In the case of Brontë, literal nature has the effect of blocking creativity by making her feel that anything she writes about it will be secondary. I am not attempting here to psychoanalyze the biographical Emily Brontë; I am referring to the psyche that is available to the reader, Brontë as she presents herself in the text, intentionally or not. If actual people repress threatening drives by abstaining from those activities, or repress dangerous memories by forgetting them, then the corresponding act of repression for the literary psyche would be to keep the dangerous element out of the text, which is that psyche's version of consciousness. Brontë must repress literal nature by not naming it directly, in order to write.

In Freud, "successful" repression, repression that succeeds in driving the threatening force underground forever, is not as desirable as certain kinds of unsuccessful repression, if the repressed material returns in a different and unthreatening form. This is one of Freud's definitions of sublimation, and that is what Brontë's conversion of literal nature into figuration accomplishes: repressed material returns in a form useful to her, radiantly creative because it has been tamed, made tertiary, deprived of its threatening independence of meaning and subservient to imposed meaning. The energy cathected to one has been transferred to the other. This is why there is an absolute difference between primal nature, whose lurking presence is only implied, and figurative nature, which appears so abundantly: when the repressed material returns, it must be cleared of original or literal meaning. (Sublimation is distinct from reaction-formation, which is the substitution of something harmless for something too potent. Here, sublimation offers an altered version of the same, not a substitution.)

In *The Problem of Anxiety* and *Three Essays on the Theory of Sexuality* Freud proposes a model for sublimation, which may describe the process as it functions in *Wuthering Heights*. An activity that is not inherently erotic can become eroticized and, once it has taken on the force of a sexual drive, the individual will then abstain from it just as if it were actually dangerous. This takes place because of excessive eroticization of the part of the body that performs the activity. Freud's image for this process is the path: a path is broken in the psyche, allowing too great contact between sex and the fingers or writing or between sex and the feet or walking. If the process is one of pathbreaking, then it should be possible to reverse the direction of the path or to travel psychically in the opposite direction, away from rather than toward eroticization. To take this path backward, to desexualize a function in order that it cease to require repression, is to sublimate. On the basis of this model, it could be said that there is a psychic path in Brontë between nature and some primal force, not necessarily sexual, which could be called her sense of the literal, or whatever it is that threatens to preempt her power to write or to imagine. Fearing that it is nature that threatens creativity, she abstains from bringing nature into her novel as an unmediated presence. In Cathy's diary fragment, an experience in nature does not need to be written about, but the reader also suspects it could not be written about. Perhaps Brontë's fear is that, if she were to attempt to write nature directly into her book, the attempt would produce silence, because reality can never enter a text without mediation. Her figurative uses of nature suggest that the path can be and is reversed. Instead of associating nature with the force of the literal, she associates it with that which is purely nonliteral, her invented characters. Nature is deprived of its primacy, or de-eroticized on the Freudian model; yet the sublimation into figure making cannot have redirected all the energy attached to the repressed material—or the path is at best a two-way street—because she still cannot write a scene in nature that does not testify to constant vigilance, and the lacunae show that repression is still at work. In some of the symbolic landscapes we have seen how she verges on affording the image some degree of independence from her characters, but her inability to sustain this for long is the trace of a repression not wholly cured or emptied out.

It is important to point out that she is repressing, not nature, but what nature has come to represent or to be associated with; nature is a vehicle for something else. In one paper on repression Freud makes a distinction between the instinct and its "ideational representative." The repressed itself cannot be named because as such it never enters consciousness at all. Nature does enter consciousness, or the present time of the narrative (in the form of Lockwood's fearful snowstorm), and is then driven out again, to be sublimated later. We must take the nature that is absent from *Wuthering Heights* as the ideational representative of something inherently unnamable, perhaps what we call reality, perhaps something else. What Freud is saying is that a process like sublimation, the process of finding a name for the feared thing, takes place even before repression proper can begin. Repression appears to be directed at the nature that is omitted in Brontë's lacunae, but there is an even more threatening force behind that nature, for which nature is only the representative.

When Cathy is sick with her fatal "madness" she speaks the only direct or scenic presentation in the novel of any part of her and Heathcliff's childhood on the moors. Pulling the feathers out of her pillow, she finds a lapwing's, which looses a flood of memory:

> "Bonny bird; wheeling over our heads in the middle of the moor. It wanted to get to its nest, for the clouds touched the swells, and it felt rain coming. This feather was picked up from the heath, the bird was not shot—we saw its nest in winter, full of little skeletons. Heathcliff set a trap over it, and the old ones dare not come. I made him promise he'd never shoot a lapwing, after that, and he didn't."

The description is made possible by her derangement. Such direct narration of an episode in nature, which amounts to reliving it, is not possible in a healthy state. Even if it were possible, the repression and sublimation of nature in the rest of the novel suggest that such a description could bring on madness. It is the return of repressed material not sublimated into figures but whole, direct, and all at once. It is as though, on the "path" model of the eroticization and subsequent sublimation, or desexualization, of a function, Cathy were dying of her inability to reverse the path. Only nature has become not eroticized (though that may be part of it, in that, in her love for Heathcliff and in her association of Heathcliff with nature, she may have transferred erotic longings to nature), nor is it the ideational representative of what Brontë herself is repressing. For Cathy, nature is dangerous because it is so totally identified with Heathcliff. When she returns from her first visit to Thrushcross Grange, her initial reaction of repulsion toward Heathcliff comes from his dirt and his wildness, in other words, from his life as a savage in nature. She has learned, as part of the civilizing influence of the Lintons, that dirt is bad and that therefore her own savage past was bad and that therefore any relic of that past, such as Heathcliff's perennially dirty person, is to be avoided. Nature, Heathcliff, and her former delight in nature are all rejected at once, as a complex of associated repressions. Later, when Heathcliff has come to be the most threatening of those repressed functions, the other two, nature and her memories of the past, are repressed all the more forcefully for their continued association with Heathcliff. The association becomes a representation. During Heathcliff's absence and her marriage to Linton she successfully repressed her love for Heathcliff, but, when Heathcliff returns, the personification of a repressed instinct bursting through the barriers of her repression, the psychic health of her tranquil life with Linton is destroyed by a resumption of the unresolvable mental strife between her conflicting loves, or rather, more specifically, by the need for a fresh effort of repression. Heathcliff, the past, and nature were repressed together. The return of one brings with it the return of the associated repressions, and the flooding return of the story of the lapwing is evidence that all those barriers have collapsed. During her illness her chief desires are to be outside on the moors and to return to her childhood, without much specific reference to a longing for Heathcliff himself. Those repressed desires might come back harmlessly if they were not still tied to her desire for Heathcliff, if she could reverse the path and undo their association with Heathcliff. But every memory of the past, specifically the lapwing story, undoes her efforts to regain psychic health.

Looking closer at the lapwing story, the reader finds a particular reason for the anxiety caused by memories such as this one that tie nature and Heathcliff together. There is something suspect about the absence of Heathcliff from her other memories. She fantasizes that she is back at Wuthering Heights, in her own room, and her constant refrain is the wish to be outside on the moors and to be her former self, but the strength-giving recollections that provoke such desires do not seem to include Heathcliff:

> "Oh if I were but in my own bed in the old house!" she went on bitterly, wringing her hands. "And that wind sounding in the firs by the lattice. Do let me feel it—it comes straight down the moor. . . . I wish I were out of doors—I wish I were a girl again, half savage and hardy, and free. . . . I'm sure I should be myself were I once among the heather on those hills."

Waking from her first fit of unconsciousness, she finds she had forgotten (or repressed) all of her life since the last occasion of being at one with Heathcliff, just before their last expedition to spy in the windows at the Grange, the history of her defection from Heathcliff. Her remembrance of the separation ordered at that time between her and Heathcliff is extremely painful, but the recollected tears are nothing compared to the agony of the fruits of her own willing separation, when memory comes rushing back: "My late anguish was swallowed in a paroxysm of despair." She is portraying to herself a memory of childhood that now seems relatively idyllic, because its only sorrowful moments came from an external and readily detestable agent. Regression to childhood is her escape from, and refutation of, a difficult adult present that is of her own making. Yet the story about the lapwing feather belies the idealization of her childhood of which Cathy would convince herself. She scans her real memories of childhood and finds a vision that is neither innocent nor curative, but nightmarish. The illogical order of the events in her account shows her mind moving nervously, too quickly, over memory. She should tell about the trap before she tells about the "little skeletons," for example. The setting is the onset of a storm. The episode reveals acutely what the reader suspected but never could verify from previous episodes: that Heathcliff was as sadistic in his relatively happy childhood as he is as an adult. Further, the motif of abandoned infants is a recurrent one. Heathcliff himself was left to starve by his own parents, and, orphaned again by Mr. Earnshaw's death, he was subject to the cruelty of another parent figure. In addition to being cruel, Heathcliff is already a symbol maker, old beyond his years, imposing the horrors of his own experience on a helpless world of things. The picture of the children's experience of nature is hardly as innocent as Cathy might have led herself and the reader to believe, during her outbursts of longing for the past.

The story is also not about Heathcliff alone. The most curious fact about it is Cathy's half-willing complicity in its events. She finds her reward for the painful memory in the recollection of Heathcliff's sweet obedience to her request not to shoot any more lapwings and takes it as evidence of a harmonious childhood. However, her interdict on shooting extends only to lapwings, and, by distinguishing shooting as the form of killing of which she disapproves, she half admits an attraction to the far more perverse technique that Heathcliff did use. Where spots of blood as evidence of shooting would upset her, the trap placed over the nest causes her no special distress; and there is clearly a macabre fascination in the tone of "full of little skeletons," a mixture of attraction and repulsion. After all, if her reaction had been one of complete distaste, she would have made him promise never to kill any birds, or any animals, using whatever weapon. But she does not. The memory, almost blurted out, testifies to why she is really so afraid, to the point of madness. Real memories such as that one, memories that balance Heathcliff's sweet submission with his diabolical cruelty and implicate her in a similar way, preempt her reconstructed memories, which are as secondary as any figure or other deviation from literal truth. Any effort to recreate a nicer childhood and so attain some degree of psychic health for the present is ruined by such influxes of the literal.

It is not Brontë's but her fictional character's repressions that have so disastrously returned. Nature and her memory of the past are Cathy's ideational representatives for Heathcliff, or for that in her which "is" Heathcliff, and that repression is distinct from Brontë's repression. Nevertheless, Cathy's experience must be analogous to Brontë's own. The lapwing story is just such a narrative as we might have expected to find in the part of the book about Cathy and Heathcliff's childhood, and its late appearance, out of sequence, suggests that it functions for Brontë as a return of her own narrative omissions, a return of her own repressed. It is, of course, impossible to know whether Brontë consciously determined this pattern or whether it is truly a welling up of unconscious elements; in either case, the reader's experience is the same. The analogy between Cathy and her creator may help to designate what it is about literal nature that Brontë finds necessary (intentionally or not) to repress. Cathy represses nature as a representative of that in her which "is" Heathcliff, because, like anything that claims primacy in the psyche, it blocks her efforts to reimagine the past. This aspect of the analogy only confirms what the reader already knows about Brontë's avoidance of the literal in order not to let her own writing appear secondary. In this she is successful, because, even though nature is presented almost exclusively in overt figures, those figures give the reader the impression of a much more literal depiction of nature.

Cathy also represses the Heathcliff-nature complex because of the content of that primal memory, as well as because of its effect of primacy. The memory is cruel to her because it is a memory of cruelty, Heathcliff's and her own. The lapwing story shows that love and violence, love and death are identified in him and in the medium of their relationship; it gives her to herself suicidally. Nature, or the literal as it is represented by nature, appears to provoke a similar attitude in Brontë, whether that attitude becomes part of a conscious strategy of writing or remains unconscious. Not only is nature's literality destructive to creative energy, but nature is also literally destructive. Lockwood's snowstorm erases nature's readability, but, beyond that, nearly kills that reader, Lockwood, himself. To try to name literal nature in the novel after that, aside from the technical difficulty of doing so, would make it necessary to inflict harm on her characters in addition to the harm they do to each other. Nature, or "reality," just like Heathcliff in Cathy's memory, cuts off relations between parents and children, between those who love one another, and causes distress, starvation, and death. Nature's truth is death, and only when reimagined does it approach neutrality or beneficence.

The lapwing story, paired with the fragment of Cathy's diary, also presents an alternative paradigm for the relation between nature and writing. The diary omits an episode in nature, for the sake of not distorting nature, and the primary experience of nature, with inadequate language, while Cathy's madness produces a story that distorts her psychic health. The two stories are paradigms for narrative options or poles at the extremes of a narrative axis: blank spaces at one end and confused, fevered talk at the other. That Brontë creates a large figure for her own repressed condition, as well as making constructive figurative language out of the repressed material itself, shows that figuration is her best outlet for repression. But the difference between herself and Cathy, the eccentricity in the analogy, gives her even more than does the initial similarity. If the analogy to the diary fragment were carried out fully, then, in addition to drawing inferences from what Cathy leaves out, we would be obliged to take as a paradigm what Cathy does write about and to suggest that Brontë, too, writes as a solace for moments of solitude or sorrow. That would produce a reductive theory of therapeutic writing, which is certainly not applicable to so powerful a novelist. Similarly, the analogy drawn from the lapwing story would lead to a theory of passive or stream-of-consciousness writing or to a theory identifying fiction with dreams. Brontë can reverse the psychic path and avoid the extremes of Cathy's condition, and the diary and the lapwing story are there to admonish and to mark outer limits, rather than to provide exactly tailored paradigms. Making the figures is only part of the process of recovery; surpassing them is even better. To be tied down to a figure would only be to instigate a new cause for repression.

SANDRA M. GILBERT
AND SUSAN GUBAR

The Genesis of Hunger
According to Shirley

I was, being human, born alone;
I am, being woman, hard beset;
I live by squeezing from a stone
The little nourishment I get.
——ELINOR WYLIE

There is nothing to be said against Charlotte's frenzied efforts to counter
the nihilism of her surroundings, unless one is among those who would
find amusement in the sight of the starving fighting for food.
——REBECCA WEST

In times of the most extreme symbols
The walls are very thin,
Almost transparent.
Space is accordion pleated;
Distance changes.
But also, the gut becomes one dimensional
And we starve.
——RUTH STONE

Where *Jane Eyre* has an Angrian intensity that compelled even the most hostile
of its early readers to recognize its story as radical and in some sense "mythic,"
Charlotte Brontë seems, with *Shirley* (1849), to have retreated to the heavier disguises and more intricate evasions of *The Professor*. But while in that first novel
she strove for realism by literally attempting to impersonate a man—and an aus-
tere, censorious man at that—in *Shirley*, as if reacting against the flames of rage

From *The Madwoman in the Attic: The Woman Writer and the Nineteenth-Century
Literary Imagination* by Sandra M. Gilbert and Susan Gubar. © 1979 by Yale University. Yale University Press, 1979.

released in *Jane Eyre*, she seems at first glance to be trying for objectivity, balance, restraint, by writing a novel of private, lonely struggle in an historical setting with public references which seem to dictate that her central characters will lose potency and withdraw rather than advance as the story unfolds.

Brontë herself was ambivalent about her use of this narrative strategy, and astute contemporary readers—G. H. Lewes for one—seem to have perceived her discomfort. "There is no passionate link [in *Shirley*]," Lewes wrote, "nor is there any artistic fusion, or undergrowth by which one part evolves itself from another." While it is true that *Shirley* fails to develop organically, this is at least partially because, in trying to create the calm objectivity she associated specifically with the magisterial omniscience of a "Titan" like Thackeray, Brontë becomes enmeshed in essentially the same male-dominated structures that imprison the characters in all her books. Certainly, in trying to deal historically with a caste denied any public existence, Brontë is committed to exploring the distance between historical change and the seemingly unrelated, lonely struggles of her heroines. When this generic incongruity results in a loss of artistic fusion, as Lewes complained, we can see from our vantage point that the pain of female confinement is not merely her subject in *Shirley*; it is a measure or aspect of her artistry.

Significantly, the novel begins with a distinctively male scene, the sort of scene Jane Austen, for instance, notoriously refused to write. Three clergymen are at a table: complaining that the roast beef is tough and the beer flat, they nevertheless swallow enormous quantities of both, calling for "More bread!" and ordering their landlady to "Cut it, woman." They also consume all her vegetables, cheese, and spice cake. The voracious curates are not, as many of Brontë's critics have claimed, merely a bit of local color, or an irrelevant digression. With them commences a novel very much about the expensive delicacies of the rich, the eccentric cookery of foreigners, the food riots in manufacturing towns, the abundant provisions due soldiers, the scanty dinner baskets of child laborers, and the starvation of the unemployed. Indeed, the hunger of the exploited links them to all those excluded from an independent and successful life in English society: one of the workers lucidly explains that "starving folk cannot be satisfied or settled folk" (chap. 18). And since, as in *Jane Eyre*, hunger is inextricably linked to rebellion and rage, it is hardly surprising that contemporary reviewers discovered in *Shirley* the female identity of Currer Bell. For, despite its omniscient and pseudo-masculine point of view, Charlotte Brontë's third book is far more consciously than either of her earlier works a novel about the "woman question." Set during the wartime crisis in England's depressed mercantile economy of 1811–12, the novel describes how the wrath of the workers does the work of destruction for all those exploited, most especially (as our epigraphs imply) for those women famished for a sense of purpose in their lives.

Describing the same hunger that troubles the dispossessed characters of Jane Austen, Mary Shelley, and Emily Brontë, Charlotte Brontë also implies that women are as famished for food as they are for sustaining fictions of their own devising. Therefore, when introducing the "unromantic" scene of the greedy curates at the beginning of the novel, the narrator explains that "the first dish set upon the table should be one that a good Catholic—ay, even an Anglo-Catholic —might eat on Good Friday in Passion Week: it shall be unleavened bread with bitter herbs, and no roast lamb" (chap. 1). Of course, from Fielding to Barth, novelists have set their fictional repasts before readers whose palates they have tried to tantalize and satiate, but in *Shirley* Brontë begins with so unappetizing a first course because she wants to consider why the curates' feast initiates her heroines' fasts. Indeed, in *Shirley* Brontë portrays not only how the hunger of women is, in the words of Dickinson, "a way / Of Persons outside Windows—," but also why "The Entering—takes away—" desire, since the foods and fictions that sustain men are precisely those that have contributed to the sickening of women. The word these "Apostolic" curates furnish is one reason why women are famished, or so Brontë seems to imply in this feminist critique of the Biblical myth of the garden.

We have already seen how Shirley's attack on Milton—"Milton was great; but was he good?"—is related to the fictional strategies of Brontë's female predecessors. But Brontë is far more pessimistic about the results of revisionary poetics, although in *Shirley* she is presumably depicting an Emily Brontë born under happier circumstances. Thus, focusing upon a world already inalterably fallen, she suggests that the private broodings of women writers cannot eradicate the powerful effect of public myths. During the writing of *Shirley*, Brontë witnessed the decline and death of Branwell, Emily, and Anne, and we sense great despair at her own isolation in a novel that attests to her imprisonment within her own narrative structures. Like Elizabeth Barrett, who set her postlapsarian "A Drama of Exile" (1844) directly outside the locked garden gates, Charlotte Brontë studies the self-inflicted punishments of Eve's exiled daughters.

Since *Shirley* is about impotence, Brontë had to solve the problem of plotting a story about characters defined by their very inability to initiate action. As we shall see, every class in this novel has been affected by the inability of the English to win their war against France. In Yorkshire, the manufacturers, the clergy, and the workers suffer because the Orders of Council have cut off the principal markets of trade. To underline this point, the book begins with the curates called away from their meal to help mill-operator Robert Moore, who is waiting for the arrival of machinery that finally appears smashed to pieces by the angry workers. Throughout the novel, Moore waits, hoping to alter his waning fortunes but unable to take any real initiative. Finally he is reduced to the morally reprehensible and pitifully ineffective decision not to marry Caroline Helstone because she is poor, and instead to propose to Shirley Keeldar because she is rich. The novel is centrally concerned with these two young women and the inauspicious roles assigned them. But while none of the characters can initiate effective action because of the contingencies of a costly war abroad, Brontë's heroines are so circumscribed by their gender that they cannot act at all. Though many readers have criticized *Shirley* for a plot which consistently calls attention to its own inorganic development, we shall see that Brontë deliberately seeks to illustrate the inextricable link between sexual discrimination and mercantile capitalism, even as she implies that the coercion of a patriarchal society affects and infects each of its individual members. With this the case, it is not easy to provide or describe escape routes.

The best of the Yorkshire leaders, those most dedicated to shaping their lives through their own exertions, are two men who are bitter political enemies. Hiram Yorke, a rebellious blasphemer, rants against a land "king-ridden, priest-ridden, peer-ridden" while Mr. Helstone, an ecclesiastic, defends God, king, and "the judgment to come" (chap. 4). Each thinks the other damned. They are barely on speaking terms, yet they share uncommon personal courage and honesty. Yorke's democratic and blunt generosity is as admirable as Helstone's loyal fearlessness. Whig and Tory, manufacturer and clergyman, family man and childless widower, one a wealthy landowner and the other comfortably well-off from a clerical living, these two pillars of the community remain unaffected by the poverty and bankruptcy of their neighbors. Moreover, secure about their future, representative of the best in their society, they share a common past, for early in the novel we discover that they were rivals in their youth for "a girl with the face of a Madonna; a girl of living marble; stillness personified" (chap. 4).

This "monumental angel" is ominously named Mary Cave, reminding us of the parables of the cave that spell out how females have been entrapped in immanence, robbed of all but secondary arts and of their matriarchal genealogy. Indeed, because she was a kind of angel of death, Mary Cave was completely ignored by her clergyman-husband. We are told that, belonging as she did to "an inferior order of existence," she was evidently no companion for Mr. Helstone, and we learn that, after a year or two of marriage, she died, leaving behind a "still beautiful-featured mould of clay . . . cold and white" (chap. 4). Marriage to Yorke, we later learn, would also have led to her suffering, for neither of these men respects or likes the female sex, Helstone preferring women as silly as possible, and Yorke choosing a morose, tyrannical wife to breed and rear his brood. Even the noblest patriarchs are obsessed with delusive and contradictory images of women, Brontë implies, images pernicious enough to cause Mary Cave's death. She is therefore an emblem, a warning that the fate of women inhabiting a male-controlled society involves suicidal self-renunciation.

Understandably, then, she haunts the imagination of Caroline Helstone, who has taken her place in her uncle's house, where she too lives invisibly. Unable to remember her mother, Caroline seems as vulnerable and lonely as her aunt had been. But her life with Helstone is at least calmer than her past existence with her father, who had shut her up day and night, unattended, in an unfurnished garret room where "she waited for his return knowing drink would make him a madman or senseless idiot" (chap. 7). Helstone, at least, merely ignores her, always supplying adequate physical surroundings. And she can visit her cousins, the Moores, until her uncle's political feuding, coupled with Robert's rejection of her, makes these visits impossible.

Caroline's escape into the Moore household is by no means a liberation, however, since she is tortured by her cousin Hortense as she is initiated into the "duties of women," which consist of grammatical problems in French, incessant sewing, and eye-straining stocking-mending, inflicted because Hortense is convinced that this decorous girl is "not sufficiently girlish and submissive" (chap. 5). And certainly, although she seems exceptionally docile, Caroline does know her own mind; she knows, for instance, that she loves Robert Moore. Although demure and neat, moreover, she criticizes Robert's cruelty toward the workers and tries to teach him the evils of pride, drawing lessons from *Coriolanus*. Perhaps because of the examples of Mary Cave and of her own father, Caroline also knows from the first that she would be better off if she were able to earn her own living. Realizing that her cousin is dedicated to getting and spending, so much so that he will not allow himself to marry a portionless girl, she has little difficulty interpreting his mere glance, distant and cousinly, as a rejection of her.

As a female who has loved without being asked to love, therefore, Caroline is chastized by the narrator. Spurned, she is admonished to "ask no questions; utter no remonstrances" (chap. 7). The narrator's comments are pitiless, couched in all the imagery that has developed around the opposition of food and stone, as well as the necessity of self-enclosure and self-containment for women:

> Take the matter as you find it; ask no questions; utter no remonstrances: it is your best wisdom. You expected bread, and you have got a stone; break your teeth on it, and don't shriek because the nerves are martyrised: do not doubt that your mental stomach—if you have such a thing—is strong as an ostrich's: the stone will digest. You held out your hand for an egg, and fate put into it a scorpion. Show no consternation: close your fingers firmly upon the gift; let it sting you through your palm. Never mind: in time, after your hand and arm have swelled and quivered long with torture, the squeezed scorpion will die, and you will have learned the great lesson how to

endure without a sob. For the whole remnant of your life, if you survive the test—some, it is said, die under it—you will be stronger, wise, less sensitive.

(chap. 7)

Infection is surely breeding in these sentences spoken by the voice of repression we might associate with Nelly Dean or Zoraïde Reuter, for the assurance that "the stone will digest" or "the squeezed scorpion will die" is contradicted not only by the images themselves, but also by the grotesque transubstantiation from bread to stone, from egg to scorpion, which is prescribed as a suitable punishment for someone "guilty" of loving. Like the ballad heroine of *Puir Mary Lee*, Caroline can only withdraw into her imprisonment with the ambiguous solace that comes of being hidden:

> And smoor me up in the snaw fu' fast,
> And ne'er let the sun me see!
>
> Oh, never melt awa' thou wreath o' snaw
> That's sae kind in graving me;
>
> (chap. 7)

One of the damned, brought from Miltonic "Beds of raging Fire to starve on Ice," Caroline is plagued with "pining and palsying faculties," because "Winter seemed conquering her spring; the mind's soil and its treasures were freezing gradually to barren stagnation" (chap. 10). Withdrawing first into her room and then, more dangerously, into herself until she begins literally to disappear from lack of food, Caroline *Hel/stone* is obsessed with a "deep, secret, anxious yearning to discover and know her mother" (chap. 11). But as a motherless girl she is helpless against male rejection, and so she follows the example set by Mary Cave: standing in shadows, shrinking into the concealment of her own mind, she too becomes "a mere white mould, or rigid piece of statuary" (chap. 24).

As a ghost of herself, however, Caroline has nothing left but to attempt the rites and duties of the lady at her uncle's tea table and Sunday school. To emphasize this fact, the first scene after Robert's look of rejection pictures Caroline tending the jews-basket, "that awful incubus" (chap. 7), while entertaining the community's paragons of propriety in her uncle's parlor. Wearied by such pointless activity, tired of the lethargy caused by the tasteless rattle of the piano and the interminable gossip, Caroline retreats to a quieter room only to be caught unexpectedly in a meeting with Robert. There is something foreboding in her warning that his harshness to the mill laborers will lead to his own destruction. She wants him to know "how the people of this country bear malice: it is the boast of some of them that they can keep a stone in their pocket seven years, turn it at the end of that time, keep it seven years longer, and hurl it and hit their mark at last" (chap. 7). The man who offers stones instead of bread in return for the woman's love will receive as his punishment the rocks and stones cast by the other victims of his competitive egotism, the workers.

That Robert can offer Caroline nothing but stones becomes even clearer when we learn that he is himself "a living sepulchre" dedicated to trade (chap. 8), and that he feels as if "sealed in a rock" (chap. 9). Caroline recognizes the hardness in him that allows him to believe and act as if he and all men should be the free masters of their own and society's future. Priding himself on his own exertions, on work and self-reliance, Robert embodies the faith of English tradesmen and shopkeepers who view all activity except business as "eating the bread of idleness" (chap. 10). Given this credo, he necessarily despises women; but he also condescends to his own workers. With nothing but his own economic interests to guide him, moreover, he even opposes the continuation of a war that he knows must be fought to insure British liberty. Thus Brontë implies through him and the other manufacturers that the work ethic of self-help means selfishness and sexism, and, linking the exploitation of the workers with the unemployment of women, she further indicates that the acquisitive mentality that treats both women and workers as property is directly related to disrespect for the natural resources of the nation.

While Robert Moore is quite sure of his course of action, however—a revengeful attempt to exert control over his mill, the wares in it, his workers, and his women—Caroline must study the "knotty" problem of life (chap. 7). "Where is my place in the world?" is the question she is puzzled to solve (chap. 10). Curbing her remembrances of a romantic past, forcing herself to return to her present lonely condition, she tries to replace visions of feeding Moore berries and nuts in Nunnely Wood with a clear-sighted recognition of her own narrow chamber; instead of the songs of birds, she listens to the rain on her casement and watches her own dim shadow on the wall. Although she knows that virtue does not lie in self-abnegation, there do not seem to be other answers in her world. The bitten who survive will be stronger because less sensitive, like Miss *Mann*, the exemplary spinster Caroline visits in order to learn the secrets of old maids. But what she discovers on that occasion is a Medusa whose gaze turns men to stone, a woman to whom "a crumb is not thrown once a year"; a woman who exists "ahungered and athirst to famine" (chap. 10). And Miss Ainely, the other local spinster, manages to live more optimistically only through religious devotion and self-denial. Scorned by Robert, these lives are not attractive to Caroline either, but she nevertheless sees no other option because "All men, taken singly are more or less selfish; and taken in bodies they are intensely so" (chap. 10).

With clenched hands, then, she decides to follow Miss Ainely's example: to work hard at keeping down her anguish, although she is haunted by a "funereal inward cry" (chap. 10).

Just as *Jane Eyre* is a parable about an Everywoman who must encounter and triumph over a series of allegorical, patriarchal perils, Caroline Helstone's case history provides proof that the real source of tribulation is simply the dependent status of women. Unlike Jane, however, Caroline is quite beautiful, and she is protected from penury by the generosity of her uncle, who promises an annuity to provide for her even after his death. But Jane has at least mobility, traveling from Gateshead to Lowood, from Thornfield to Marsh End, and finally to Ferndean, while Caroline never leaves Yorkshire. Caroline, in fact, would welcome what she knows to be an uncomfortable position as governess because it would at least alleviate the inertia that suffocates her. But of course such an option is rejected as improper by her "friends," so that her complete immobility finally begins to make it seem quite probable that her "mental stomach" cannot "digest the stone" nor her hand endure the scorpion's sting. Significantly, it is only at this point of total paralysis that Brontë introduces Shirley Keeldar, a heroine who serves in all ways as a contrast to Caroline.

As brilliant as Caroline is colorless, as outgoing as Caroline is retiring, Shirley is not a dependent inmate or a passive suppliant, not a housekeeper or a housewife. She is a wealthy heiress who owns her own house, the ancestral mansion usually allotted to the hero, complete with old latticed windows, a stone porch, and a shadowy gallery with carved stags' heads hung on its walls. Almost always pictured (when indoors) beside a window, she enters the novel that bears her name through the glass doors of the garden. As "lord" of the manor she scorns lap dogs, romping instead with a huge mastiff reminiscent of Emily's hound Keeper. And she clearly enjoys her status as well as its ambiguous effect on her role in society:

> Business! Really the word makes me conscious I am indeed no longer a girl, but quite a woman and something more. I am an esquire! Shirley Keeldar, Esquire, ought to be my style and title. They gave me a man's name; I hold a man's position: it is enough to inspire me with a touch of manhood, and when I see such people as that stately Anglo-Belgian—that Gérard Moore before me, gravely talking to me of business, really I feel quite gentleman-like.
>
> (chap. 11)

Part of this is teasing, because Shirley is speaking to Mr. Helstone, who is unsympathetic to her independence. But the passage also reflects Brontë's recurrent and hopeless concern with transvestite behavior: Mr. Rochester dressing up as a gypsy, Shirley preening as a gallant cavalier, Lucy Snowe flirting as a fop for the hand of a coquette in a theatrical production, and Charlotte herself impersonating Charles Wellesley or William Crimsworth—all show a fascination with breaking the conventions of traditional sexual roles to experience the liberating and (especially in Victorian England) tantalizingly mysterious experiences of the other sex. When Shirley plays the captain to Caroline's modest maiden, their coy banter and testing infuses the relationship with a fine, subtle sexuality that is markedly absent from their manipulative heterosexual relationships. Yet, given that Shirley's masculine name was bestowed by parents who had wished for a son, there is something not a little foreboding about the fact that independence is so closely associated with men that it confines Shirley to a kind of male mimicry.

A true Lady Bountiful, strong yet loving, Shirley is never except playfully a male manqué. Laying out impromptu feasts in the garden or banquets in the dining room, she owns the dairy cows that supply the cottagers with milk and butter, and she pays exorbitant bills for bread, candles, and soap, although she suspects that her housekeeper must be cheating her. Shirley manages to give sustenance to Caroline, not only because she has meat and wine for Moore's men or sweet cake in her reticule to throw to chickens and sparrows, but also because she is blessed with the capacity for delight that poetic imagination can inspire: in moments of "fulness of happiness," Shirley's "sole book . . . was the dim chronicle of memory, or the sibyl page of anticipation . . . round her lips at moments played a smile which revealed glimpses of the tale or prophecy" (chap. 13). To Caroline, this gift promises to save Shirley from the grotesque dependence she herself feels upon men and their approval, for Caroline is convinced that even extreme misery when experienced by a poet is dissipated by the creation of literature: Cowper and Rousseau, for instance, certainly "found relief in writing . . . and that gift of poetry—the most divine bestowed on man—was, I believe, granted to allay emotions when their strength threatens harm" (chap. 12). Such a poet does not need to be loved, "and if there were any female Cowpers and Rousseaus, I should assert the same of them" (chap. 12). In other words, Caroline hopes that in Shirley she has found a woman free from the constraints which threaten to destroy her own life.

And, certainly, the fact that Shirley emerges only when Caroline has been completely immobilized through her own self-restraint and submission is reminiscent of the ways in which Bertha Mason Rochester offers a means of escape to the otherwise boxed-in Jane Eyre. But here repression signals the emergence of a free and uninhibited self that is not criminal. That Shirley is Caroline's double, a projection of all her repressed desire, becomes apparent in the acts she performs "for" Caroline. What Shirley *does* is what Caroline would like to do: Caroline's secret hatred for the curates is gratified when Shirley angrily throws them out of her house after they are attacked by her dog; Caroline needs to move Helstone, and Shirley bends him to her will; Caroline wishes early in the novel that she could penetrate the business secrets of men, while Shirley reads the newspapers and letters of the civic leaders; Caroline wants to lighten Robert's financial burden and Shirley secures him a loan; Caroline tries to repress her desire for Robert, while Shirley gains his attention and proposal of marriage; Caroline has always known that he needs to be taught a lesson (consider her explication of *Coriolanus*) and Shirley gives it to him in the form of a humiliating rejection of his marriage proposal. Caroline wishes above all else for her long-lost mother and Shirley supplies her with just this person in the figure of Mrs. Pryor.

Paradoxically, however, for all the seeming optimism in this depiction of a double, as opposed to the earlier portrait of self-destructive and enraged Bertha, Shirley does not provide the release she first seems to promise Caroline. Instead, she herself becomes enmeshed in a social role that causes her to duplicate Caroline's immobility. For example, she gratuitously flirts, thereby inflicting pain on Caroline, who is tortured by her belief that Shirley is a successful rival for Robert Moore's love. Indeed, Shirley manages to rob Caroline of even a modicum of pleasure from Moore's presence: "Her famished heart had tasted a drop and crumb of nourishment . . . but the generous feast was snatched from her, spread before another, and she remained but a bystander at the banquet" (chap. 13). Furthermore, Shirley begins to resemble Caroline in the course of the novel until she finally succumbs to Caroline's fate. And, for all her assertiveness, she is shown to be as confined by her gender, as excluded from male society, as her friend. Brontë traces the origin and nature of this imprisonment through the juxtaposition of two central episodes, the Sunday school feast and the attack on the mill.

Looking "very much like a snow-white dove and gem-tinted bird-of-paradise" (chap. 16), Caroline and Shirley head the Briarfield contingent of women and children in the Whitsuntide celebration. When, in a narrow lane in which only two can walk abreast, they confront an opposition procession of Dissenters, Shirley very accurately terms them "our doubles" (chap. 17). Since Helstone and Shirley force the Dissenters to flee, the final feast becomes more a victory celebration than a Christian rite of piety. Even if Brontë had not linked this scene to the defense of the mill, its military and national overtones would have been apparent: not only is the church an arm of the state; both church and state depend on exclusion and coercion which are economic, social, and sexual. Or so the taking of toast and tea imply, for in the midst of merriment and cheer, Shirley has to resort to the most inane feminine wiles to preserve a seat, while Caroline is silently tortured by her friend's intimacy with the man she secretly loves. Above all the imbibing, suspended in at least twenty cages, sit an incongruous flock of canaries placed there by a clerk who "knew that amidst confusion of tongues they always carolled loudest" (chap. 16). A mocking symbol of the heroines' chatter and finery, the caged birds are just as decorative and irrelevant as Caroline and Shirley, who are excluded from the plans for defense of the mill and only able to watch the historic conflict between mill owners and workers from a nearby hill. When the workers, their "doubles," break down gates and doors, hurling volleys of stones at the windows of the mill, Caroline and Shirley are divided in sympathy between owners and workers and effectively prevented from any form of participation.

To understand the workers' violent wrath at the mill in terms of the women's revenge, it is necessary to recall the meditations of Shirley and Caroline after they refuse to follow the rest of the Sunday school into the church at the close of the day and before the nighttime battle. For it is in this scene that, moved by the beauty of nature, Shirley offers Caroline the alternative to Milton's story of creation that we discussed in our consideration of "Milton's bogey." Shirley describes not the domesticated housekeeper pictured by Milton, but "a woman-Titan" who could conceive and bring forth a Messiah, an Eve who is heaven-born, yet also an Amazon mother originally called "Nature" (chap. 18). And, as we have already observed, Charlotte Brontë's portrait of her sister links Emily to a character who makes Nature her goddess. Throughout *Shirley*, Shirley's green thoughts in a green shade are "the pure gift of God to his creatures," but they are also, significantly, "the free dower of Nature to her child" (chap. 22). Finally, in fact, Shirley's capacity for joy is not unrelated to her intimate awareness of the fertility, the felicity, and the physicality of her own Titan-Eve. But this means that, for Shirley, the goddess of nature supplants the god of spirit, as she did at times for Emily Dickinson, whose belief that " 'Nature' is what we see— / . . . Nature is what we know" resulted in her complementary feeling that "the Bible is an antique Volume— / Written by faded Men." At the same time, however, both Brontë and Dickinson imply that the male-created word, the book of books, is powerful enough to cause women to "forget" both their past and their power. Although Eden is only "a legend—dimly told—," it obscures the tunes women originally heard, specifically the melodies of their own special glee, their unfallen nature.

Just in case we have forgotten how radical a departure is Shirley's Titan from the Biblical Eve, Brontë almost immediately introduces Moore's foreman to remind us. This censorious workman quotes the second chapter of Saint Paul's first epistle to Timothy: " 'Let the woman learn in silence, with all subjection. . . . For Adam was first formed, then Eve,' " and when Shirley does not receive the lesson immediately, he continues: " 'Adam was not deceived; but the woman, being deceived, was in the transgression'" (chap. 18). Clearly there is a confusion of tongues here, for Shirley can no more accept this Eve than the foreman could have understood her Titan-woman. Neither Shirley nor Caroline can really make any headway with the man, however. Shirley is "puzzled" by the Biblical injunctions, and Caroline can only feebly resist them with the defense that Dorothea Brooke exploits against her Milton: "if I could read the original Greek," she speculates hopefully, ". . . It would be possible, I doubt not, with a little ingenuity, to give the passage quite a contrary turn" (chap. 18).

It was precisely this "ingenuity" in giving the passage "quite a contrary turn" that Elizabeth Cady Stanton and her "Revising Committee" attempted in the nineties in their feminist commentaries on the word of God. Considered by more than one clergyman the "work of women and the devil," their *Woman's Bible* begins to confront Paul's injunctions in the epistles to Timothy by modestly explaining that "it cannot be that Paul was inspired by infinite wisdom in this utterance." But Stanton's feminists go on to reveal how Paul's misogyny is related to male attempts to control not only women's speech, but their property and their persons.

Although Brontë exposes the ways in which the exploitation of women that the Bible seems to justify perpetuates mercantile capitalism and its compulsive manipulation of human and physical nature, her characters cannot escape the confinement of Biblical myth: haunted by Eden, Caroline wants to return to Hollow's Cottage "as much almost as the first woman, in her exile, must have longed to revisit Eden" (chap. 13); but she and Shirley, knowing the power of Paul's use of the story of the garden, also realize that men imagine women as either angels of submission or monsters of aggression:

> The cleverest, the acutest men are often under an illusion about women: they do not read them in a true light: they misapprehend them, both for good and evil: their good woman is a queer thing, half doll, half angel; their bad woman almost always a fiend.
>
> (chap. 20)

Increasingly aware that instead of inhabiting Eden they actually live on the edge of Nunnwood with its ruins of a nunnery, Shirley and Caroline feel that men do not read women in a true light and that the heroines of male-authored literature are false creations. But Shirley knows as well how subversive her critique of male authority is, explaining to Caroline that if she were to give her "real opinion of some [supposedly] first-rate female characters in first-rate works, " she would be "dead under a cairn of avenging stones in half-an-hour" (chap. 20).

Shirley is also conscious that her own and other women's silent acquiescence to such debilitating images helps foster female rage. While planning a trip for herself, her governess, and Caroline, Shirley describes a mermaid that she dreams of encountering in the far reaches of the North Atlantic:

> I show you an image, fair as alabaster, emerging from the dim wave. We both see the long hair, the lifted and foam-white arm, the oval mirror brilliant as a star. It glides nearer: a human face is plainly visible; a face in the style of yours, whose straight, pure (excuse the word, it is appropriate), —whose straight, pure lineaments, paleness does not disfigure. It looks at us, but not with your eyes. I see a preternatural lure in its wily glance: it beckons. Were we men, we should spring at the sign, the cold billow would be dared for the sake of the colder enchantress; being women, we stand safe, though not dreadless.
>
> (chap. 13)

Not merely parodying stereotypical male images of women as unnatural (but seductive) monsters, Shirley is also describing the effect such images have on women themselves. Locked into her unnatural, desexed body, the mermaid works her cold enchantment in order to destroy the men who have enslaved such pure women as Caroline and Shirley. A portrait of Gorgon-Medusas like Miss Mann, Miss Moore, and Mrs. Pryor, the mermaid is also a revisionary avatar of Sin, Eve's precursor, and a "monstrous likeness of ourselves" who exacts the revenge of nature against culture; for "the treacherous mermaid," as Dorothy Dinnerstein has shown, is the "seductive and impenetrable female representative of the dark and magic underwater world from which our life comes and in which we cannot live." Unable to become a "female Cowper," since her identification with biological generativity excludes her from cultural creativity, Shirley can only envision a silent oceanic punishment for those castaways who have denied the validity or even the possibility of her self-definition.

Because she so consciously experiences herself as monstrous, deviant, excluded, powerless, and angry, Shirley sees through the coercive myths of her culture that imply and even condone inequality and exploitation. Because she understands the dehumanizing effect of patriarchal capitalism, moreover, she is the only wealthy person in the novel who "cannot forget, either day or night, that these embittered feelings of the poor against the rich have been generated in suffering" (chap. 14), for her experience of her gender as it is circumscribed by available sexual roles gives her insight into the misery of the poor. This does not mean, however, that she has a solution to the class conflict she watches with such ambivalence. Sympathizing with Moore as he defends her property, she knows that his cruelty and the workers' misery have erupted in violence she can only deplore, and although her own rather matriarchal relationship with the laborers allows for more kindness between classes, it too is fraught with potential violence, since she retains economic control over their lives and they, in their masculine pride, are angered by what they see as her unnatural authority.

Still, she alone rejects "all arraying of ranks against ranks, all party hatred, all tyrannies disguised as liberties" (chap. 21). But her revolt against patriarchal injustice only causes her neighbor, Hiram Yorke, to try to deflate her political ardor by defining it as amorous passion in disguise. Shirley's proud self-defense baffles him since he feels that he cannot read the untranslatable language of her look, which seems to him to be a "fervid lyric in an unknown tongue" (chap. 21). It is during this most interesting impasse that we learn a fact never developed in the novel but highly suggestive: Shirley's father's name was Charles *Cave* Keeldar. Mary Cave, symbol of female protest through suicide, is one of Shirley's ancestors and yet another link with Caroline.

Although Shirley lives a pastoral life of freedom reminiscent of the mythic existence of her own Titan-woman, there *is* something untranslatable not only about her fervid lyrics but about all her gestures and talk. Whether she is the courtly gentleman, the courageous captain, the coy coquette, the Lady Bountiful, the little lady, or the touched bard, Shirley seems condemned to play the roles she parodies. That she is continuously hampered in this way makes less surprising her mysterious decision to invite the Sympson family, with its "pattern young ladies, in pattern attire, with pattern deportment" (chap. 22), into her home. Although neither Caroline nor the reader yet realizes that she is using the Sympsons to obtain the presence of their tutor and her lover, Louis Moore, his appearance is one more step in Shirley's subjugation. When Shirley keeps secret her wiles to gain the presence of a suitor, her lack of freedom affects Caroline's further decline.

Not merely lovesick, Caroline is profoundly discontent, her illness the result of her misery at what she terms her own impotence. Her mentor Mrs. Pryor has already assured her that neither the married state nor a job as governess would offer relief from tedium and loneliness. Into the mouths of the wonderfully named Hardman family (who employed Mrs. Pryor when she was the governess Miss Grey) are placed all the criticisms leveled against Charlotte Brontë by the reviewers of *Jane Eyre*. But Miss Grey's story of her governess days also recalls Anne Brontë's *Agnes Grey*, as if Charlotte needed to deflate the romantic happy ending envisioned there. In the name of Christian resignation, Miss Hardman tells Miss Grey what Miss Rigby had said of Jane Eyre and what Agnes Grey's employers told her: "You are proud, and therefore you are ungrateful too" (chap. 21). And Mrs. Hardman warns Miss Grey to quell her ungodly discontent because it can only lead to death in a lunatic asylum (chap. 21). Both Caroline and Mrs. Pryor agree that this is the religious faith of an elitist and exploitative pharisee. Yet

Caroline seems to have no alternative except to sit resignedly "still as a garden statue" (chap. 22). Perceiving the unmarried women she knows as nuns trapped in close cells, robes straight as shrouds, beds narrow as coffins, Caroline is repelled by a society that demands that "old maids, like the houseless and unemployed poor, should not ask for a place and an occupation in the world" (chap. 22). It is the "narrowness" of the woman's lot that makes her ill and causes her to scheme in the "matrimonial market" where she is as much a commodity as the workers are in the mercantile market. But Caroline's thoughts about the woman question conclude pitifully, with an impassioned plea directed, of course, to the "Men of England!" It is they who keep female minds "fettered," and presumably it is only they who have the power to unlock the chains.

Directly after this outburst, almost as if her own anger is taken up and expressed in another's voice, Caroline is verbally attacked by Rose Yorke. Using language that exploits all the imagery of imprisonment in a context that illustrates how the woman's domestic lot enlists her as a jailor of herself, Rose proclaims her refusal to live "a black trance like the toad's buried in marble," for she will not be "for ever shut up" in a house that reminds her of a "windowed grave":

> "And if my Master has given me ten talents, my duty is to trade with them and make them ten talents more. Not in the dust of household drawers shall the coin be interred. I will *not* deposit it in a broken-spouted tea-pot, and shut it up in a china-closet among tea-things. I will *not* commit it to your work-table to be smothered in piles of woollen hose. I will *not* prison it in the linen press to find shrouds among the sheets; and least of all, mother" — (she got up from the floor) — "least of all will I hide it in a tureen of cold potatoes, to be ranged with bread, butter, pastry, and ham on the shelves of the larder."
>
> (chap. 23)

The pun on the word *talent* is a functional one since Rose's point is precisely the connection between the financial dependence of women and the destruction of their creative potential: each and every one of the housekeeper's drawers, chests, boxes, closets, pots, and bags represents the very skill that insures suicidal "feminine" service, self-burial, and silence.

A model "lady" (chap. 9), Caroline Helstone has buried her talents, so she is consumed in the same "well-lit fire" that destroyed Helen Burns, and, as Helen did, she seems to fade away "like any snow-wreath in thaw" (chap. 21). Consumed by sorrow, she cannot eat, reminding us again of the prominence of anorexia nervosa as a female dis-ease and as a theme in women's literature:

Caroline has received stones instead of bread, and she has been deprived of maternal care and nourishment, so she denies herself the traditional symbol of that love. But of course, like so many other girls suffering from this disease (all of whose case histories reveal a paralyzing feeling of ineffectiveness), Caroline has good reason to believe that the only control she can exert is over her own body, since she is completely ineffectual at altering her intolerable lot in the world. Like other anorexics, she has been rewarded only for her compliant attractiveness and "feminine" docility, so her self-starvation is, ironically, an acceptance of the ideal of self-denial. And she has also experienced male rejection, which has obviously contributed to a debilitating sense of her own low worth. For Caroline is ashamed at Robert's rejection, not angry or sorry, and her sense of inadequacy becomes therefore a justification for self-punishment, as the initial admonishment to endure meals of stone and the scorpion's sting illustrated.

Caroline's self-starvation is even more symbolically complex than these parallels with contemporary anorexics suggest, however. Earlier in the novel, as we have seen, Brontë carefully associated food with the voracious curates, the Sunday school feast, Mr. Helstone's tea table, and Shirley's supplies for the mill owners. In some ways, then, Caroline's rejection of food is a response not only to these characters but also to their definitions of communion and redemption. Shirley has already attacked the Christian version of Genesis. But now it becomes clearer how the myth of origins, in which a woman is condemned for eating, reflects male hatred of the female and fear of her sustaining or strengthening herself. Caroline has internalized the injunction not to eat, not to speak, and not to be first. And Brontë's portrayal of her self-inflicted torture is strikingly similar to Elizabeth Barrett Browning's dramatization of the guilt of Eve, who asks Adam in "A Drama of Exile" to "put me straight away, / Together with my name! Sweet, punish me!" Admitting that "I, also, after tempting, writhe on the ground, / And I would feed on ashes from thine hand," Barrett Browning's Eve resembles Caroline, who also accepts the necessity for feeding on ashes because, like Eve, she feels "twice fallen . . . From joy of place, and also right of wail, / 'I wail' being not for me—only 'I sin.' " In other words, Caroline's silent slow suicide implies all the ways in which she has been victimized by male myths.

On the other hand, like Catherine Earnshaw Linton, Caroline Helstone is also using her hunger strike as a kind of protest. Catherine had rejected her "confinement" as a woman, and her refusal to eat was, we saw, partially a rejection of pregnancy. But anorexia nervosa even more frequently occurs in virgins, and it can be viewed as a protest against growing up female, since self-starvation returns such girls to the physical state of small children, just as it interrupts the menstrual cycle which has been defined for them as a "curse." Finally, Caroline's self-starvation is also a rejection of what her society has defined as nourishing. As an act of revolt, like that of the lady in *Castle Rackrent*, fasting is a refusal to feed on foreign foods. Since eating maintains the self, in a discredited world it is a compromise implying acquiescence. Women will starve in silence, Brontë seems to imply, until new stories are created that confer upon them the power of naming themselves and controlling their world. Caroline's fasting criticizes female providing and male feasting, even as it implies that a Father whose love must be earned by well-invested talents is not worth having.

And so, meaningfully, it is at this point that she begins to question the existence of the other world and the purpose of this one. As Dickinson observed, the precious "Word made Flesh" is often only "tremblingly partook" by women, it seems, since they are far from certain that it is suited "To our specific strength—." Like Shirley's, Brontë's style becomes more rhapsodic and fervid, more exotic, as her writing progresses and she seeks to create a new word, a new genre for her sex. In *Shirley* as in *Jane Eyre* one heroine silently starves while the other raves. Both are involved in a militant rejection of the old myths and the degrading roles they provide. But unlike *Jane Eyre*, *Shirley* is very consciously an attack on the religion of the patriarchs. Caroline, in her illness, searches for faith in God the Father. She finds instead the encircling arms of her mother.

Mrs. Pryor is a suitable mother. Aloof and withdrawn in public, she has survived the test of "a man-tiger" (chap. 25) whose gentlemanly soft speech hid private "discords that split the nerves and curdled the blood—sounds to inspire insanity" (chap. 24). Formal and reticent, she is the prior woman, prior to Shirley as well as Caroline, because her experience, not the woman-Titan's, is typically female in the society these young women inhabit. Like most girls, Caroline and Shirley will grow into womanhood through marriage, which, Mrs. Pryor warns, is a horrible, shattering experience; although she never details the terror of male potency, it seems all the more dreadful here for remaining so mysterious. Her pain in marriage and eventual flight from it, moreover, are central to the initial split between Caroline and Shirley, the split between suicidal "feminine" passivity and "masculine" self-assertion. Mrs. Pryor has in some sense perpetuated this dichotomy, even as she herself exemplifies it, because her dread of her husband has caused her to reject his daughter, but Caroline is also her daughter and part of herself. Thus Mrs. Pryor contributes to Caroline's passivity because she has withheld from her daughter the love that allows for a strong sense of self. Further, by experiencing men as evil, by seeing herself as a victim who can only submit to male degradation or flee from it, she defines the woman's role as a tragic one. Finally, Shirley's surrogate mother and Caroline's biological mother, she proves that the heroines are similarly circumscribed. At this point, therefore, both heroines—now sisters—are wooed by the brothers Moore, and it seems clear that their initiation into their own sexuality is bound to be humiliating.

After the emergence of Mrs. Pryor, Shirley increasingly shows herself to be as reticent and discreet as that severe lady could have wished. Not only does Shirley refrain from communicating to Caroline her suspicions about Mrs. Pryor's real identity, she is quite secretive about the existence of Caroline's cousin Louis Moore. When Louis does finally appear, Shirley persists in treating him with cold formality, and her reserve reaches its heights when she is bitten by a dog she believes to be mad. Caroline was admonished to show no consternation over the figurative bite of the scorpion, but it is Shirley who fully epitomizes the horror of self-repression when she actually remains silent about her fears of hydrophobia and begins to waste away from sheer anxiety. The cauterized wound is only the outward mark of her pain at this fall which is so similar to the dog bite that initiates Catherine Earnshaw into the prison of gender. For even as she becomes more reserved, Shirley also grows docile in the schoolroom with her old tutor. When she tries to study French, she actually finds "lively excitement in the pleasure of making his language her own" (chap. 27). Returning her, as one chapter title puts it, to "Old Copy-Books," Shirley's fate also recalls Frances Henri's destiny. Gifted as she is with extraordinary visions, Shirley represents one more attempt on Brontë's part to come to terms with the silences of even the most inspired women.

If Shirley, a romantic visionary, had had "a little more of the organ of acquisitiveness in her head—a little more of the love of property in her nature" (chap. 22), the narrator speculates, she might have taken pen to paper. Instead, she will "die without knowing the full value of that spring whose bright fresh bubbling in her heart keeps it green" (chap. 22). Without an adequate language at her disposal, Shirley never experiences "the strong pulse of Ambition." For "Nature is what we know— / Yet have no art to say—," as Dickinson explains, "So impotent Our Wisdom is / To her Simplicity." But Shirley also seems hampered because, like Elizabeth Barrett's Eve, she is afraid to speak again, having spoken "once to such a bitter end." Shirley's final return to the rhetoric of the classroom only confirms and completes her fall. But Brontë does not, as some critics suggest, condone Shirley's submission; instead, she repeatedly calls attention to her buried talents. The Titan-woman has been subdued, and by no one less than the first man. "With animals," Louis declares proudly, "I feel I am Adam's son: the heir of him to whom dominion was given over 'every living thing that moveth upon the earth'" (chap. 26).

As we observed in our discussion of "Milton's bogey," Shirley's old devoir, an essay entitled "La Premiere Femme Savante," differs drastically from her previous descriptions to Caroline of a Promethean Titan-woman since this alternative myth countenances female submission. Here in Shirley's homework for her teacher we find a hungry, cold orphan girl who is first fostered by the earth but who ultimately responds to a male master, called Genius, who finally takes his dying bride into "his home—Heaven," where he "restored her, redeemed, to Jehovah—her Maker" (chap. 27). While Shirley presumably begins by celebrating a sexual union in which the female is infused with the godly power of creativity, she ends up telling what we saw was the embedded myth of *Wuthering Heights*: how the child of physical maternal Nature is seduced or abducted into the Father's deathly realm of spirit. As well as providing a sensitive appreciation of Emily's art, Charlotte's elegy for her sister mourns the diminishment she feels at Emily's absence, even as it pays tribute to Emily's triumphant resistance against the forces that finally seduce Shirley, as they had Catherine Earnshaw before her.

Like Brontë herself, then, Shirley begins with a new story, a female myth of origin; but she too finds herself repeating an old tale of "Eve—and the Anguish —Grandame's story," even as she tries to remember her own melody: "But—I was telling a tune—I heard—." For although Brontë had begun this novel with what seemed like a radical intent, she capitulates to convention. Brontë undercuts traditional expectations by presenting a fair, pale heroine full of rage at the men of England and a dark, romantic woman who is self-contained and silent about her true feelings, but she also seems to describe how Shirley and Louis Moore reverse novelistic conventions. Indeed, these lovers at first seem to reverse the types exploited in *Jane Eyre*: just as Shirley possesses all the accoutrements of the aristocratic hero, Louis Moore—like the young clerk William Crimsworth—is the male counterpart of a governess. A private tutor who is invisible and hungry (chap. 36), he feels his faculties and emotions are pent in, walled up (chap. 26), and in his locked desk he keeps a journal to record a hopeless passion which at one point causes him to fall ill of a fever. He himself refers to this exchange of traditional roles when he remembers "the fable of Semele reversed" (chap. 29). Yet, despite this apparent role reversal, Louis loves Shirley because she requires his mastery, his advice, and his checking. As an older and wiser teacher, he values the perfect lady in her, as well as her need to be curbed. By the end of the novel, therefore, Shirley is a "bondswoman" in the hands of " a hero and a patriarch" (chap. 35).

It looks as if Brontë began *Shirley* with the intention of subverting not only the sexual images of literature but the courtship roles and myths from which they derive. But she could find no models for this kind of fiction; as she explains in her use of the Genesis myth, the stories of her culture actively endorse traditional sexual roles, even as they discourage female authority. In spite of all the rationales Brontë provides, therefore, the absence and inactivity of her heroes seem contrived, just as the problems faced by her heroines seem unrelated to the particular historical framework in which they are set, in spite of the fact that at least one of her major statements in *Shirley* concerns the tragic consequences of the inability of women to shape the public history that necessarily affects their own lives. The tension between Brontë's personal allegiances and the dictates of literary conventions is especially evident when she seeks to write a story of female strength and survival. She has herself explained to the reader in the course of the novel why the only "happy ending" for women in her society is marriage. She gives us that ending, but, like Jane Austen, she never allows us to forget that marriage is a suspect institution based on female subordination, and that women who are not novel heroines probably do not fare even as well as Caroline and Shirley.

More specifically, having recognized that inherited generic conventions assign characters a degree of freedom that contradicts her own sense of the female condition, Brontë can only call attention to this disjunction by describing remarkably improbable escape routes for her heroines. At least part of what makes the ending of *Shirley* seem so unreal is the way in which the plot metes out proper rewards and punishments to all the characters with an almost cynical excess of concession to narrative conventions. Robert Moore, for instance, has erred both in his cruelty to the workers and in his mercenary proposal of marriage to Shirley, so he is shot down "like some wild beast from behind a wall" (chap. 31) by a half-crazed weaver. Robert has made himself into a business machine so he must be taught the limits of self-reliance, the need for charity. Imprisoned at Briarmains, the Yorkes' home, he finds himself at the mercy of a female monster; locked up in an upstairs bedroom, he is taught docility by the terrible Mrs. Horsfalls. Robert's indifference has made Caroline ill; he now wastes away at the hands of a woman who is said to starve him.

The entire episode recalls childhood fantasies and fears that are further emphasized by the introduction of Martin Yorke, a young boy who is enthralled by a contraband volume of fairy tales. An adolescent misogynist, Martin seems endowed with puckish powers since he is able to cast the entire household under a spell, and thereby make possible Caroline's trip upstairs to awaken the sleeping invalid of *Briar*/mains. It is because he is still only a boy that Martin has the sympathy and the imagination to help the lovers. But as a sort of parody of the author, he is corrupt enough to enjoy controlling them with his fictions by viewing them as characters in a romance of his own making. Robert manages to evade Mrs. Horsfalls and Martin only by returning to Caroline, his sister Hortense, and the house he now recognizes for the first time as a home. But by returning to the fairy tale motifs of *Jane Eyre* in this new historically defined context, Brontë marks the redemptive education of the manufacturer as mere wish-fulfillment.

Shirley's path to happiness is no less amazing than Caroline's. Just as Caroline employs Martin, Shirley uses poetic Henry Sympson's admiration to enchant

Louis. She rejects three marriage proposals of increasing material advantage, until Louis seems finally transformed from an ugly old duck into a youngish swain. In a set-piece of passion, Shirley rebukes her wicked stepfather Mr. Sympson, who cannot understand why she has rejected all her suitors and questions whether she is really "a young lady." Defiantly she claims to be something a thousand times better—"an honest woman" (chap. 31)—and with the forces of propriety so easily silenced, the time is obviously ripe for union. Presumably Louis's age and intelligence balance off Shirley's wealth and beauty: their only remaining problem is determining who shall speak first. The fact that Louis is the one to break the silence is one more sign of his mastery. "As cool as stone" (chap. 36) even when angry, Louis looks like "a great sand-buried stone head" (chap. 36) of an Egyptian god. By Shirley's own admission he is her "keeper," and she has become a "Pantheress" so that he, the first man, must prove his dominion over her as "She gnaws at the chain" (chap. 36) At the very end of the novel, Brontë qualifies her emphasis on Shirley's submission by quoting her claim that she "acted on system," since Louis "would never have learned to rule, if she had not ceased to govern" (chap. 37). But, whether tactical or obsessive, her submission is the complete and necessary prelude to their marriage.

Brontë calls attention to the ridiculous fantasy that is the novel's end by entitling her final chapter "The Winding-Up." As if that were not enough to qualify the happy ending, she ties up loose ends and proclaims, "I think the varnish has been put on very nicely" (chap. 37). With Shirley on the brink of marriage, it is no surprise that Robert Moore starts perceiving Caroline's resemblance to the Virgin Mary, although for those readers who remember Mary Cave the echo is ominous. Brontë is careful to develop the imagery she has established from the beginning of the novel, most especially the connection between stones and male lovelessness. The scene of the marriage proposal is set near a wall, next to the fragment of a sculptured stone, perhaps the base of a cross, a fitting symbol in this novel of female dispossession. Characteristically, Robert asks, "Is Caroline mine?" He wonders if she can care for him, "as if that rose should promise to shelter from tempest this hard, grey stone" (chap. 37). Still unable to love anyone except himself, he pictures Caroline as the perfect Sunday school mistress for the cottagers he will employ at his expanded mill.

And Robert's is the spirit of the nineteenth century, that "Titan-boy" who "hurls rocks in his wild sport" (chap. 37). That salvation of England has been effected by a similar "demigod," named Wellington. But Brontë implies that the final victory and vision are Robert's. He describes how the "green natural terrace shall be a paved street: there will be cottages in the dark ravine, and cottages on the lonely slopes: the rough pebbled track shall be an even, firm, broad, black, sooty road" (chap. 37). The future has been won by and for men and their industrial patriarchy. The narrator confirms the truth of the prophecy, returning to the Hollow to describe the stones and bricks, the mill as ambitious as a tower of Babel. "His" account ends with a conversation with "his" housekeeper whose mother "had seen a fairish (fairy) in Fieldhead Hollow; and that was the last fairish that ever was seen on this country side" (chap. 37). The absence of fairies, like the repudiation of the fairy tale at the end of this novel, implies that the myth of Mother/Nature has been betrayed in mercantile, postlapsarian England. Happy endings, Brontë suggests, will not be quite so easily arranged in this fallen world, for history replaces mere romance in a world of stony facts.

JANICE CARLISLE

The Face in the Mirror:
Villette *and the Conventions*
of Autobiography

Recounting one of the more famous anecdotes of the fabled life at Haworth parsonage, Patrick Brontë once described the result of his desire to know what his very young children were thinking: "happening to have a mask in the house, I told them all to stand and speak boldly from under the cover of that mask." The father suspected that the everyday behavior of his children was itself a mask, an assumed pose of innocence that veiled "more than [he] had yet discovered." By means of his ruse he hoped to counter that deception; the mask would conceal the face and identity of the speaker in order to reveal the child's heart. The episode is one of those telling revelations of both character and the forces that mold character. Even at the age of eight, Charlotte Brontë was being encouraged to adopt subversive modes of self-expression. The form of this little drama would become the form of her art. Like Thackeray, who fled the responsibilities of speaking *in propria persona* by creating narrators such as Barry Lyndon or Arthur Pendennis, Brontë was most comfortable when presenting narratives mediated through a consciousness other than her own; from the earliest extant juvenilia to the fragment of the novel begun just before her death, she spoke with most freedom when she spoke through the voices of characters like Captain Tree or Charles Wellesley Townshend, Jane Eyre or Mrs. Chalfont. This mode was never more central to Brontë's art than in the case of *Villette*. Lucy Snowe is the mask under cover of which Brontë conceals her identity in order to reveal the unappealing reality of her emotional life and its central figures, M. Heger and George Smith. The mask, however, performs this function in the service of art. The novel is a mirror in which reality is transformed to grant the emotional and aesthetic satisfactions that life invariably withholds.

From *ELH*, no. 2 (Summer 1979). © 1979 by the Johns Hopkins University Press.

Villette, the result of this process, is indeed a private document, but its privacy is a function of Lucy Snowe's life and character, not its author's. Brontë was able to distance herself from her own experience and even from facets of her own personality so that we do not need the facts of her life to explain or justify the novel. Yet *Villette* is genuinely puzzling, and it presents mysteries that we might be tempted to unlock with the key of biography. Its first reader, George Smith, responded to the manuscript with a pained silence so prolonged that it almost induced Brontë to journey to London to discover what had gone amiss. Even she seemed at least partially unaware of the implications of her novel. Like Lucy naively suggesting that her cold exterior represents her true identity, Brontë commented soon after finishing *Villette*, "Unless I am mistaken the emotion of the book will be found to be kept throughout in tolerable subjection." She was, of course, mistaken, and one might say of Charlotte and *Villette* what Charlotte said of Emily and *Wuthering Heights*, "Having formed these beings, she did not know what she had done." Charlotte Brontë firmly believed that writers are mastered by a force that they themselves do not comprehend — "something that at times strangely wills and works for itself" — but even the powers of unconscious creative agency do not explain the questions the novel raises. What are we to make of its disjointed chronology, its shifts of tone and subject, its patent evasions, and the inconclusiveness of its ending? Does the novel reveal the view of a women who accepts suffering as the dispensation of a just Providence? Or does it, in Matthew Arnold's words, display the author's "hunger, rebellion, and rage"? On a first reading, the novel almost always seems as "preternatural in its power" as George Eliot found it, but most readers — and here I speak for myself and my students — wonder if its power is not the result of emotions profoundly confused and confusing. Yet if we begin to look more closely at Lucy Snowe, at the shape and form of Brontë's mask, what has seemed perplexing or contradictory about her story reveals a clarity and persuasive emotional logic that shine through even the most apparently trivial or irrelevant detail.

The qualities that Lucy displays as the narrator of her own life and the qualities of *Villette* as the mirror of her experience are most easily defined if we set the novel in the context of its contemporary tradition, the art of autobiography at the Victorian midcentury. As Leigh Hunt noted in 1850, autobiography had "abounded of late years in literary quarters," and the trend only continued to increase in the early years of the 1850s. The popularity of *Jane Eyre* (1847) had been an important impetus to the widespread adoption of the form. Because of the generous gifts of books from her publishers and a growing circle of literary friends, Charlotte Brontë was well aware of this development. During the fall of 1849, when *Shirley* was being published, she began reading Dickens's *David Copperfield*, the first in a number of autobiographical works that she read before starting *Villette*. If "autobiographical" is defined formally in terms of first-person narration, then this group of works includes memoirs and poetry as well as fiction: the "Recollections" that preface Southey's *Life and Correspondence*, Hunt's *Autobiography*, and Tennyson's *In Memoriam*. The most significant work, however, was the posthumous 1850 edition of Wordsworth's *Prelude*. In all the autobiographical works that Charlotte Brontë read in 1849 and 1850, the central issues of memory and the past are treated in a highly self-conscious manner. To each of these writers, memory is the source and proof of personal identity: as Southey comments, "at two years old . . . my recollection begins; prior identity I have none" ("Recollections"). The effect of this widespread emphasis on memory seems clear. Though Jane Eyre had been called upon to recount her past experience, only in *Villette* and one of the sketches that preceded it does Brontë treat memory as a problematic function. *Henry Esmond*, a novel that Brontë read in manuscript as she was writing *Villette*, testifies to the predominance of the same concerns: for the first time in Thackeray's career, memory itself becomes the subject of analysis and description.

Autobiography is, almost by definition, a form that strives to accommodate fact and desire, circumstances as they actually occurred and the longing that they —or oneself—had been somehow different. The complexity of memory is beautifully imaged in Wordsworth's well-known comparison of the man who looks through the "surface of the past" to a man looking over the side of a boat on a still lake: he

> often is perplexed and cannot part
> The shadow from the substance, rocks and sky,
> Mountains and clouds, reflected in the depth
> Of that clear flood, from things which there abide
> In their true dwelling; now is crossed by gleam
> Of his own image, by a sun-beam now,
> And wavering motions sent he knows not whence.
> (*Prelude* IV, 263–69)

The past self is the product of a number of refracted images: the uneven mirror of the lake reflects the sky, the sun, and the face of the watcher as it communicates the ever-moving objects on its bottom: shadow and substance merge indistinguishably. Most potent are the shadows cast by the longing to perceive an image of self that is acceptable if not flattering. Biographical research has shown us the extent to which such feelings can shape the "facts" recorded in autobiographical documents. Wordsworth omits the story of Annette Vallon from *The Prelude*, perhaps because she had little relevance to the account of his poetic discipline, more probably because his own part in the affair involved unattractive qualities that he did not care to reveal. In his *Confessions* Rousseau similarly distorts the chronology of his sojourn at Les Charmettes so that he does not have to acknowledge the quality of Mme. de Warens's less than exclusive affection for him. Not constrained even as much as Wordsworth or Rousseau by the need to be faithful to actual events, Brontë uses the freedom of her fictional autobiography to increase the complexity of interpenetrating and refracted images of self. Why she would need to do so seems clear. For neither Brontë nor Lucy Snowe can the facts or circumstances of experience offer any satisfaction. Family is gone; suitors have disappeared. M. Paul is dead; Graham Bretton, married to another woman, is dead to Lucy. Memory can only reveal a past of promise and hope turned to present deprivation; it is primarily a record of losses and humiliations. David Copperfield or Jane Eyre can see every untoward event in their lives as a step in the direction of the happy resolution of past difficulties—Agnes and Rochester wait at the end of their narrative journeys. No such consolation is available to Lucy. Her dilemma is like that of *In Memoriam*: events can yield fulfillment only through a change in the perspective of the individual who has suffered through them. Lucy must find the little satisfaction that her life affords through the pattern which she imposes on it, through the way in which she chooses to relate events: memory must mold experience into a form that is acceptable, a form that will "suffice," if not actually console. Lucy must depend on essentially subversive ways of appeasing memory.

Commenting on other people and their petty vanities, Lucy notes "wherever an accumulation of small defences is found . . . there, be sure, it is needed." *Villette* is a carapace of defenses against the almost intolerable pain of memory, and the first of the ways in which Lucy tries to assuage that pain is the simplest: she ignores one of the most prominent themes of midcentury autobiography by flatly refusing to acknowledge the cost of retrospection. Even in a treatment of the past as unremittingly cheerful as Leigh Hunt's, the writer still looks back on his narrative and notes, "I can never forget the pain of mind which some of the passages cost me." Likewise, Southey claims with calm satisfaction, "I have lived in the sunshine, and am still looking forward with hope," while he speaks of the "courage" he has had to find "to live again in remembrance with the dead, so much as I must needs do in retracing the course of my life." The pain of loss is the predominant tone in much of David Copperfield's narrative, and the valiant, but futile efforts of Mr. Dick illustrate the frustrations faced by any man who tries to write "a Memorial about his own history." But Lucy does not deal with the problem so directly. Indeed she never lets us know that for her recollection is something less than an occasion for tranquillity. In the context of her character, such evasions make sense. She has been trained by untoward circumstances to hide her feelings, to pretend that she is the "unobtrusive article of furniture" that the other characters take her to be. Throughout her earlier experience in Bretton and at Mme. Beck's, she has learned the benefit of "telling tales," of presenting elliptical accounts of events that do not involve any embarrassing revelations of her feelings. In one rather comically self-conscious instance, she tells Ginevra that her callous mockery of Graham and his mother has caused him acute suffering — she has told a tale, a lie, to satisfy Ginevra's expectations. Lucy often treats the reader and his conventional demands for a gratifying story as cavalierly as she has treated Ginevra. She buries her feelings in her "heretic narrative" as surely as she has buried her affections in the jar she entombs beneath the pear-tree in Mme. Beck's garden. She tells us that one must struggle "with the natural character, the strong native bent of the heart," that one must follow the dictates of Reason rather than Feeling and present to the world a surface that is "regulated," quiet, and "equable." To see beyond the supposedly imperturbable, opaque surface of Lucy's story is the reader's most challenging responsibility. Only by examining a crucial event from the narrator's earlier experience can we begin to understand the pain she inevitably feels whenever she thinks of her past.

At the opening of volume 2, Brontë presents one of the most complete of Victorian speculations on the dangers and terrors of memory, but her analysis is as remarkable for its indirection as for its power. Instead of letting the older Lucy tell us what it means to revive thoughts of the past, Brontë subjects the younger Lucy to a literal return of the "scenes and days" of her "girlhood." The effect is something like watching Alice fall down the rabbit-hole of imagination: mental phenomena are rendered as physical objects and sequences of narrative. Brontë sets this scene in "Auld Lang Syne" at a moment of crisis. Lucy has been left to spend the long vacation alone at Mme. Beck's *pensionnat*. After fainting in a street beyond the church where she has attended confession, she wakes to experience an involuntary and unexpected rebirth into a strangely familiar world. "With pain, with reluctance, with a moan and a long shiver," Lucy finds herself in an environment that seems ghostlike. At one of those oddly resonant moments so frequent in *Villette*, Lucy faces a mirror and sees the skull-like image of a dead self: "In this mirror . . . I looked spectral; my eyes larger and more hollow, my hair darker than was natural, by contrast with my thin and ashen face." As she begins to recognize the objects in the drawing room as the furniture from her godmother's house in Bretton, Lucy becomes increasingly skeptical about her own identity or sanity. She then falls asleep—only to wake in another room that intensifies her earlier sense of uncanny recognition. Again, Lucy looks into a mirror; instead of seeing a ghostly image of herself, she sees the past: "Bretton! Bretton! and ten years ago shone reflected in that mirror. And why did Bretton and my fourteenth year haunt me thus? Why, if they came at all, did they not return complete?" To return to the past, as Lucy literally does here, is to journey into a world that is spectral because it is dead, a world that calls into question the stability and substantiality of one's identity.

There is, of course, a logical explanation for Lucy's hallucinatory vision of "auld lang syne." After recognizing a portrait of Graham Bretton, Lucy soon discovers his mother sitting by her bedside. Although Lucy chooses not to reveal her identity, she learns that the past has been revived in the present simply because the Brettons have moved themselves and their belongings from England to Labassecour. As she becomes accustomed to her reinstatement in the world of her childhood, she describes even its comforts in a way that again suggests the emotional cost of memory. She rests in her bedroom and thinks of her "calm little room" as a "cave in the sea":

> There was no colour about it, except that white and pale green, sug-gestive of foam and deep water; the blanched cornice was adorned with shell-shaped ornaments, and there were white mouldings like dolphins in the ceiling-angles. Even that one touch of colour visible in the red satin pincushion bore affinity to coral; even that dark, shin-ing glass might have mirrored a mermaid. When I closed my eyes, I heard a gale, subsiding at last, bearing upon the house-front like a setting swell upon a rock-base. I heard it drawn and withdrawn far, far off, like a tide retiring from a shore of the upper world—a world so high above that the rush of its largest waves, the dash of its fiercest breakers could sound down in this submarine home, only like mur-murs and a lullaby.

La Terrasse literally offers Lucy a refuge in the past. The scene evokes some of the most eloquent language in *Villette*, yet its lyrical qualities are themselves warnings against the seductive and potentially dangerous powers of memory. Like other Victorian descriptions of the past, this passage is an image of a withdrawal that is also a regression. In the womblike "submarine home" of memory, one is protected from the storms of adult experience; there the sound of conflict is magically transformed into a lullaby. The context of the passage offers further warning that the peace of this withdrawal is deceptive and its comfort merely temporary. Like every other retreat Lucy finds, it must be abandoned; like every moment of calm, it will be disturbed. Only four chapters later, Lucy suffers a "Reaction" when she returns to Mme. Beck's school: the responsibilities of maturity must inevitably replace the joys and security of childhood. Lucy now must live by "imperious rules, prohibiting under deadly penalties all weak retro-spect of happiness past; commanding a patient journeying through the wilderness of the present."

From these events the twenty-three-year-old character learns an impressive lesson that the older narrator is not likely to overlook. To relive the sorrows of the past is to revive their pain; to relive its joys is to relinquish them once more. Though Lucy's retreat to La Terrasse, to the cave in the sea, is a time of peace and fulfillment, it renders more unbearable the present solitude and struggle which she must endure. Like Vashti, Lucy remembers the heaven she has left, and "Heaven's light" can only serve to disclose the "forlorn remoteness" of her "exile." By making a narrative return to the scenes of her past, the older Lucy is forcing herself to do what Graham unwittingly does to her when he brings to La Terrasse the sick English schoolteacher he does not recognize. In the face of such difficulties, simple reticence is no adequate defense. Without giving the reader any direct indication of the principles that underlie her treatment of the past, the narrator responds to the events or characters she recalls in ways that vary according to the emotional challenges they entail. Like the young woman responding to the unfolding revelations of her stay at La Terrasse, the older woman allows her attitudes toward the past to develop according to a coherent "plot" roughly equivalent to the volume divisions of the novel: her visit to Bretton when she was fourteen and her first term at Mme. Beck's *pensionnat* in volume 1; her renewed acquaintance with the Brettons and the Homes in the second volume; and the relationship with M. Paul that dominates the action of the third volume. But the narrator never acknowledges that such a development is taking place. The reader must discover for himself how and why these psychological processes are at work. Again the practice of Brontë's contemporaries helps define Lucy's more unconventional modes of dealing with the past.

Dickens, Hunt, Southey, Wordsworth, and Tennyson all agree on the central problem that memory presents: the difficulty of defining one's temporal perspective on the past. Wordsworth is, of course, the subtlest commentator on this question. As he explains, the man who tells his own story may feel that the difference between his past and present selves creates in him "two consciousnesses," separate identities with no relation to each other. Conversely, these two selves may interpenetrate. Speaking of his undergraduate days, Wordsworth admits: "Of these and other kindred notices / I cannot say what portion is in truth / The naked recollection of that time, / And what may rather have been called to life / By after-meditation" (*Prelude* III, 612–16). The narrator may present his "naked recollection"—his initial impressions of an event—or the product of his "after-meditation": his first impressions may be altered or effaced by his knowledge of later events or his more mature understanding of himself. Although they may not be as dismayed by their autobiographical tasks as Mr. Dick, all these writers openly admit that they are often baffled by the relation between their past and present selves. Like Wordsworth, they conscientiously warn us when, in Hunt's words, they "bring [their] night-thoughts into the morning of life." Southey, for instance, speaks of an acquaintance: "I look back upon his inoffensive and monotonous course of life with a compassion which I was then not capable of feeling." The Prologue to *In Memoriam* notifies the reader that the present-tense lyrics that follow are actually records of the first impressions of a past experience of grief. Dickens's careful handling of tenses is an even more remarkable indication of the care with which an author may balance the presentation of the narrator's first impressions against his later understanding of them. The use of the historical present is, of course, frequent in *David Copperfield*, especially in the first half of the novel as David tries to recapture the feelings of childhood. David's evolving identity is defined by present-tense chapters such as "I Observe" and his various "Retrospects." Yet the use of the tense can also express the strength of older narrator's feelings about his past experience: the warehouse where David works as a child contains "things, not of many years ago, in my mind, but of the present instant." Dickens is exceedingly careful to distinguish between the historical present of the revivified past and the present tense appropriate to his narrative activity. David adds qualifications such as "according to my present way of thinking" whenever his "later understanding comes . . . to [his] aid." At one point, he even employs the two uses of the tense in one sentence so that he can distinguish between them: "I am a sensible fellow [at seventeen years], I believe—I believe, on looking back, I mean—." Here irony emphasizes the demarcation between past and present; the narrator's "I believe" becomes a telling comment on the sense with which the seventeen-year-old credits himself.

Such self-conscious treatments of memory and its perplexing effects are characteristic of the autobiographical works Charlotte Brontë read as she approached the writing of *Villette*. By comparison Lucy Snowe's attitude toward her retrospective activity seems almost naive. Again she simply avoids the issue. Her reticence about her narrative role suggests that, for her, memory involves neither pain nor complicated temporal perspectives. Indeed her most straightforward comment on the question—the one too often accepted as definitive—implies that *Villette* is entirely the product of mature "after-meditation": "(for I speak of a time gone by: my hair which till a late period withstood the frosts of time, lies now, at last white, under a white cap, like snow beneath snow)." Lucy, now an old woman, tells the story of her younger self. The passage is reminiscent of Southey's comments on his old age or David's reference to the twenty years that separate his present self from the events he recounts. We are asked to believe that Lucy brings to the story of her youth all the serenity and calm resignation implicit in the image of her whitened hair. As we have learned from "Auld Lang Syne," however, memory has not always been a capacity that Lucy has been able to exercise with such painless ease. In another passage describing the attitudes of her younger self, Lucy has noted, "Oh, my childhood! I had feelings: passive as I lived, little as I spoke, cold as I looked, when I thought of past days, I *could* feel." The older narrator differs in no essential way from the young woman who makes this statement. A look at the first three chapters of *Villette* reveals the complex distortions of temporal perspective that her feelings create.

As conventional autobiography, these chapters are woefully inadequate. As an indication of the essential qualities of Lucy's relation to her past, they display an admirable degree of emotional logic. Reticence, of course, predominates. Neither the narrator's past nor present self is the ostensible subject here. Lucy refuses to tell us about her own childhood; rather she depicts her adolescent acquaintance with the child Paulina Home. We are asked to assume that Lucy offers us her first impressions on this relationship. Her apparently detached, yet ultimately hostile attitude toward this child creates the main difficulty. In Lucy's view of her, Paulina is scarcely human. She arrives in Bretton a "shawled bundle"; even when she emerges, Lucy repeatedly calls her "it" or the "creature" or a "mere doll." She continually views Paulina's love for her father or Graham as "absurd" or grotesquely dehumanizing. At one point Lucy even suggests that Paulina, the "little Odalisque," is faintly immoral. We might be tempted to attribute these shrewish comments to Lucy's adolescent jealousy. There is reason enough for that response. Before Paulina arrives, Lucy reigns supreme in Mrs. Bretton's affections. Paulina causes a "change" in this situation that is all the more disturbing because it is so "unexpected." This quaint child takes Lucy's place, and Lucy is forced to watch as Mrs. Bretton lavishes her attention on Paulina. Lucy finds the reunion between Paulina and her father "oppressing" simply because she is excluded from that or any other scene of parental fondness. Yet there are at work here forces—covert emotions, confused perceptions—that simply cannot be explained as the first impressions of even the most jealous of fourteen-year-old girls.

Though the narrator betrays no emotional involvement in the Bretton scenes she recalls, we need to know why she would begin her own story at that point in her experience. One answer is obvious: like the vignettes of the child and nature in *The Prelude*, like David Copperfield's precocious fascination with the subject of marriage, Paulina's stay in Bretton has a central thematic role in *Villette*. It illustrates what Lucy knows to be the basic structure of human relationships: emotional bonds are forged by the pressure of a woman's great need, and they are inevitably disrupted by "fate" or a man's fickle indifference. More importantly, Lucy's depiction of Paulina defines a central quality of her own memory: the emotional resonance of a particular scene often has little relation to Lucy's "naked recollection," and the narrator's temporal perspective on an event usually becomes apparent only after she has moved on to recount later incidents in her

life. Without giving the reader any warning, Lucy allows her "later understanding" to efface her first impressions of Paulina. Only after we have read well into
the second volume of *Villette* do we realize that Lucy's memory of the Bretton
scenes elicits an extremely defensive response because they prophesy the most
disturbing crisis in her later experience.

The events of volume 2 recapitulate those in the first three chapters and
explain why Lucy should find those earlier events significant. The incidents that
occur when Lucy is fourteen are exactly reenacted when she is twenty-three. After
the distressing isolation of the long vacation—comparable to the "unsettled sad-
ness" of her kinfolk's home when she is fourteen—Lucy again finds herself with
her godmother, "happier, easier, more at home" than she has been for years.
Bretton and the past have been revived for her. She is again pampered by Mrs.
Bretton and treated to sight-seeing and entertainments by John. Again Paulina
usurps Lucy's place. When Graham first meets the Homes at the theatre, he tells
them that the lady with him, Lucy, is "neither hindrance nor incumbrance." She
is certainly no incumbrance on his affections. She is completely forgotten for
seven weeks after the renewal of the relationship between the Brettons and the
Homes. Even the seemingly insignificant details of the second volume have their
precursors in the first three chapters. When Lucy finally returns to her "own little
sea-green room" at La Terrasse, she finds that Paulina has installed herself there
and that she is herself the "intruder," just as she has earlier gone up to her bedroom at Bretton and found, without warning, that a crib and a chest have been
added for another child's use. Paulina's sewing, her lisping speech, her servile and
tender doting on the men, all repeat her earlier behavior. Lucy even uses the same
allusion to describe the two episodes in her life. Her visits in Bretton "resembled
the sojourn of Christian and Hopeful beside a certain pleasant stream." Later,
Graham's attention is "a goodly river on whose banks I had sojourned, of whose
waves a few reviving drops had trickled to my lips." In both cases the comfort is
taken away: the river "bend[s] to another course," Paulina. Lucy's treatment of
the earlier Bretton scenes must bear all the weight of a mature woman's jealousy,
yet she cannot admit to herself—much less to her reader—that she has ever
experienced such feelings.

To reticence, then, Lucy adds a second defense against her memories of the
past: even the indirect revelation of both the narrator and the character's emotional involvement may be transferred from the scene which elicited it to another,
less painful scene. Because the events recorded in the second volume of *Villette*
are ultimately more significant than the events of Lucy's adolescence, she dis-
places her feelings about Paulina's second entry into her life onto the story of her
first intrusion into the Bretton world of security and affection. The scene at Bretton, for all its pretence of calm objectivity, is a scene recollected so much in the
light of later events that the initial emotions are ignored while the narrator tries

to avoid depicting her own present response to her memory of the scene. The result of this process is a curious sort of freedom. By attributing to her adolescent experience all her harsh attitudes toward Paulina, Lucy can recount her rival's later role in the second volume as if it had no relation to her own hopes and desires. She can ignore the cruelty of Graham's indifference. The emotional energy appropriate to the later event has already been expended. The reader's response to this complex interweaving of temporal perspectives must be less immediately productive. The reader can begin to understand the considerations that have shaped Lucy's account of an event only long after she has finished relating that part of her story. *Villette* would seem to be a novel that must be read backwards or, at very least, reread if one is to judge the narrator's perspective accurately.

Lucy's unacknowledged love for Graham Bretton is, of course, the reason for her evasive treatment of the past in volume 2. Like Pauline, Lucy is naturally reticent about affection that is not reciprocated. In a characteristically deceptive parenthetical statement, she denies entertaining any "warmer feelings" for Graham. Even years later when her hair has turned to gray, Lucy abides by the convention that a woman should not speak of love until she has been spoken to. Beyond such social prohibitions there is a more important reason for Lucy's silence. The memory of this unrequited love, the mere thought of which carries with it the certain knowledge of unfulfilled desires and wasted emotions, is so painful that it cannot be confronted openly. Like Paulina's letters to Graham, however, Lucy's narrative does "glow" with the "unconfessed confession" of her love. Indeed, Thackeray, confusing Lucy with Charlotte Brontë, felt moved to make a condescendingly amused comment on the author's "naive confession of being in love with 2 men at the same time." Only as the novel reaches its conclusion, do we discover the full extent of the narrator's involvement with these concealed past emotions and, therefore, the justice of Thackeray's comment.

Four chapters before the end of *Villette*, when Lucy is describing her hallucinatory responses to the characters gathered at the fête in the park, she refers in an uncharacteristic fashion to events that occur after the close of her story. Here, for the first and only time in the novel, she confesses to the reader her past love for Graham Bretton and, more importantly, her present undiminished capacity to love him:

> I believe in that goodly mansion, his heart, he kept one little place
> under the skylights where Lucy might have entertainment, if she chose
> to call. It was not so handsome as the chambers where he lodged his
> male friends . . . still less did it resemble the pavilion where his mar-
> riage feast was splendidly spread; yet, gradually, by long and equal
> kindness, he proved to me that he kept one little closet, over the door
> of which was written "Lucy's Room." I kept a room for him, too—

a place of which I never took the measure, either by rule or compass: I think it was like the tent of Peri-Banou. All my life I carried it folded in the hollow of my hand—yet, released from that hold and constriction, I know not but its innate capacity for expanse might have magnified it into a tabernacle for a host.

As Lucy has said of her younger self, "I *could* feel." This confession completely invalidates her earlier claim to the resigned objectivity of old age. At any time, presumably even as she tells her story, Graham could find in her heart a place splendid enough for a god. Coming as late as it does, offset by its placement among opium-induced visions, this avowal merely highlights the disconcerting complexity of the temporal perspectives in *Villette*.

This confession gives us the clue we need if we are to understand the narrator's earlier attitudes toward Graham and his place in her past. Because her feelings are so often at stake, she can never present her "naked recollections" of these events. The excessive emotions that typify her responses to Graham can be explained only by the later feelings she never mentions. Although her first meeting with Dr. John is too brief to allow her to realize that he is Graham Bretton, she reacts to this stranger who leads her through Villette with all the exaggerated trust that a Victorian wife might place in the husband who will lead her through life: "as to distrusting him, or his advice, or his address, I should almost as soon have thought of distrusting the Bible. There was goodness in his countenance, and honour in his bright eyes . . . . I believe I would have followed [his] frank tread, through continual night, to the world's end." The tone here is clearly inappropriate. Lucy's response seems proof of almost hysterical desperation or a naive adoration of "bright eyes." Many chapters later we learn that her extravagant claims of faith in this stranger can be attributed to her later recognition of him as the man she would marry if she could. Memory has clearly responded to the pressures exerted on it by the knowledge of later events. The reader, however, is asked to accept this passage as the rendering of a first impression; there are no clues to the perspective from which the event is actually viewed. Such evasions continue. The most obvious was noticed by E. M. Forster. Lucy violates the one essential convention of autobiographical form—if the reader does not demand to share the narrator's sense of later events, he does have the right to know what the character realizes at the time of any given event. For six chapters before she finds herself at La Terrasse, Lucy refuses to tell us that she knows that Dr. John and Graham Bretton are one and the same character.

In volume 2 the pressures of memory result in the confusing gyrations in attitude that typify Lucy's comments on Dr. John. She often takes pleasure in rehearsing the shortcomings of this bright-eyed John Bull—his "cruel vanity," his "levity," and his "masculine self-love." The man we see beyond her biased presentation of him deserves perhaps better treatment. He may indeed be un-imaginative, even sometimes unfeeling, but he can also be kindly, generous, and charming. His greatest shortcoming seems to be his failure to recognize just how attractive he is. Lucy surely is making him pay for his "frozen indifference" to her. Only once in the second volume does she come close to describing her origi-nal estimate of John. When he becomes disenchanted with Ginevra, when there is no other woman to claim his attention, Lucy allows herself another excessive statement, "I remember him heroic. Heroic at this moment will I hold him to be." Such ardor fades as soon as another woman arrives to captivate Graham's interest.

What Lucy recognizes as the "seeming inconsistency" of her treatment of John in volume 2 disappears when she comes to describe the hero of volume 3, Paul Emanuel. M. Paul is the only character in *Villette* who is treated in any-thing like a consistent fashion by Lucy's memory. His avowed love for her is the confirmation and fulfillment that she has sought, and one would expect her to present him entirely from the perspective of "after-meditation." Quite the oppo-site is true. Paul's characterization depends on the attitudes and judgments of the younger Lucy Snowe. We learn to value Paul just as Lucy has done. At first he is hostile, malicious—an intriguer, a despot, "not at all a good little man." Slowly, however, a "face" replaces this "mask," and we are allowed to see his good quali-ties as Lucy discovers them. Because the narrator can take comfort in looking ahead to the declaration of their mutual love in volume 3, she can afford to describe, with honesty and immediacy, those times in their relationship when even friendship seemed an impossibility. Paul's effect on Lucy has been not only to make her behavior in the past "placid and harmonious," but also to offer her a memory that she can later view in a placid and harmonious manner.

Lucy herself seems to understand that Paul's love has freed her from the emotional restraints that Graham's indifference has imposed on her. M. Paul, she tells the reader, "deserved candour, and from me always had it." When they reach the Faubourg Clotilde, she gives him a complete and accurate account of her feelings:

> "I want to tell you something," I said; "I want to tell you all." . . . I spoke. All leaped from my lips. I lacked not words now; fast I nar-rated; fluent I told my tale; it streamed on my tongue. . . . All I had encountered I detailed, all I had recognized, heard, and seen . . . the whole history, in brief, summoned to his confidence, rushed thither truthful, literal, ardent, bitter.

This description of Lucy's communication with M. Paul—"truthful, literal, ar-dent, bitter"—is an accurate account of the way she tells the part of the story in which he is involved. Again the quality of Lucy's initial behavior toward a character determines the quality of her memories. At the end of *Villette*, Lucy is finally able to be candid with both herself and the reader. She can say openly, "I loved him . . . with a passion beyond what I had yet felt." W. S. Williams had complained that the break between the second and third volumes of *Villette* marks a transfer of interest from one set of characters to another. Such, indeed, is the case. Yet there is a more significant change: from one mode of memory—painful, evasive, confused—to another mode that permits an honest return to first impressions. The third volume of *Villette* is one of the finest achievements in Charlotte Brontë's fiction. For once the characters, not the attitudes of the "morbid" narrator, dominate and determine the action. The passion and the comedy that characterize the love between Lucy and Paul are given room to expand and develop. For once a clarity of tone, based on a secure temporal perspective, puts the reader at his ease.

David Copperfield provides a suggestive counterpoint here. Throughout David's "written memory," the narrator is simultaneously "looking back" to the past and looking forward to a time "thereafter, when all the irremediable past [is] rendered plain." Although he never offers more information than he as a character would have had at the time of any particular event, the whole narrative is dominated by his awareness of a future in which that event becomes part of the "irremediable past." We can accept David's frequently excessive responses because we know that he is aware of implications to which we are necessarily blind. Before he describes Steerforth's seduction of Emily, he speaks of the "dread" with which his narrative "journey" fills him: "I cannot bear to think of what did come, upon that memorable night; of what must come again, if I go on." We may disagree with the judgments and attitudes that result from David's basic conventionality, but we trust him to define his perspective on his past. Yet even David can be evasive. His love for Agnes, "the most secret current of [his] mind," is a secret kept from the reader's view. Because he knows that his feelings for Agnes are not merely sibling affection even while Dora is alive, he cannot reveal them until long after he has recounted the event of Dora's death. The older narrator cannot acknowledge a love which even his younger self represses; as Thackeray said of Brontë, David has loved two women at the same time. Lucy's difficulties are even more complex—she seems to look back on an isolated moment in the past as if nothing precedes or follows it simply because each event leads to Graham's ultimate rejection of her—but the basic pattern of reminiscence is the same. Evidences of guilty love, be it love for Agnes or Graham, must be suppressed. The narrator can afford to revive his first impressions only when his love has been the function of his innocence—as is David's infatuation with Dora—or when it has found later confirmation—as Lucy's does when M. Paul proposes to her.

Yet even Paul's response to the intensity and purity of Lucy's love does not account for the emotional clarity that the narrator achieves in volume 3. Here we find the direct and unrestrained honesty that is one of Jane Eyre's most attractive qualities. Here Lucy is able to confess her love for Graham. We are forced to recognize that Lucy has managed to put considerable distance between her narrating self and her earlier emotions; paradoxically, this distance allows a revival of first impressions. At first this paradox seems inexplicable. The facts of Lucy's experience have again become an insurmountable barrier to emotional satisfaction. Unlike David, who writes his story with Agnes seated next to him, Lucy is another Miss Marchmont, alone with her memories. Yet she recounts the marriage of Paulina Home and Graham Bretton with such calm disinterest one might think that it causes her no pain. How does this situation come about? In one sense the answer to this question is very simple. Lucy's writing of her story in the first and second volumes is itself the activity that allows her to triumph over her earlier inability to confront the implications of memory. Both *The Prelude* and *In Memoriam* attest to the way in which the expression of confusion or sorrow may become the means to certainty or consolation. Unlike Wordsworth, however, Lucy can take no comfort in an artistic self that is the source of imperishable art. Nor is her perspective like Tennyson's; her focus, more comparable to that of Wordsworth's political hopes, is fixed on this world, "the place where, in the end, / We find our happiness, or not at all" (*Prelude* XI, 143–44). As Lucy tells us, if she were a nun, she would have no reason to write her confessions. The act of recording her past must, therefore, provide Lucy with the specifically temporal satisfactions that this world has denied her. The process by which this unlikely end is attained is again illuminated by an event from her earlier experience.

During her first term at Mme. Beck's, Paul forces Lucy to perform a man's role in a vapid comedy, and she turns an incident which seems to promise only embarrassment into an emotional harvest. This scene has made numbers of readers uneasy. It is less important, however, as a demonstration of covert androgyny or sexual peversity than as a key to the way in which Lucy's imagination allows her to triumph over apparently intractable circumstances. At this point in the story, Dr. John is in love with Ginevra, a woman Lucy judges unworthy of his affections. The role that M. Paul asks Lucy to play before an audience which includes Dr. John allows her to reverse the roles of actual experience. If Lucy cannot be successful as Ginevra's rival for Dr. John's affections, then she will become the image of Colonel de Hamal, Dr. John's rival for Ginevra. Here Lucy is fully aware of what she is doing: "my longing was to eclipse the 'Ours:' *i.e.*, Dr. John." Lucy's "idea" has "half-changed the nature of the rôle" and "recklessly altered the spirit" of the play. She proves that Ginevra can be attracted to a "butterfly, a talker, and a traitor" by accepting that characterization as her own.

She finds immense personal satisfaction in her part: "warming, becoming interested, taking courage, I acted to please myself." She mocks the facile nature of both John's love and its object. The "facts" of the play's script have been retained, but they have been molded to offer Lucy precisely the gratifying self-justification they would seem to preclude.

This incident is a remarkably clear emblem of the way in which Lucy recalls the most potentially painful junctures of her experience. She finds consolation in an otherwise barren past by systematically and continuously reversing the roles which the facts of her story impose on herself and her fellow characters. Particularly in volume 2, each of the major characters becomes an objectified version of Lucy's personality or experience—until together they become a way of positing at least a symbolic or vicarious fulfillment of her desires. *Villette* is less a narrative in which other characters are granted an autonomous existence than a hall of mirrors in which they are allowed to appear because they serve as facets reflecting the affective truth of Lucy's life. This process allows Lucy to set her identity at a distance for the purposes of honest scrutiny while she transforms that image of self into an emotionally satisfying prospect. Memory, for Lucy, achieves all the status that the Romantics attribute to the imagination. Indeed, Lucy's narrative is proof of the mental capacities whose power De Quincey found so overwhelming: "I feared . . . that some . . . tendency of the brain might thus be making itself . . . *objective*; and the sentient organ *project* itself as its own object." The recreative power of Lucy's memory has precisely this effect: by "projecting" her past and present needs onto the portions of the narrative ostensibly concerned with other lives, her "sentient organ," her memory of the past finally achieves expression.

The role of Paulina de Bassompierre is central to the transformations wrought by Lucy's memory. The childhood scenes of the novel contain hints of a mysterious emotional identification between the two characters. At one point, Lucy notes, "I wished she would utter some hysterical cry, so that I might get relief and be at ease." Paulina is the main defense created by the quality of Lucy's vision because she is a projection of Lucy's most gratifying self-image. In an idealized and literally beautified manner, Paulina's "hoar-frost" and "pure, fine flame" recapitulate the fire and ice of Lucy's nature. The narrator explains, "In speaking of her attractions, I would not exaggerate language; but, indeed, they seemed to me very real and engaging." Indeed they should—for they are the attractions of sensibility and character that Lucy knows to be her own. If we take the assumptions behind the illusion of autobiographical fiction seriously, we must accept the premise that Lucy has no control over the action. John and Paulina will marry, whatever Lucy may feel about that event. By defining Paulina as a second self, Lucy can find satisfaction in the attraction that John feels for the qualities she shares with Paulina—even as she offers implicit criticism of his inability to recognize them in herself.

This process, however, would not work if Lucy's memory did not have another counter with which to work: Ginevra Fanshawe. During the action of the first volume, Ginevra serves as a way of putting Graham in his place—or, more precisely, of putting Graham in Lucy's place. Like Graham in his responses to Lucy, Ginevra dismissed his affection because he has none of the glamour of Colonel de Hamal; she claims, "Les penseurs, les hommes profonds et passionnés ne sont pas à mon gout," but her characterization of Graham is more appropriate to Lucy than to the charming young doctor. At the beginning of the second volume, just as Graham suffers his final disillusionment about Ginevra, Lucy describes him in a way that exactly defines her own situation: "His lady-love beamed upon him from a sphere above his own: he could not come near her; he was not certain that he could win from her a look." Like Lucy, Graham finds himself loving someone both unattainable and worthless. Including Ginevra in her story is Lucy's way of making Graham suffer the pain that his indifference causes her. Here, perhaps, is one reason behind the inconsistency of Lucy's behavior when she responds to Graham's suspicions about Ginevra by becoming her "advocate." Here, as well, is the emotional logic behind the unacknowledged bond of intimacy between the spoiled schoolgirl and the reserved teacher at Mme. Beck's.

When Paulina enters the action in the second volume, Lucy's memory of events must again "half-change" and "alter" the roles of the various characters if this process of emotional fulfillment is to continue. If Lucy is not to hate her new rival Paulina—and she cannot hate the woman who is a perfected version of herself—then Lucy must attribute to Ginevra all the jealousy she cannot allow herself to feel. Ginevra therefore learns to value Graham's attentions only when he no longer feels anything for her. Like the Lucy who narrates the first three chapters of *Villette*, Ginevra dismisses Paulina as a "conceited doll" and finds "sickening" the domestic scenes enacted by the Brettons and the de Bassompierres. Lucy's evaluation of Ginevra's petulance is shrewd. She tells Ginevra, "It would not have been so [sickening] if the object of attention had been changed: if *you* had taken Miss de Bassompierre's place." Lucy, of course, is right about Ginevra's jealousy. Here temporal perspectives become complex indeed; the narrator's younger self is indirectly commenting on her own later attitude toward Paulina, an attitude that has made itself apparent in the earlier childhood scenes. Because Ginevra is acting out Lucy's jealousy, the narrator can understand its implications. Later when Ginevra expresses her disdain for Graham, a "hatred . . . expressed in terms so unmeasured and proportions so monstrous," she gives the schoolgirl a "sound moral drubbing." Ginevra receives the "taming" that Lucy's Jael so often must administer to the Sisera of her affections. To complete this circle of identifications, Paulina must assume the burden of Lucy's earlier jealousy of Ginevra. Long after Graham's actions cease to justify the fear, Paulina worries that he loves Ginevra. At the end of chapter 26, she confesses this fear to Lucy. Lucy now can answer with all the calm and generous candor of the celibate who has been freed from the pressures of earthly desires—only because Paulina is acting out those desires for her. As the story of Graham and Paulina's engagement develops along the periphery of the central action of volume 3, Lucy can tell that part of the story with dignified objectivity—not because she is now the "mere looker-on at life" that she has claimed to be, not because the older woman no longer feels any love for Graham, but simply because she sees herself so thoroughly involved in Paulina's unquestionable triumph over Graham's heart.

Finding such fugitive modes of self-expression is a central convention of nineteenth-century autobiography. The writer whose work is a mirror of his experience naturally emphasizes those events or characters within it which serve as miniature reflections of self. The pretence of distance between the writer and his reflection is, however, absolutely essential to the success of this kind of self-analysis. Wordsworth, for instance, inserted in *The Prelude* a description of himself that he had written earlier, but he found he had to conceal it as a meditation on the dead Winander boy if he were to acknowledge that a facet of himself had likewise perished. One another occasion he refers to the story of Vaudracour and Julia because Vaudracour is a repressed version of the self who fell in love with Annette Vallon. *In Memoriam* is the record of similar processes. Tennyson continuously seeks out analogues for his feelings—he is variously defined as the widow, the linnet, the expectant or disappointed lover—and he explains this proliferation of analogues by noting that the love he feels "sees himself in all he sees" (XCVII, 4). In one passage he recalls a dream in which he has seen Hallam's troubled face. He wakes and realizes, "It is the trouble of my youth / That foolish sleep transfers to thee [Hallam]" (LXVIII, 15–16). The art of autobiography, like Tennyson's dream, rests on such projections of self. Patrick Brontë's mask, seemingly the bright idea of a concerned parent, is a device that has a natural role in autobiography. By exploring self as if it were another identity, the autobiographer can confront its hidden facets with honesty and often profoundly acute scrutiny. Lucy's use of this device is unusual only because it invariably achieves for her an otherwise unattainable emotional gratification.

Brontë defines even more clearly the tradition behind *Villette* when Lucy says of Paulina, "I wondered to find my thoughts hers: there are certain things in which we so rarely meet with our double that it seems a miracle when that chance befals." Lucy uses precisely the right word here. Paulina is her double, but that fact is a function of her own perception, not the result of the workings of Providence or fortune. Unlike Lucy, Brontë would not be blind to the psychological implications of that term. In *The Spell*, one of the more coherent works of the juvenilia, she had followed the model of Hogg's *Confessions of a Justified*

Sinner (1824) when she created for the Duke of Zamorna a twin brother, an "alter-ego" and "repetition" to explain his "unfathomable, incomprehensible nature." Lucy, a character considerably more advanced in complexity than even Zamorna, deserves and indeed requires a *doppelgänger*. Paulina, Ginevra, and even Vashti are extensions of a technique that Brontë would have remembered from her early reading of Romantic fiction and from her own adolescent Angrian works. Yet the psychological process involved in the creation of doubles is as much akin to the conventions of autobiography as it is characteristic of the Gothic or Romantic imagination expressed in *The Devil's Elixir* or Hogg's *Confessions*. Otto Rank defined the link between doubles and narcissism as the desire to perceive a version of self that triumphs over mortality; autobiography, by definition a narcissistic endeavor, would seem the genre particularly suited to such modes of perception. In fact, both *David Copperfield* and *Villette* attest to the vitality and significance of the double in midcentury autobiography.

Like Tennyson and Wordsworth, both David and Lucy share the propensity to project versions of themselves onto other characters such as Steerforth, Traddles, Ginevra, or Miss Marchmont, but they also refuse to recognize the doubles who figure forth their own sexual identities—Uriah Heep and the Nun. This situation is not at all surprising. Both David and Lucy suffer from a similar inability to recognize themselves when they literally look into a mirror. David's hatred for Uriah is the only expression he can give the "secret current" of his emotions, his love for Agnes. Uriah's role in his story is consistently tied to David's attitude toward his adopted "sister." Uriah takes over David's bedroom in the Wickfield household; he aspires to Agnes's hand in marriage—all when David himself is involved in his courtship of Dora and their subsequent marriage. David acts out his self-disgust and punishes his own hidden desires when he slaps Uriah. If there were any question about the nature of David's feelings, it would be swept away by his response when Uriah announces his plan to marry Agnes:

> I believe I had a delirious idea of seizing the red-hot poker out of the fire, and running him through with it. It went from me with a shock, like a ball fired from a rifle: but the image of Agnes, outraged by so much as a thought of this red-headed animal's, remained in my mind . . . . He seemed to swell and grow before my eyes . . . and the strange feeling . . . that all this had occurred before, at some indefinite time, and that I knew what he was going to say next, took possession of me.

David, of course, knows what Uriah will say next because Uriah expresses what he feels; the concatenation of libidinal energies in this passage is attributed to both characters, not just to Uriah. Interestingly, Brontë inverts this use of the double—and indeed the larger tradition of which it is an example—in her treatment of the nun. While Dickens uses Uriah to objectify the sexual impulses that David must deny, Lucy Snowe's nun projects the refusal to express such energies: the sin in *Villette* is not desire, but the repression of desire. The nun first appears when Lucy receives a letter from Graham, when she is trying to summon reason to restrain emotion. As Graham quite accurately comments, the nun is specifically his enemy. Only after she has buried Graham's letter and her hope that he might reciprocate her feelings does Lucy welcome and even reach out to touch the spectral figure she has earlier fled. David leaves the side of Dora's deathbed so that he can travel to Dover and aid in the defeat of Uriah's ambitions; when it seems most likely that Dora's death will render his feelings for Agnes acceptable, David literally puts them in prison. Lucy, however, destroys her double when she recognizes the strength of her love for M. Paul; after seeing Justine Marie in the park with Paul, she can express her jealous desire to possess him and, later that evening, tear to pieces the clothes worn by the nun.

Yet memory must further complicate these earlier psychological processes. Brontë gives the tradition of the double a final and unconventional twist by turning Lucy's lover into yet another of her second selves. Paul is, first and foremost, Graham's replacement. If Graham is the romantic hero of *Villette*, Paul is its "Christian hero." Patterned after the initial tie between Lucy and Graham, Paul's love first finds expression in the idea of a sibling affection. Just as the Frenchman represents a more satisfying version of the young English doctor, he is also another Lucy. At one point he even forces her to look in a mirror so that she can see the "affinity" between them. His irritable actions, like Lucy's reserve, conceal the "inner flame" he shares with both Lucy and Paulina. This identification, in turn, affects Lucy's position. Paul's love, his frequently demonstrated jealousy, his fiery nature allow Lucy to assume the role that Graham has played in volumes 1 and 2. Like the earlier Graham, she becomes the unresponsive object of love: she is "placid" in the face of Paul's tempestuous emotions; she experiences "a certain smugness of composure, indeed, scarcely in my habits, and pleasantly novel to my feelings." That Paul, playing Lucy's earlier role, wins her affection and respect, is, by analogy, a final triumph over Graham's indifference. By describing Paul as if he were going through a course of emotions that she herself has previously experienced, Lucy manages to have it both ways. Because Paul is a man, he can reveal his feelings and therefore act out the responses that Lucy has previously denied. Even the quality of Paul's speech depends on Lucy's actions and characterization. When he explains that his capacity for love "died in the past— in the present it lies buried—its grave is deep-dug, well-heaped, and many winters old," he is recapitulating the scene in which Lucy buries the symbol of her love for Graham under the pear-tree in the garden. Paul's exaggerated jealousy also reveals Lucy's carefully concealed responses to Graham. As Lucy allows herself to play the roles of both Paulina and Graham, Paul's character becomes identified with those of Graham and Lucy.

Late in *Villette* Lucy makes what seems to be a wholly gratuitous and nearly absurd statement that again emphasizes the transformations that her imagination perpetually effects. After asking Lucy for her friendship, Paul fails to meet her at their usual hour for lessons. Instead he works in the garden outside the schoolroom and "fondles" the spaniel Sylvie, "calling her tender names in a tender voice." Lucy describes the dog and then comments, "I never saw her, but I thought of Paulina de Bassompierre: forgive the association, reader, it *would* occur." This strange "association" is explained in the next sentence: "M. Paul petted and patted her; the endearments she received were not to be wondered at; she invited affection by her beauty and her vivacious life." Paulina must appear one more time as a threat to Lucy's hold on a man's affections. Here, however, her rival for Paul's love is no more likely to succeed than she herself could have succeeded against Paulina's claims on Graham. Her apology for this "association" is either disingenuous or naive. Such associations, doublings, and identifications are the distinguishing characteristic of a narrative which constantly mirrors back the images of Lucy's suppressed emotional life. At one point she says of Graham, "He was a born victor, as some are born vanquished." Lucy consistently sees herself as one of the vanquished. But if some victors are born, Lucy's narrative proves that others can be made. During the course of the third volume, the fact of Paul's love allows Lucy to triumph. More importantly, the way in which she describes that love, the form that memory imposes on events through "associations," allows her to triumph one last time over that "born victor," Graham Bretton.

During their first meeting at La Terrasse, Paulina explains herself to Lucy by paraphrasing a line from Wordsworth: "The child of seven years lives yet in the girl of seventeen." The rest of the epigraph to the "Intimations of Immortality" ode is equally applicable to Paulina: "And I would wish my days to be / Bound each to each by natural piety." Paulina's quite Wordsworthian sense of the past—as opposed to Graham's propensity to live in and for the present moment—elicits Lucy's unqualified approval and admiration: "Her eyes were the eyes of one who can remember; one whose childhood does not fade like a dream, nor whose youth vanish like a sunbeam. She would not take life, loosely and incoherently, in parts, and let one season slip as she entered on another: she would retain and add; often review from the commencement, and so grow in harmony and consistency as she grew in years." This passage recalls Wordsworth's desire to use the narration of his past experience to "understand [him]self":

"my hope has been, that I might fetch / Invigorating thoughts from former years; / Might fix the wavering balance of my mind" (*Prelude* I, 627, 620–22). Memory, for both Paulina and Wordsworth, is literally a source of integrity, that sense of a self that is "consistent," "harmonious," and unwavering. The connections between past and present selves that are wrought by memory are proof of the organic growth of a distinct identity. Addressing Venus, the morning and the evening star, Tennyson makes the same point: "Thou, like my present and my past, / Thy place is changed; thou art the same" (*In Memoriam* CXXI, 17–20). By the end of *David Copperfield*, the narrator can claim a similar faith in the coherent patterns that memory imposes on his life. Earlier he has seen an absolute division between the young boy he was and the man he has become: "That little fellow seems to be no part of me; I remember him as something left behind upon the road of life—as something I have passed, rather than have actually been—and almost think of him as of some one else." By the time he proposes to Agnes, however, his narrative "journey" has linked the two selves: "Long miles of road then opened out before my mind; and, toiling on, I saw a ragged way-worn boy forsaken and neglected, who should come to call even [Agnes's] heart now beating against mine, his own." Paulina's sense of the past, then, embodies a common nineteenth-century ideal, one that would appear again as the central piety of *The Mill on the Floss*.

Paulina's ability to give "a full greeting to the Past" is yet another way in which she is a refined version of Lucy's less than ideal self. Lucy has said of her younger self that she has lived "two lives"; that sense of division is appropriate to her narrative activity as well. The moments of clarity she achieves in volume 3 fade in the "Finis" with which *Villette* ends. Here again memory too painful for expression must be evasively cloaked in vague generalizations and patently ironic statements of resolution. Earlier Lucy's childhood, unlike Paulina's, has "fade[d] like a dream." At the end of the novel, Lucy lets another "season slip" because its revival would be unbearable. Though the evasions at the end of *Villette* were a response to Patrick Brontë's demand for a happy ending, Charlotte Brontë's attempt to "veil the fate in oracular words," as Elizabeth Gaskell called the process, is an appropriate final demonstration of the nature of Lucy's memory. The workings of memory implicit in her narrative correspond to the stages depicted in "Auld Lang Syne." During the childhood sections of *Villette*, Lucy is a ghost-like presence on the periphery of the action. Later she finds herself "happier, easier, more at home" in the past as she has felt during her stay at La Terrasse. But the comfort offered by memory is a promise of inevitable dispossession. The fact of Paul's death makes the past as uninhabitable as Lucy's earlier need to earn a living has made La Terrasse. Yet in the interval before she must acknowledge the fact of her ultimate and continuing deprivation, Lucy makes at least partial peace

with her past. In her hands the already highly developed conventions of autobiography reach a new level of complexity and subtlety. Both character and creator construct a narrative mirror in which self appears vindicated against the
slights experience has dealt them and consoled for the indifference with which
others have treated them.

ROSEMARIE BODENHEIMER

Jane Eyre in Search of Her Story

O‍n the first page of *Jane Eyre*, Jane is ordered to keep silent; at the end of the novel her voice becomes the central source of perception for her blind and captive audience, Mr. Rochester, "impressing by sound on his ear what light could no longer stamp on his eye." How Jane acquires and uses the power of speech, and with whom, are subjects that bear both upon the story of her development as a character and upon the first-person narrative stance that Charlotte Brontë invented for her first successful novel. At many points in the telling, Jane's story calls attention to the questions, "How shall I learn to tell the story of my life?" and "What kind of a story is it?" And her narrative is persistently set in relation to other, more conventional kinds of stories—not only the fairy tales, Gothics, and "governess tales" which have received critical attention, but also the internal, interpolated narratives like Rochester's story about his affair with Céline Varens, St. John Rivers's version of Jane's inheritance story, or the innkeeper's tale about the burning of Thornfield. Jane's insistence on the originality of her character and voice must therefore be seen as taking shape in a world full of fictions, which often prove to be in curiously unstable relations with her own.

"Until you can speak pleasantly, remain silent," Mrs. Reed says to Jane in the opening scene; the words quite precisely reverse Brontë's private formulation of the heroics of narration:

The standard heroes and heroines of novels are personages in whom I could never from childhood upwards take an interest, believe to be natural, or wish to imitate. Were I obliged to copy these characters I

From *Papers on Language and Literature* 16, no. 3 (Summer 1980). © 1980 by the Board of Trustees of Southern Illinois University.

> would simply not write at all. . . . Unless I have the courage to use
> the language of Truth in preference to the jargon of Conventionality,
> I ought to be silent.

And, in fact, Jane Eyre's history may be read as the story of an empowered
narrator, which describes her gradual, though partial release from conventional
bondages, both social and fictional. Such a reading, emphasizing the literary self-
consciousness of *Jane Eyre*, shows that the "problem" of speaking out in a single
and singular voice is not only Brontë's narrative voice, but an explicit and com-
plexly argued theme in the substance of the fiction.

In one of the moments so frequent in self-conscious narratives, Brontë gives
us an embedded image of the fiction-maker herself. Restless at Thornfield, be-
lieving in "the existence of other and more vivid kinds of goodness," Jane stands
on the roof of Rochester's house and indulges the "bright visions" of her imagination,

> to let my heart be heaved by the exultant movement, which, while it
> swelled it in trouble, expanded it with life; and, best of all, to open
> my inward ear to a tale that was never ended—a tale my imagination
> created, and narrated continuously; quickened with all of incident,
> life, fire, feeling, that I desired and had not in my actual existence.

The temptation to read this as an uncritical image of Jane's all-devouring fantasy
has been well argued away by critics who show how little we can identify Jane's
romantic daydreams with the vision of the novel. But the passage raises a number
of points which have, finally, to be understood in the entire context of Jane's role
as the teller of her life. First, the creations of Jane's imagination have already
been made suspect during the childhood scene in the red room, where her fantasies overwhelm and overpower her. The scene of Jane's Thornfield fantasy life
—pacing the third story, within earshot of the mysterious laughter—links it, as
well, with the inarticulate sounds that signify Bertha Mason's imprisonment in
her own passions. The inward tale is clearly presented as a substitute for the life
of social observation and action that Jane wants; and as soon as a real relation
presents itself—as Rochester conveniently does two pages on—Jane stops needing the relief, though she does not stop the habit of transforming actual experience into narrative.

But it is exactly the curious conflation of heroine, teller, and audience that
is crucial to the state Jane describes, and that makes it an image of imprisonment rather than one of romantic escape. This tale, a transaction between Jane's
"imagination" and her "inward ear," is inaudible, untestable; it seems to have no
beginning or end because of its function as daydream, and because there is no

audience. Jane's progress in the novel is in opposition to this state, and has to do with finding a fit audience for whom she can give a proper shape to her own story.

Much of the drama in the Gateshead section of the novel is created through the tension between Jane's—and our—listening in outraged silence to the versions of her offered by members of the Reed household, and Jane's explosive outbreaks into speech. The novel begins where it does to emphasize exactly this: "that day" so casually introduced in the first sentence is the day on which Jane first talks back to John Reed, her accustomed and quite involuntary words articulating "parallels" drawn "in silence, which I never thought thus to have declared aloud." Jane's frantic comparison of John Reed with the Roman emperors of her reading is comic, and lightly suggests the imbalance between her interior life and social reality that results from her long-withheld resentment. The immediate effect of the outbreak is the famous red-room scene, which teaches Jane that passion vented leads to imprisonment—a major theme of the novel. Yet the real climax of the Gateshead section is the scene in which Jane lashes out at Mrs. Reed, achieving a taste of the power of speech and a brief sensation of victory. That scene gathers up many of the implications of "tale-telling" as it is treated in the first section.

Jane's pain and confusion is established from the beginning as a response to the disjunction between the descriptions she must listen to and the truth of her character. Her first spoken words are, "What does Bessie say I have done?" Requiring evidence for crime, and getting none, she has already a touch of skepticism about the accuracy even of the relation between Bessie's saying and her own doing. Mrs. Reed's culminating blow is to publicize Jane to Brocklehurst as a liar. The accusation could not be more wrong; it attacks Jane at her tenderest spot, on the matter of false and true speaking. Her subsequent outburst at Mrs. Reed is finally effective at quenching her antagonist because Jane asserts for the first time a reciprocal power of tale-telling, and an equivalent power to defame Mrs. Reed's character: "I will tell anybody who asks me questions this exact tale. . . . I'll let everybody at Lowood know what you are, and what you have done." The triumph in a victory won with weapons of the oppressor is soon corroded, and the narrator makes a statement that sets up for the next stage of Jane's learning: "I would fain exercise some better faculty than that of fierce speaking." It has become necessary that Jane find a life, and a way of telling it, that does not equate truth-telling with revenge.

Though less dramatic than the "fierce speaking" sequence, Jane's relationships with Mr. Lloyd and Bessie are also full of attention to how she talks. The doctor is Jane's first sympathetic audience, but the narrative emphasis during his dialogue with her is on her ineptitude at putting her woes into words. During the first half of the scene Bessie answers for Jane most of the time, frustrating our desire for Jane to take charge of her own story; when the doctor maneuvers Bessie's departure, the narrative pauses to announce the importance of the theme: "Children can feel, but they cannot analyze their feelings; and if the analysis is partially effected in thought, they know not how to express the result of the process in words." Jane's "bungling" pauses and "meagre" truths are meant to show again the imbalance between Jane's words and her thoughts and so to establish the terms for her future growth. A similar focus on Jane's way of talking informs her dialogue with Bessie after the outburst at Mrs. Reed; here Jane dares more gentle frankness, with more reward, than ever before, and Bessie exclaims, "You little sharp thing! you've got quite a new way of talking."

Once at Lowood, Jane has a "story," and how she tells it becomes an explicit issue. Helen Burns is Jane's first literary critic. To her, Jane pours out "the tale of my sufferings and resentments. Bitter and truculent when excited, I spoke as I felt, without reserve or softening." She then expects Helen to agree to her tale's moral: " 'Well,' I asked impatiently, 'is not Mrs. Reed a hard-hearted, bad woman?' " Helen chastises Jane for wasting her energy "registering wrongs"; she makes it clear that the tale-teller chooses her story. Though Helen's own focus on heaven is never Jane's own, Helen's admonitions modify Jane's tale when she comes to tell it to Miss Temple. The description of that process is fascinating for its emphasis on art and credibility:

> I resolved in the depth of my heart that I would be most moderate: most correct; and, having reflected a few minutes in order to arrange coherently what I had to say, I told her all the story of my sad childhood. Exhausted by emotion, my language was more subdued than it generally was when it developed that sad theme; and mindful of Helen's warnings against the indulgence of resentment, I infused into the narrative far less of gall and wormwood than ordinary. Thus restrained and simplified, it sounded more credible: I felt as I went on that Miss Temple fully believed me.

The episode marks the socialization of Jane's narrative style; the moment when she realizes the power of conscious control over sequence, diction, and tone. Unlike the warlike power to threaten that she uses with Mrs. Reed, this deliberate restraint gets her what she has always wanted: the power to make others believe her. It is especially important here that at the moment when Jane's internal life finally finds a fair hearing, Brontë should stress the complicated artfulness required by Jane's double awareness of story and listener, the interdependence of art and audience. At the same moment, however, Brontë offers to us—her audience—a similarly double position, for we have experienced the rage as well as the restraint; and are allowed to feel the difference between the "credible story" Miss Temple hears and the personal sources or original truths of the experiences themselves. In this way a crucial tension is established between Jane's moral progress in designing her story and the novel's implicit assertion that "truth" is not credibility, that it is made of different, less coherent stuff. My point here is less to emphasize Brontë's own ambivalence about "Truth versus Art" than to point out her artfulness in setting up the dialectic between Jane's "internal" progress as a narrator and the "external" narrative, which creates in the reader a dramatic sense of the tension. As audience to Jane's audiences, we are required to maintain a strenuous consciousness of the pressures in the process of turning experience into story.

Jane's primary audience is Rochester; in that relationship the dynamic of "fierce speaking and credible narrative" is revived and expanded. The "rightness" of Rochester as Jane's lover is initially dramatized through Jane's freedom to speak frankly with him and their shared distrust of conventional social languages. This is made plain in the opening of one of their important early dialogues when Rochester asks Jane if she thinks him handsome. Her response sets up both the beauty of the relationship and its danger: "I should, if I had deliberated, have replied to this question by something conventionally vague and polite; but the answer somehow slipped from my tongue before I was aware:—'No sir.'" The dialogue (which is, again, about the subject of how Jane and Rochester are to speak) becomes the brusque flirtation which is to characterize and validate the love affair; but the involuntary aspect of Jane's answer is a two-sided token, recalling her helpless, uncontrolled early outbursts as well as offering a new freedom. The manipulative character of Rochester's power to move Jane to involuntary speech is underlined in his attempt to trick her into self-revelation by disguising himself as a gypsy fortune-teller; and it comes to a head in the garden proposal scene when he successfully precipitates Jane into speech by threatening her with jealousy and loss. The moment echoes Jane's scene with Mrs. Reed ("*Speak* I must: I had been trodden on severely, and *must* turn: but how?"); Jane is again mastered by repressed feelings: "In listening, I sobbed convulsively; for I could repress what I endured no longer: I was obliged to yield; and I was shaken from head to foot with acute distress. . . . The vehemence of emotion, stirred by grief and love within me, was claiming mastery, and struggling for full sway; and asserting a right to predominate: to overcome, to live, rise, and reign at last; yes,—and to speak."

Raised to something like passion," Jane asserts her equality with Rochester in a new kind of "fierce speaking." Interestingly, the idea of freedom arises, again, from that stance: "I have spoken my mind, and go anywhere now. . . . I am a free human being with an independent will; which I now exert to leave you." It is a rehearsal in miniature for her later actual leaving, after another fervent moment of speaking her mind releases her to do what she knows to be necessary for the preservation of her integrity. The recurrent conjunction of impassioned speech and liberation from a social tie is an important one. "Speaking the mind" is not storytelling; it lacks the artistic control and the awareness of audience that precede social integration. The opposition between these two kinds of speech is crucial to an understanding of Jane's final return to Rochester.

At the end of the novel, Rochester's blindness leaves Jane in sole command of the narrative field; she becomes the single source of evidence, the voice which tells what her audience cannot see, and the arbiter of what is and is not to be told. This rather absolute overturning of the power situation at the end of the novel has generated a good deal of critical eyebrow-raising. Of course it is true that Brontë defines relationships as power struggles, that her imagination tends to work between extreme poles. But it is hardly an imagination that knows not what it does. The narrative here is completely forthright about Jane's new position: "His countenance reminded one of a lamp quenched, waiting to be relit — and alas! it was not himself that could now kindle the lustre of animated expression: he was dependent on another for that office! I had meant to be gay and careless, but the powerlessness of that strong man touched me to the quick." What Brontë is interested in dramatizing in the last scenes is not that Jane has the power, but how she is to use it. And the power she takes to "rehumanize" and "rekindle" is defined precisely as the power of storytelling.

When Jane first sees Rochester at Ferndean, she immediately describes her reactions in terms of the restraint associated with "credible narrative": "I had no difficulty in restraining my voice from exclamation, my step from hasty advance." She arranges, of course, that Rochester recognize her by her voice. Most importantly, she manipulates the telling of her adventures in ways which are carefully designed to "cure" Rochester's despair; she becomes "the instrument for his cure," not in the way he had earlier intended, but through the powers of the storyteller to move her audience. On the first night, she gives "very partial replies" to his questions because she wishes "to open no fresh well of emotion in his heart: my sole present aim was to cheer him." She banks on the suspense of a half-told tale to keep his hopes going overnight, and so realizes the power at her command: " 'I see I have the means of fretting him out of his melancholy for some time to come.' " Her presentation of her relationship with St. John draws out the suspense to exactly that end; while Jane plays on Rochester's jealousy as he had earlier played on hers, she does so with a full moral control of its effect. "The narrative of my experience" is "softened considerably" to avoid inflicting "unnecessary pain"; and in that description we hear the final stage of the mediation between "truth" and "audience" that Jane began to learn in telling her story to Miss Temple. Having then discovered art as a means to credibility, she now uses it for the moral and emotional amusement, relief, and animation of her audience.

Brontë's interest in stressing Jane's responsibility to her audience is particularly clear when she makes a special point of telling us that Jane withholds the "supernatural" experience of hearing Rochester's voice calling her. Even though she has earlier proclaimed the belief that the event was nature doing "her best," Jane feels that Rochester's tendency to "gloom, needed not the deeper shade of the supernatural." The passage seals Jane's commitment to "credible narrative," and to the shaping and pruning of experience that it demands. The implication for her development is clear: Jane has grown up into a purveyor of tales realistic and moral, suspenseful and heartwarming. Since the time of her lonely pacing in Thornfield's third story, her tale has acquired form and social content, while she has acquired an endless supply of audience and the concomitant power and responsibility to shape a vision of the world for him.

A private and dependent audience of one in a secluded manor may not seem so triumphant a development from that internal continuous narrative—though it is not a bad image for the single and private relationship of novelist and reader. But in Jane's career the search for audience is essentially a search for love and human connection. And maintaining the connection means withholding some truths. Thus, the act of withholding so curiously stressed at the end of the novel is a guarantee of the social connection of Jane and Rochester, even as it suppresses the mystic connection implied by the supernatural calls through the night. It is Jane's assertion of control, both over Rochester and over forces in the universe, and in the psyche, that belie the desire to shape and control experience.

While the "internal" plot presents Jane's repression as a moral choice, the larger narrative remains in command of both the shapely story and what it leaves out. Jane is represented as having been moved to find Rochester by that "supernatural" event for which she claims full reality; the fact that she rejects it as material to be told to Rochester shows again the tension between Brontë's character and her narrative, which retrieves and includes the irrational sources that Jane learns to repress in order to achieve her social, loving, and controlling ends. If Jane grows up to be a successful narrator, she is not—at least not yet—the narrator of *Jane Eyre*, whose vision depends on the tense truth of the discontinuity between fierce feeling and credible story.

Brontë's linkage of controlled, artful narrative with loving sociality also takes the more negative form of a linkage between stereotypical social behavior and recognizably conventional narrative modes. Conventional characters think of their lives as conventional stories; in this way they are effectively deprived of inner reality. Against that world of social and narrative convention, Jane devotes herself to the notion of originality, which becomes, in her hands, a moral attribute.

Brontë continually asks us to think about typical plots in order to disengage them from her own. Georgiana and Eliza Reed function, for example, as parody heroines of other and lesser stories. After relating the history of Jane's parents (in a paragraph that is a masterpiece of conventional plot summary, complete with wife "cut off without a shilling") Bessie and Abbot decide that "a beauty like Miss Georgiana" would be a more "moving" heroine of that tale than Jane could be. And Georgiana herself tries to see her life in novelistic conventions; when Jane revisits Gateshead at the time of Mrs. Reed's death, Georgiana confides in her: "in short, a volume of a novel of fashionable life was that day improvised by her for my benefit." Eliza parodies, in a different way, the choice of religious sacrifice more seriously depicted in the careers of Helen Burns and St. John Rivers. But those stories too—and it is notable that the novel ends with St. John's—function as roads not taken, choices against which the originality of Jane's history is to take form.

The moral status of originality is also apparent in Jane's judgments. Her indictment of Blanche Ingram takes this form: "She was not good; she was not original: she used to repeat sounding phrases from books; she never offered, nor had, an opinion of her own." The sentimental phrases with which the other ladies of the Thornfield party respond to the stranger Mason are also used as evidence against their powers of accurate moral judgment. Even the banality of charming Rosamond Oliver is most effectively set in the observation that she imagines that Jane's "previous history, if known, would make a delightful romance."

Jane's own story is forever veering into one or another recognizable literary mode, only to be brought up short in a comic deflation. A few examples must stand in for the rest: when Jane is nervously waiting in the Millcote Inn for a carriage to take her to Thornfield for the first time, the moment of uncertainty brings on the rather grandiose diction of adventure: "It is a very strange sensation to inexperienced youth to feel itself quite alone in the world: cut adrift from every connection; uncertain whether the port to which it is bound can be reached, and prevented by many impediments from returning to that which it has quitted." After waiting an unheroic half-hour, Jane ventures to ring the bell, only to find that the carriage is already there, responsibly waiting. In a similar and more central moment, Rochester's entrance is elaborately, romantically set in a description of the landscape—and the hero's first act is to fall down in the middle of it. Later, after the first major burst of "Gothic," the fire set to Rochester's bed, Jane's practical efforts wake him, "fulminating strange anathemas at finding himself lying in a pool of water. 'Is there a flood?' he cried." The language is a literal douse of comedy, acting like the others to jolt characters and reader out of that other sort of story into which we have, momentarily, been lulled.

In its most direct form, the standard of originality is used to deny a full life to the minor characters by having them think of themselves as "characters" in bad fictions. Yet this quiet but constant undertow of concern to claim originality for Jane's character and narrative actually takes the form of using, then apparently disengaging from, literary models, as though the only possibility of originality in a world full of other stories were the ability to draw back and recognize them as conventions. The stance is really a dependent position of independence; but it is certainly a self-conscious one, containing and making a subject of the stresses Brontë must have felt as she worked out the narrative of *Jane Eyre* in full awareness of the conventional fictions she scorned.

The sorts of stories that Jane does not tell herself are put into mouths of other characters. These narratives within the narrative work as measures for Jane's art, and also raise questions about exactly what kind of a story Jane's life might be. Rochester is, of course, the most important secondary narrator. At first he is represented as a deserving lover because of his own unconventionality and because his interest in Jane is sparked by his sense that she is "singular." In the central portion of the novel, however, his ways of describing his life, and Jane's role in it, show a desperate reliance on conventional stories which are used to mask the "true story" of his marriage.

When Rochester appears at Thornfield, he conceals a history which makes him "interesting"—a word which shares honors with "original" throughout the novel. The narrative in the Thornfield section is set up to engage both Jane and the reader in working out the solution to Rochester's mystery; at this point Jane herself has no comparable "interesting story" to speak of. Jane is offered a series of evasive accounts before she finally hears Rochester's own truthful narrative on the night of the intended wedding day. The first narrative, Mrs. Fairfax's, suggests that Rochester's story is one about the trials of a second son in a proud, wealthy family. The second, Rochester's story of his affair with Céline Varens, begins with a piece of ironic apology for having been so conventional: "In short, I began the process of ruining myself in the received style; like any other spoonie. I had not, it seems, the originality to chalk out a new road to shame and destruction, but trode the old track with stupid exactness not to deviate an inch from the beaten centre." Rochester is capable of as much literary self-consciousness about the telling of his life as Jane is herself. Yet the tale of Céline is in fact full of conventional language, and is organized to show that Rochester's cynical rendition of that cheap melodrama is actually a digressive maneuver. The expostulations to Thornfield which burst out in his dramatic interruption reveal that he is inwardly writing quite another tale—"arranging a point with my destiny"—that concerns him far more deeply: the story of a bigamous marriage.

The sense that Jane is living amidst a set of manufactured tales becomes explicit in her dialogue with Grace Poole after the fire in Rochester's bed; Grace's version of what has happened is designed to make Jane doubt the evidence of her senses and to write her out of the story. Rochester's houseparty stages a novel of fashionable life in an episode which is saturated on every level of narrative with theatrical metaphor. It is the final, major production in the series of cover stories —except, of course, for the proposed wedding to Jane. All of these incidents demonstrate Rochester's belief that he an arrange his destiny, act simultaneously as production manager and fortune-teller, and write both the beginnings and the ends of his life plans as though they were stories. In every case, his scenes are interrupted by extrusions of his real "story," the marriage with Bertha. In this carefully orchestrated presentation of Rochester as narrator, or playwright, the linkage between conventional plots and untruthfulness is firmly forged.

Rochester's ways of imagining Jane in his projected romance also show how he betrays his own recognition of Jane's originality; in attempting to describe his feeling about Jane's place in his life, he falls into traditional or fashionable modes of fantasy. When he tries to load Jane with clothes and jewels, his words debase even the notion of originality itself. In an exchange remarkable for its explicit "story" metaphors, Jane protests Rochester's possessive looks: " 'You need not look in that way;' I said: 'if you do, I'll wear nothing but my old Lowood frocks to the end of the chapter.' " Rochester answers as though Jane were the latest fashionable delight of the social stage: " 'Oh, it is rich to see and hear her! . . . Is she original? Is she piquant? I would not exchange this one little English girl for the grand Turk's whole seraglio; gazelle-eyes, houri-forms and all!' " In the context established, he could hardly commit a more devastating lapse of imagination as to the kind of story he might compare Jane's to. At other moments, Jane is a combination of fairy-elf and heavenly messenger ("the instrument for my cure"), presumably in a spiritualized version of the reformed rake's tale.

Brontë underlines the irresponsibility of this state of mind in the fairy tale Rochester tells Adèle about "taking mademoiselle to the moon." Adèle will have none of it; she points out that Rochester will be depriving Jane of food, clothing, and shelter. It is a lovely narrative move, suggesting the sinister undercurrents of fantasy-play that even a child can hear. Rochester's refusal to imagine Jane as a social being in these stories is as childish as Jane's childhood rages and fantasies and as dangerous. Jane's subsequent refusal to play out his idea of her part is, among other things, a refusal to be a supporting character in a dubious—and irresponsible—tale of someone else's invention.

The most remarkable piece of evidence for the complexity of Brontë's interest in the issue of storytelling and truth is the single scene in which Jane herself becomes a set narrator within her own narration. This occurs on the eve of the interrupted wedding, when Jane tells Rochester the story of Bertha's nocturnal appearance in her room, and the tearing of the wedding veil. The scene represents so many tiers of stories within stories that it might almost stand for a miniature model of the novel as a whole. To begin with, the tale is elaborately set up as a ghost story: despite the fear and anguish which Bertha's visit would presumably have caused, Jane waits until the stroke of midnight to begin her tale and creates a shaped, suspenseful narrative by prefacing her account of Bertha's visit with two dream sequences. In them she fearfully imagines Rochester riding away into the romantic landscape (as he had ridden into it, in the earlier narrative), and sees a preliminary vision of the destroyed shell of Thornfield. In itself, this highly stylized and manipulated Gothic tale suggests several layers of confusion between fiction and lived experience, and between Jane's midnight tales and the tale of *Jane Eyre* she tells to us. The point of the scene is exactly that multiplication of confusion: it allows Rochester to maintain his hold over Jane's imagination by convincing her that Bertha's visit was "half dream, half reality." Jane's appearance as a Gothic narrator, so carefully "set" to emphasize the point, is clearly a dangerous position.

Even more fascinating is the way that, early in the scene, Jane talks about Rochester as though she were creating his character in her imagination:

> I smiled as I unfolded the wedding veil, and devised how I would teaze you about your aristocratic tastes, and your efforts to masque your plebeian bride in the attributes of a peeress. I thought how I would carry down to you the square of unembroidered blonde I had myself prepared as a covering for my low-born head, and ask if that was not good enough for a woman who could bring her husband neither fortune, beauty, nor connections. I saw plainly how you would look; and heard your impetuous republican answers, and your haughty disavowal of any necessity on your part to augment your wealth, or elevate your standing, by marrying either a purse or a coronet.

The overt point here is simply that Jane knows Rochester so well that she can imagine scenes between them, and her version of their relationship is certainly more accurate—to the "external" fiction—than are his stories about "mademoiselle on the moon." But this passage does two other things as well. It multiplies the layers of fiction-making again, showing Jane telling Rochester a story about making up scenes in which she invents his character, as though to say, "You are nothing more than a character in my fiction." It also introduces Jane's view of the story-pattern that she and Rochester belong to; it is the *Pamela* pattern of class fantasy: aristocrat marries dependent girl. Jane's discomfort with that story is clear enough in the dreams that follow, depicting abandonment and desolation. The position of dependency that the *Pamela* story implies will not do for her, and a good deal of the rest of the novel is designed to rewrite the scenario in her favor.

It is important throughout the scene that Jane thinks of the marriage as a way of dissolving into Rochester's life: "the life that lay before me—*your* life, sir—an existence so much more stirring and expansive than my own." That Jane should present herself as a Gothic tale-teller on the eve of a fraudulent wedding to Rochester's "story" suggests that she is in the position of losing control of her own story. Her flight from Rochester might thus be read as a search for a true and equivalent story of her own.

When Jane leaves Thornfield to become the heroine of her own life, her own story is conventional and fantastic enough. She sets forth like any picaresque hero, loses her last shilling in the first scene, discovers her true family, and inherits a fortune. The difference between this and Rochester's story is that it is not a romance, and that Jane is the hero of it; now she is the one who appears at Moor House with a story to conceal and a mystery to solve. That we are to experience all this as "story" is apparent when Brontë puts the tale of Jane's inheritance into the mouth of St. John Rivers—not without having him point out its conventionality: " 'I spoke of my impatience to hear the sequel of a tale: on reflection, I find the matter will be better managed by my assuming the narrator's part, and converting you into a listener. Before commencing, it is but fair to warn you that the story will sound somewhat hackneyed in your ears: but stale details often regain a degree of freshness when they pass through new lips.' " St. John suggests that a new teller might reanimate an old tale, yet making Jane into an audience to her own story is another of Brontë's distancing moves: no, even this is not the main story; Jane is its passive heroine but not its narrator. The whole scene is particularly delightful because Jane keeps interrupting with questions about Rochester; in her version of her life he would clearly have to be a major figure, while St. John chides her for forgetting "essential points in pursuing trifles"; he would have her rejoice properly in her role as missing heiress. In this way Brontë succeeds in using the story-pattern of the inheritance plot to Jane's advantage, while refusing to allow us to think of Jane—or Jane to think of herself—as "that kind of heroine."

When Jane leaves Moor House to find Rochester again, she does not know what has happened to him and dreads knowing the outcome of his part of the plot. She finds out from yet another outside narrator, the "respectible-looking, middle-aged" host of "The Rochester Arms." What has happened to Rochester attains in this way the same "story" status as Jane's inheritance plot. Once again, the metaphor is clearly worked: when Jane sees the burnt shell of Thornfield, she responds as she did to the pictures of her youth: "What story belonged to this disaster?"; now, of course, the pictures are scenes in her own life. Prepared for "a tale of misery," Jane's concern during the dialogue is to prevent the innkeeper from telling her part in the story. The scene is a funny counterpart to the one with St. John, for Jane wants to put Rochester into her story, but does her best to keep herself out of his.

But the host cannot and will not keep her out; his narrative insists that Jane is part of Rochester's story, moving back and forth from his eyewitness account of the "Gothic" fire to a more "moral" internal tale—the effect on Rochester of Jane's leaving. His version, fully sympathetic to Rochester, testifies to Jane's overwhelming power to affect Rochester's life: " 'a more spirited, bolder, keener gentlemen than he was before that midge of a governess crossed him, you never saw, ma'am . . . for my part I have often wished that Miss Eyre had been sunk in the sea before she came to Thornfield Hall.' " He also describes Rochester as having become "savage" in self-imposed isolation—in the state of asocial imprisonment in overwhelmed feeling that Jane has worked against since the time of the red-room.

Like St. John's version of Jane's story, the innkeeper's tale does the work of setting Jane into a pattern without identifying her with it. Most dramatically, it makes Jane into the villain; she appears as the character who walked into Rochester's life, ruined it, and then rode off into the distance. We cannot, knowing Jane's internal experience, assent to this glimpse in a different mirror any more than Jane can. But even the inclusion of a suggestion—that her story could be read in quite another way that stresses Jane's responsibility for Rochester's pain— indicates Brontë's vigilant efforts to represent the choices in storytelling.

At the same time, the innkeeper's story prepares the way for Jane's return to be read as a mission of salvation: she alone, like the fairy-tale prince, can release Rochester from the prison of despair he as locked himself into. Since the novel has established that state of moral isolation as its most dangerous pole, Jane's return is thus defined not as another fall into fantastic and excessive feeling, but as a reasonable extrication from its extremes.

So Rochester's idea of Jane as his fairy-tale instrument of salvation comes true—but not until it has been rewritten in Jane's terms. Again, the peculiar dependent independence from conventional story-patterns comes up; by the end of the novel Jane has figured in so many different kinds of stories that it is difficult to characterize the novel in any one way. And that multiplicity may finally be the most important point. It is not enough to say that Brontë reanimated the

Gothic, or that *Jane Eyre* takes its place among patterns established by fairy tales or "governess novels," though these arguments are important contributions to an appreciation of Brontë's art. For at every turn the novel is conscious of its status among fictions, and of the difficulty of describing personal history in any way that does not turn it into one pattern or another. The many kinds of stories that are explicitly brought up in the text are there partly to be used, party to be exorcised and denied as limitations in the scope of Jane's character or Brontë's narrative powers. In the end it becomes impossible to answer the question "Then what kind of story is Jane's life?" For it is the life of a storyteller in a world full of fictions, a teller whose claim to originality as a character rests in her ability to take charge of so many kinds of stories in a narrative that seems both to credit and to quarrel with them all.

J. HILLIS MILLER

Wuthering Heights:
Repetition and the "Uncanny"

"I don't care—I will get in!"
—EMILY BRONTË, *Wuthering Heights*

Lockwood's "ejaculation," as Brontë calls it, when he tries to get back into the Heights a second time, might be taken as an emblem of the situation of the critic of *Wuthering Heights*. This novel has been a strong enticement for readers. It exerts great power over its readers in its own violence, and in its presentation of striking psychological, sociological, and natural detail. It absorbs the reader, making him enwrapped or enrapt by the story. In spite of its many peculiarities of narrative technique and theme, it is, in its extreme vividness of circumstantial detail, a masterwork of "realistic" fiction. It obeys most of the conventions of Victorian realism, though no reader can miss the fact that it gives these conventions a twist. The reader is persuaded that the novel is an accurate picture of the material and sociological conditions of life in Yorkshire in the early nineteenth century. The novel to an unusual degree gives that pleasure appropriate to realistic fiction, the pleasure of yielding to the illusion that one is entering into a real world by way of the words on the page.

Another way the novel entices the reader is by presenting abundant material inviting interpretation. Like *Lord Jim*, it overtly invites the reader to believe that there is some secret explanation which will allow him to understand the novel wholly. Such an interpretation would integrate all the details perspicuously. It is in this way chiefly that the first, grounded form of repetition is present in this novel. The details, the reader is led to believe, are the repetition of a hidden explanatory source. They are signs of it. By "materials inviting interpretation" I

From *Fiction and Repetition: Seven English Novels.* © 1982 by J. Hillis Miller. Harvard University Press, 1982.

mean all those passages in the novel which present something evidently meaning more than what is simply present. The surface of "literal representation" is rippled throughout not only by overtly figurative language but also by things literally represented which at the same time are signs of something else or can be taken as such signs. Examples would be the three gravestones by which Lockwood stands at the end of the novel, or the "moths fluttering among the heath, and harebells" and the "soft wind breathing through the grass" as he stands there. Such things are evidently emblematic, but of what? Passages of this sort lead the reader further and further into the novel in his attempt to get in, to reach the inside of the inside where a full retrospective explanation of all the enigmatic details will be possible. Nor is this feature of style intermittent. Once the reader catches sight of this wavering away from the literal in one detail, he becomes suspicious of every detail. He must reinterrogate the whole, like a detective of life or of literature on whom nothing is lost. The text itself, in its presentation of enigmas in the absence of patent totalizing explanation, turns him into such a detective.

The reader is also coaxed into taking the position of an interpreting spectator by the presentation in the novel of so many models of this activity. Lockwood, the timid and civilized outsider, who "shrunk icily into [himself], like a snail" (I, chap. 1) at the first sign of warm response demanding warmth from him, is the reader's delegate in the novel. He is that familiar feature of realistic fiction, the naive and unreliable narrator. Like the first readers of the novel, like modern readers, in spite of all the help they get from the critics, Lockwood is confronted with a mass of fascinating but confusing data which he must try to piece together to make a coherent pattern. I say "must" not only because this is what we as readers have been taught to do with a text, but also because there are so many examples in the novel, besides Lockwood, of texts with interpretation or commentary, or of the situation of someone who is attempting to make sense of events by narrating them.

Lockwood establishes the situation of many characters in the novel and of its readers as interpreting witnesses in a passage near the start of the novel. He first boasts of his ability to understand Heathcliff instinctively, and then withdraws this to say he may be merely projecting his own nature: "I know, by instinct, his reserve springs from an aversion to showy displays of feeling—to manifestations of mutual kindliness . . .—No, I'm running on too fast—I bestow my own attributes over liberally on him. Mr Heathcliff may have entirely dissimilar reasons for keeping his hand out of the way, when he meets a would be acquaintance, to those which actuate me" (I, chap. 1). The second chapter gives additional examples of Lockwood's ineptness as a reader of signs or as a gatherer of details into a pattern. He mistakes a heap of dead rabbits for cats, thinks Catherine Linton is Mrs. Heathcliff, and so on. His errors are a warning to the over-confident reader.

Lockwood is of course by no means the only interpreter or reader in the novel. Catherine's diary is described by Lockwood as "a pen and ink commentary —at least, the appearance of one—covering every morsel of blank that the printer had left" (I, chap. 3) in all the books of her "select" library. That library includes a Testament and the printed sermon of the Reverend Jabes Branderham. Catherine's diary is written in the margin of the latter. Branderham's sermon is an interpretation of a text in the New Testament. That text is itself an interpretation by Jesus of his injunction to forgiveness as well as a reading of certain Old Testament phrases which are echoed, just as Jesus's interpretation (or that of the Gospel-maker) comes accompanied, characteristically, by a parable. A parable is an interpretation by means of a story "thrown beside" that which is to be interpreted, as in fact all of *Wuthering Heights* might be said to be, since Lockwood's narration is adjacent to or at the margin of the enigmatic events he attempts to understand. Branderham's sermon is "interpreted" by Lockwood's dream of the battle in the chapel, in which "every man's hand [is] against his neighbor" (I, chap. 3). The sound of rapping in the dream, in turn, is rationally "read," when Lockwood wakes, as the fir-branch scratching against the window, like a pen scratching on paper. That scratching is reinterpreted once more, in Lockwood's next dream, as the sound of Catherine's ghost trying to get through the window. Lockwood, when he wakens again, and Heathcliff, when he comes running in response to Lockwood's yell, of course interpret the dream differently. Lockwood sees Heathcliff's frantic calling out the window to Catherine (" 'Come in! come in!' he sobbed. 'Cathy, do come.' ") as "a piece of superstition" (I, chap. 3).

These few pages present a sequence of interpretations and of interpretations within interpretations. This chain establishes, at the beginning, the situation of the reader as one of gradual penetration from text to text, just as Lockwood moves from room to room of the house, each inside the other, until he reaches the paneled bed inside Catherine's old room. There he finds himself confronting the Chinese boxes of texts within texts I have just described. The reader of *Wuthering Heights* must thread his or her way from one interpretative narrative to another—from Lockwood's narrative to Nelly's long retelling (which is also a rationalizing and conventionally religious explanation), to Isabella's letter, or to Catherine's dream of being thrown out of heaven, to her interpretation of this in the "I am Heathcliff" speech, and so on.

The novel keeps before the reader emblems of his own situation by showing so many characters besides Lockwood reading or learning to read. The mystery Lockwood tries to understand is the "same" mystery as that which confronts the reader of the novel: How have things got the way they are at Wuthering Heights when Lockwood first goes there? What is the original cause lying behind this sad disappearance of civility? Why is it that the novel so resists satisfactory reasonable explanation? Lockwood, at the point of his deepest penetration spatially into the house and temporally back near the "beginning," encounters not an event or a presence open to his gaze, but Catherine's diary, another text to read. Catherine and Heathcliff, in their turns, are shown, in the diary, condemned to read two religious pamphlets, "The Helmet of Salvation" and "The Broad Way to Destruction," on the "awful Sunday" when they escape for their "scamper on the moors" under the dairy-woman's cloak. Edgar Linton reads in his study while Catherine is willing her own death. He tries to keep her in life by enticing her to read: "A book lay spread on the sill before her, and the scarcely perceptible wind fluttered its leaves at intervals. I believe Linton had laid it there, for she never endeavoured to divert herself with reading, or occupation of any kind" (II, chap. 1). Much later, the taming of Hareton is signaled by his patiently learning to read under the second Catherine's tutelage. Reading seems to be opposed to the wind on the moors, to death, and to sexual experience. Yet all the readers, in the novel and of the novel, can have as a means of access to these is a book, or some other mediating emblem.

Brontë's problem, once she had agreed with her sisters to try her hand at a novel, was to bend the vision she had been expressing more directly and privately in the Gondal poems to the conventions of nineteenth-century fiction, or to bend those conventions to accommodate the vision. Each technical device contributing to the celebrated complexity of narration in Wuthering Heights has its precedents in modern fictional practice from Cervantes down to novelists contemporary with Brontë. The time shifts, the multiplication of narrators and narrators within narrators, the double plot, the effacement of the author, and the absence of any trustworthy and knowing narrator who clearly speaks for the author are used strategically in Wuthering Heights to frustrate the expectations of a reader such as Lockwood. They are used to invite the reader to move step by step, by way of a gradual unveiling, room by room, into the "penetralium" of Brontë's strange vision of life.

The first who accepted this invitation was Brontë's sister Charlotte, or rather one should say almost the first, since the first reviews of Wuthering Heights precede Charlotte's essay. Charlotte Brontë's two prefaces, the "Biographical Notice of Ellis and Acton Bell" and the "Editors Preface to the New [1850] Edition of Wuthering Heights," are often the first thing the modern reader of the novel encounters, with the exception of some twentieth-century critic's introductory essay. The novel comes to the reader wrapped in layers of prefatory material. It is difficult to be sure where the margin of the introduction ends and where the novel "proper" begins. Where does the reader step over the threshold into the novel itself? If the modern critical essay is definitely outside, a kind of alien presence within the covers of the book, Charlotte's prefaces would seem to have privileged access to the house. They seem to be the last layer before entrance, the inside outside, or perhaps the first region actually within, the outside inside, an entrance room. Perhaps they should be thought of as liminal, as the threshold itself. In any case, the language of Charlotte's prefaces is often continuous with Emily's language, for example in its use of figures of speech drawn from Yorkshire scenery, though whether or not Charlotte's language distorts Emily's language by misusing it is another question.

Charlotte's prefaces establish the rhetorical stance which has been characteristic of criticism of this novel. This stance involves dismissing most previous critics and claiming one has oneself solved the enigma, cracked the code. Charlotte's prefaces also establish the situation of a reader confronting an enigmatic text as the appropriate emblem for those both inside and outside the novel:

> Too often do reviewers remind us of the mob of Astrologers, Chaldeans, and Soothsayers gathered before the "writing on the wall," and unable to read the characters or make known the interpretation. We have a right to rejoice when a true seer comes at last, some man in whom is an excellent spirit, to whom have been given light, wisdom, and understanding; who can accurately read the "Mene, Mene, Tekel, Upharsin" of an original mind (however unripe, however inefficiently cultured and partially expanded that mind may be); and who can say, with confidence, "This is the interpretation thereof."

Charlotte is here ostensibly praising the one previous review of which she approves, that by Sydney Dobell in the *Palladium* for September 1850. Dobell was persuaded that Charlotte Brontë had written *Wuthering Heights*. His review is by no means unintelligent, for example in what he says of Catherine Earnshaw: "in the very arms of her lover we dare not doubt her purity." In the end, however, Dobell only restates the enigma rather than solving it: "one looks back at the whole story as to a world of brilliant figures in an atmosphere of mist; shapes that come out upon the eye, and burn their colours into the brain, and depart into the enveloping fog. It is the unformed writing of a giant's hand; the 'large utterance' of a baby god." Charlotte, in spite of her praise of Dobell, means to present herself as the first genuine reader of this "unformed writing," the first true interpreter of the "Mene, Mene, Tekel, Upharsin."

Charlotte's preface of 1850 confidently tells the reader, before he has even read the novel, what the text is to mean. The difficulty is that she presents in fact at least four incompatible readings, citing chapter and verse for each interpretation she proposes, without apparent awareness that they differ from one another. Her readings, moreover, function to throw the reader off the track. They attempt to shift the blame for the novel away from Emily by reducing its meaning to something Charlotte imagines Victorian readers will accept.

Emily Brontë was in *Wuthering Heights*, says Charlotte in the first reading she proposes, simply following nature. She was warbling her native woodnotes wild. The novel is not Emily speaking, but nature speaking through her. The novel "is rustic all through. It is moorish, and wild, and knotty as a root of heath. Nor was it natural that it should be otherwise; the author being herself a native and nursling of the moors."

This reading is immediately qualified and replaced by a new one. The true source of the novel, says Charlotte now, is the actual wild way of life of the peasants of Yorkshire. The novel is sociologically accurate. Emily is merely the innocent transcriber of fact: "She knew them; knew their ways, their language, their family histories; she could hear of them with interest, and talk of them with detail, minute, graphic, and accurate . . . Her imagination, which was a spirit more sombre than sunny, more powerful than sportive, found in such traits material whence it wrought creations like Heathcliff, like Earnshaw, like Catherine. Having formed these beings, she did not know what she had done."

No, after all, this is not it either, Charlotte in effect says in proposing yet another reading. In fact Emily Brontë was a Christian. The novel is a religious allegory, with Heathcliff, for example, an incarnation of the Devil: "Heathcliff, indeed, stands unredeemed; never once swerving in his arrow-straight course to perdition." His love for Catherine is "a passion such as might boil and glow in the bad essence of some evil genius; a fire that might form the tormented centre —the ever-suffering soul of a magnate of the infernal world: and by its quench-less and ceaseless ravage effect the execution of the decree which dooms him to carry Hell with him wherever he wanders."

No, says Charlotte finally, this is not the true explanation or excuse. In fact, whatever the nature of the work, Emily is not to be blamed for it because she was not responsible for it. She was the passive medium through which some-thing or someone else spoke, just as, for Rimbaud, in "les lettres du voyant," the metal is not to blame if it finds itself a trumpet ("Je est un autre."); and just as the speaker in some of Brontë's poems is subject to a "God of visions" who speaks through her without her volition. "But this, I know," says Charlotte; "the writer who possesses the creative gift owns something of which he is not always master—something that at times strangely wills and works for itself . . . Be the work grim or glorious, dread or divine, you have little choice left but quiescent adoption. As for you—the nominal artist—your share in it has been to work passively under dictates you neither delivered nor could question—that would not be uttered at your prayer, nor suppressed nor changed at your caprice."

Charlotte's prefaces, with their multiple interpretations, each based on some aspect of the actual text of *Wuthering Heights*, establish a program for all the hundreds of essays and books on *Wuthering Heights* which were to follow. They do this both in the sense that all most readings could be lined up under one or another of Charlotte's four readings. They do it also in the sense that all these books and essays are also empirically based on the text. Each tends to be plausible, but demonstrably partial, though each also, like Charlotte's prefaces, tends to be presented with confident certainty. Each critic presents himself as the Daniel who can at last decipher the writing on the wall. Though the many essays on the novel do not exist on a common axis of judgment, that is, though they do not even raise the same questions about the novel, much less give the same answers, each critic tends to claim that he has found something of importance which will indicate the right way to read the novel as a whole.

There have been explanations of *Wuthering Heights* in terms of its relation to the motif of the fair-haired girl and the dark-haired boy in the Gondal poems; or by way of the motifs of doors and windows in the novel (Dorothy Van Ghent); or in terms of the symmetry of the family relations in the novel or of Brontë's accurate knowledge of the laws of private property in Yorkshire (C. P. Sanger); or in more or less orthodox and schematic Freudian terms, as a thinly disguised sexual drama displaced and condensed (Thomas Moser); or as the dramatization of a conflict between two cosmological forces, storm and calm (Lord David Cecil); or as a moral story of the futility of grand passion (Mark Schorer); or as a fictional dramatization of Brontë's religious vision (J. H. Miller); or as a dramatization of the relation between sexuality and death, as "l'approbation de la vie jusqu'à la mort," the approbation of life all the way to death (Georges Bataille); or as the occult dramatization of Brontë's lesbian passion for her dead sister, Maria, with Brontë as Heathcliff (Camille Paglia); or as an overdetermined semiotic structure which is irreducibly ambiguous by reason of its excess of signs (Frank Kermode); or as Brontë's effacement of nature in order to make way for specifically female imaginative patterns (Margaret Homans); or as the expression of a multitude of incompatible "partial selves" dispersed among the various characters, thereby breaking down the concept of the unitary self (Leo Bersani), or in more or less sophisticated Marxist terms (David Wilson, Arnold Kettle, Terry Eagleton).

This list could be extended. The literature on *Wuthering Heights* is abundant and its incoherence striking. Even more than some other great works of literature this novel seems to have an inexhaustible power to call forth commentary and more commentary. All literary criticism tends to be the presentation of what claims to be the definitive rational explanation of the text in question. The criticism of *Wuthering Heights* is characterized by the unusual degree of incoherence among the various explanations and by the way each takes some one element in the novel and extrapolates it toward a total explanation. The essays tend not to build on one another according to some ideal of progressive elucidation. Each is exclusive.

All these interpretations are, I believe, wrong. This is not because each does not illuminate something in *Wuthering Heights*. Each brings something to light, even though it covers something else up in the act of doing so. The essays by Bataille, Kermode, Bersani, and Homans seem to me especially to cast light, but each could nevertheless be shown to be partial. No doubt my essay too will be open to the charge that it attempts to close off the novel by explaining it, even though that explanation takes the form of an attempted reasonable formulation of its unreason.

My argument is not that criticism is a free-for-all in which one reading is as good as another. No doubt there would be large areas of agreement among competent readers even of this manifestly controversial novel. It is possible to present a reading of *Wuthering Heights* which is demonstrably wrong, not even partially right, though I believe all the readings listed above are in one way or another partially right. They are right because they arise from responses determined by the text. The error lies in the assumption that the meaning is going to be single, unified, and logically coherent. My argument is that the best readings will be the ones which best account for the heterogeneity of the text, its presentation of a definite group of possible meanings which are systematically interconnected, determined by the text, but logically incompatible. The clear and rational expression of such a system of meanings is difficult, perhaps impossible. The fault of premature closure is intrinsic to criticism. The essays on *Wuthering Heights* I have cited seem to me insufficient, not because what they say is demonstrably mistaken, but rather because there is an error in the assumption that there *is* a single secret truth about *Wuthering Heights*. This secret truth would be something formulable as a univocal principle of explanation which would account for everything in the novel. The secret truth about *Wuthering Heights*, rather, is that there is no secret truth which criticism might formulate in this way. No hidden identifiable ordering principle which will account for everything stands at the head of the chain or at the back of the back. Any formulation of such a principle is visibly reductive. It leaves something important still unaccounted for. This is a remnant of opacity which keeps the interpreter dissatisfied, the novel still open, the process of interpretation still able to continue. One form or another of this openness may characterize all works of literature, but, as I suggested [elsewhere], this resistance to a single definitive reading takes different forms in different works. In *Wuthering Heights* this special form is the invitation to believe that there is a supernatural transcendent "cause" for all events, while certain identification of this cause, or even assurance of its existence, is impossible.

Wuthering Heights produces its effect on its reader through the way it is made up of repetitions of the same in the other which permanently resist rational reduction to some satisfying principle of explanation. The reader has the experience, in struggling to understand the novel, that a certain number of the elements which present themselves for explanation can be reduced to order. This act of interpretation always leaves something over, something just at the edge of the circle of theoretical vision which that vision does not encompass. This something left out is clearly a significant detail. There are always in fact a group of such significant details which have been left out of any reduction to order. The text is over-rich.

This resistance to theoretical domination, both in the sense of clear-seeing and in the sense of conceptual formulation, is not accidental, nor is it without significance. It is not a result of Brontë's inexperience or of the fact that she overloaded her novel with elements which can be taken as having meaning beyond their realistic references. The novel is not incoherent, confused, or flawed. It is a triumph of the novelist's art. It uses the full resources of that art against the normal assumptions about character and about human life which are built into the conventions of realistic fiction. The difficulties of interpreting *Wuthering Heights* and the superabundance of possible (and actual) interpretations do not mean that the reader is free to make the novel mean anything he wants to make it mean. The fact that no demonstrable single meaning or principle of meaningfulness can be identified does not mean that all meanings are equally good. Each good reader of *Wuthering Heights* is subject to the text, coerced by it. The best readings, it may be, are those, like Charlotte Brontë's which repeat in their own alogic the text's failure to satisfy the mind's desire for logical order with a demonstrable base. *Wuthering Heights* incorporates the reader in the process of understanding which the text mimes in Lockwood's narration. It forces him to repeat in his own way an effort of understanding that the text expresses, and to repeat also the baffling of that effort.

Wuthering Heights presents an emblem for this experience of the reader in a passage describing Lockwood's reaction to Nelly's proposal to skip rapidly over three years in her narration: "No, no," says Lockwood, "I'll allow nothing of the sort! Are you acquainted with the mood of mind in which, if you were seated alone, and the cat licking its kitten on the rug before you, you would watch the operation so intently that puss's neglect of one ear would put you seriously out of temper?" (I, chap. 7). This, I take it, is an oblique warning to the reader. Unless he reads in the "mood of mind" here described he is likely to miss something of importance. Every detail counts in this novel. Only an interpretation which accounts for each item and puts it in relation to the whole will be at once specific enough and total enough. The reader must be like a cat who licks her kitten all over, not missing a single spot of fur, or rather he must be like the watcher of such an operation, following every detail of the multiple narration, assuming that every minute bit counts, constantly on the watch for anything left out. There is always, however, a neglected ear, or one ear too many.

Nelly describes Lockwood's anxiety about the neglected ear as "a terribly lazy mood," to which Lockwood replies: "On the contrary, a tiresomely active one. It is mine, at present, and, therefore, continue minutely. I perceive that people in these regions acquire over people in towns the value that a spider in a dungeon does over a spider in a cottage, to their various occupants" (I, chap. 7). The kitten's neglected ear, like the spider in the dungeon, is not a "frivolous external thing." It is a small thing on the surface which bears relation to hidden things in the depths. This opposition between surface and depth is suggested when Lockwood says people at Wuthering Heights "live more in earnest, more in themselves" (I, chap. 7). To live in oneself is to be self-contained. This is opposed to living in terms of surface change and frivolous external things. Where people live in themselves, external things are not superficial or frivolous. They are rather the only signs outsiders have of the secret depths.

Lockwood next provides a final figure for his situation and for that of the reader. This is a somewhat peculiar metaphor of eating. It defines the reader's situation in terms of a possible filling or the possible satisfaction of an appetite. It also puts before the reader the opposition between a single thing which stands for a whole, and therefore may be deeply satisfying, and a multitude of details which make a superficial, finally unsatisfying, whole. Rural life as against urban life, the spider in the dungeon as against the spider in the cottage, are compared in what might be called a gustatory parable: "one state resembles setting a hungry man down to a single dish on which he may concentrate his entire appetite, and do it justice—the other, introducing him to a table laid out by French cooks; he can perhaps extract as much enjoyment from the whole, but each part is a mere atom in his regard and remembrance" (I, chap. 7).

How can the reader interpret this parable? Is it a hunger for "experience," or for "knowledge," and if for one or the other, experience of what, knowledge of what? There is in any case a clear opposition between, on the one hand, a relatively sparse field of experience which allows an intense concentration on what is there to be assimilated, and, on the other hand, a diffuse multitude of things to taste which distracts attention and makes it superficial. The intense concentration leads to satisfaction, a filling of the mind now and in memory. It seems as if the single object intensely regarded leads beyond itself, stands for more than itself. It perhaps stands for the whole. The diffuse multitude reduces each item to something which is not attended to in itself. It therefore neither leads beyond itself nor sticks in the memory as a means of reaching a whole. Each part is a mere atom in the beholder's regard and remembrance.

This parable is a recipe for how to read *Wuthering Heights*. Each passage must be concentrated upon with the most intense effort of the interpreting mind, as though it were the only dish on the table. Each detail must be taken as a synecdoche, as a clue to the whole—as I have taken this detail.

Take, for example the following passages:

> The ledge, where I placed my candle, had a few mildewed books piled up in one corner; and it was covered with writing scratched on the paint. This writing, however, was nothing but a name repeated in all kinds of characters, large and small—*Catherine Earnshaw*, here and there varied to *Catherine Heathcliff*, and then again to *Catherine Linton*.
>
> In vapid listlessness I leant my head against the window, and continued spelling over Catherine Earnshaw—Heathcliff—Linton, till my eyes closed; but they had not rested five minutes when a glare of white letters started from the dark, as vivid as spectres—the air swarmed with Catherines.
>
> (I, chap. 3)

> I had remarked on one side of the road, at intervals of six or seven yards, a line of upright stones, continued through the whole length of the barren: there were erected, and daubed with lime on purpose to serve as guides in the dark, and also when a fall, like the present, confounded the deep swamps on either hand with the firmer path: but, excepting a dirty dot pointing up here and there, all traces of their existence had vanished; and my companion found it necessary to warn me frequently to steer to the right or left, when I imagined I was following, correctly, the windings of the road.
>
> (I, chap. 3)

> I sought, and soon discovered, the three head-stones on the slope next the moor—the middle one grey, and half buried in the heath—Edgar Linton's only harmonized by the turf, and moss creeping up its foot—Heathcliff's still bare.
>
> I lingered round them, under that benign sky; watched the moths fluttering among the heath, and hare-bells; listened to the soft wind breathing through the grass; and wondered how anyone could ever imagine unquiet slumbers for the sleepers in that quiet earth.
>
> (II, chap. 20)

These three texts are similar, but this similarity is, in part at least, the fact that each is unique in the structural model it presents the reader. This uniqueness makes each incommensurate with any of the others. Each is, in its surface texture as language, "realistic." It is a description of natural or manmade objects which is physically and sociologically plausible. Such things are likely to have existed in Yorkshire around 1800. All three passages are filtered through the mind and through the language of the narrator. In all three, as it happens, this is the mind of the primary narrator of the novel, Lockwood. As always in such cases, the reader must interrogate the passages for possible irony. This irony potentially arises from discrepancies between what Lockwood knows or what he makes out of what he sees, and what the author knew and made, or what the reader can make out of the passages as he interprets the handwriting on the wall. All of the passages possibly mean more than their referential or historical meaning. They may be signs or clues to something beyond themselves. This possibility is opened up in the fissure between what Lockwood apparently knows or intends to say, and what the author may have known or intended to say. None of these passages, nor any of the many other "similar" passages which punctuate the novel, is given the definitive closure of a final interpretation within the text of the novel. In fact they are not interpreted at all. They are just given. The handwriting on the wall is not read within the novel. The reader must read it for himself.

When he does so, he finds that each such passage seems to ask to be taken as an emblem of the whole novel. Each is implicitly an emblem of the structure of the novel as a whole and of the way that whole signifies something beyond itself which controls its meaning as a whole. Each such passage leads to a different formulation of the structure of the whole. Each is exclusive and incongruous with the others. It seems to have an imperialistic will to power over the others, as if it wished to bend them to its own shape. It expands to make its own special reading of the whole, just as each of Charlotte Brontë's four readings of the novel do, or just as each of the hundreds of readings which have followed hers have tended to do. Each such reading implicitly excludes other passages which do not fit, or distorts them, twisting them to its own pattern.

The first passage would lead to an interpretation of the novel in terms of the permutation of given names and family names. This reading would go by way of the network of kinship relations in symmetrical pedigree and by way of the theme of reading. The critic might note that there do not seem to be enough names to go around in this novel. Relations of similarity and difference among the characters are indicated by the way several hold the names also held by others or a combination of names held by others. An example is "Linton Heathcliff," the name of the son of Heathcliff and Isabella. His name is an oxymoron, combining names from the two incompatible families. How can a name be "proper" to a character and indicate his individuality if it is also held by others? Each character in *Wuthering Heights* seems to be an element in a system, defined by his or her place in the system, rather than a separate, unique person. The whole novel, such a critic might say, not only the destiny of the first Catherine but also that of the second Catherine, as well as the relation of the second story to the first, is given in emblem in Lockwood's encounter with the names scratched on the windowsill and in his dream of an air swarming with Catherines. The passage is a momentary emblem for the whole. The whole, as it unfolds, is the narrative of the meaning of the emblem.

The second passage offers a model for a somewhat different form of totalization. The passage is a "realistic" description of a country road in Yorkshire after a heavy snow. If the reader follows Lockwood's example and considers every detail as possibly a clue to the whole and to what stands behind or beneath the whole, then the passage suggests that the novel is made of discrete units which follow one another in a series with spaces between. The reader's business is to draw lines between the units. He must make a pattern, like the child's game in which a duck or a rabbit is magically drawn by tracing lines between numbered dots. In this case, the line makes a road which leads the reader from here to there, taking him deeper and deeper across country to a destination, away from danger and into safety. The only difficulty is that some of the dots are missing or invisible. The reader must, like Lockwood, extrapolate. He must make the road to safety by putting in correctly the missing elements.

This operation is a dangerous one. If the reader makes a mistake, guesses wrong, hypothesizes a guidepost where there is none, he will be led astray into the bog. This process of hypothetical interpretation, projecting a thesis or ground plan where there is none, where it is faint or missing, hypotrophied, is risky for the interpreter. He must engage in the activity Immanuel Kant, following rhetorical tradition, calls "hypotyposis," the sketching out of a ground plan where there is no secure indication of which line to follow. Such an operation gives figurative names to what has no literal or proper name. The reader's safety somehow depends on getting it right. There is a good chance of getting it wrong, or perhaps there is no secure foundation for deciding between right and wrong.

Exactly how the activity of reading *Wuthering Heights* concerns the reader remains to be seen. It is clear that Lockwood, the reader's vicarious representative in the novel, often gets it wrong. If he is the reader's representative in the novel, he is an example of how not to do it, of how not to do things with signs. His relation to Heathcliff in the second passage cited above, as he is guided toward a goal he could not reach himself, may be taken to figure the relation between Lockwood and Heathcliff in the novel as a whole. That relation, in turn, inscribes within the text a figure of the reader's relation to the violent and inscrutable events he must try to interpret. If Lockwood is the outsider, seeing events from a distance, Heathcliff is the male character who is most involved and who ultimately dies into the heart of violence and mystery. He returns whence he has come, leaving Lockwood behind as survivor to tell the tale. Heathcliff may be a trustworthy guide, but he is also a dangerous one to follow all the way where he is going.

The third passage quoted makes explicit the situation of the survivor. This too may be taken as emblematic of the whole text in relation to what lies behind the events it narrates, or as emblematic of the narrator's relation to the story he tells, or as a figure of the reader's relation to the story told. Just as many of Wordsworth's poems, "The Boy of Winander," for example, or the Matthew poems, or "The Ruined Cottage," are epitaphs spoken by a survivor who stands by a tombstone musing on the life and death of the one who is gone, so all of *Wuthering Heights* may be thought of as a memorial narration pieced together by Lockwood from what he can learn. The first Catherine is already dead when Lockwood arrives at the Heights. Heathcliff is still alive as the anguished survivor whose "life is in the grave." By the end of the novel Heathcliff has followed Catherine into death. At the end, Lockwood stands by three graves. These, like the three versions of Catherine's name in my first emblematic text, can stand in their configuration for the story of the first Catherine: Catherine Earnshaw in the middle torn by her love for Edgar Linton, in one direction, and for Heathcliff, in the other, destroying their lives in this double love and being destroyed by it.

A gravestone is the sign of an absence. Throughout the whole novel Lockwood confronts nothing but such signs. His narration is a retrospective reconstruction by means of them. This would be true of all novels told in the past tense about characters who are dead when the narration begins, but the various churchyard scenes in *Wuthering Heights*, for example the scene in which Heathcliff opens Catherine's grave and coffin, keep before the reader the question of whether the dead still somewhere live on beyond the grave. The naiveté of Lockwood, even at the end of the novel, is imaged in his inability to imagine unquiet slumbers for the sleepers in the quiet earth. The evidence for the fact that this earth is unquiet, the place of some unnamable tumultuous hidden life, is there before his eyes in the moths fluttering among the heath and hare-bells. It is there in the soft wind breathing through the grass, like some obscurely vital creature. These are figures for what can only manifest itself indirectly. If Lockwood survives the death of the protagonists and tells their story, it may be this survival which cuts him off from any understanding of death. The end of the novel reiterates the ironic discrepancy between what Lockwood knows and what he unwittingly gives the reader evidence for knowing.

Each of these three passages can be taken in one way or another as an emblem of the structure of the whole narration and of the relation of that whole to the enigmatic ground on which it rests, the origin from which it comes and the goal to which it returns. Beginning with any one as starting place the reader or critic can move out to interpret the whole novel in the terms it provides. Each appropriates other details and bends them around itself. Each leads to a different total design. Each such design is incompatible with the others. Each implicitly claims to be a center around which all the other details can be organized.

Different as are the several schematic paradigms for the whole, they share certain features. Each is a figure without a visible referent. Whatever emblem is chosen as center turns out to be not at the center but at the periphery. It is in fact an emblem for the impossibility of reaching the center. Each leads to a multitude of other similar details in the novel. Each such sequence is a repetitive structure, like the echoes from one to another of the lives of the two Catherines, or like the narrators within narrators in Lockwood's telling, or like the rooms inside rooms he encounters at the Heights. Each appearance is the sign of something absent, something earlier, or later, or further in. Each detail is in one way or another a track to be followed. It is a trace which asks to be retraced so that the something missing may be recovered.

The celebrated circumstantiality of *Wuthering Heights* is the circumstantiality of this constant encounter with new signs. The reader of *Wuthering Heights*, like the narrator, is led deeper and deeper into the text by the expectation that sooner or later the last veil will be removed. He will then find himself face to face not with the emblem of something missing but with the right real thing at last. This will be truly original, the bona fide starting place. It will therefore be possessed of full explanatory power over the whole network of signs which it has generated and which it controls, giving each sign its deferred meaning. Through this labyrinth of linkages the reader has to thread his way. He is led from one to another in the expectation of reaching a goal, as Heathcliff leads Lockwood from marker to marker down that snowcovered road.

A further feature of this web of signs behind signs is that they tend to be presented in paired oppositions. Each element of these pairs is not so much the opposite of its mate as another form of it. It is a differentiated form, born of some division within the same, as the different Catherines in the passage discussed above are forms of the same Catherine; or as Heathcliff and Lockwood are similar in their exclusion from the place where Catherine is, as well as opposite in temperament, sexual power, and power of volition; or as Cathy says of Heathcliff not that he is her opposite, other than she is, but that "He's more myself than I am"; or as, in the passage describing the three graves, Edgar on one side of Catherine or Heathcliff on the other each represents one aspect of her double nature. The novel everywhere organizes itself according to such patterns of sameness and difference, as in the opposition between stormy weather and calm weather; or between the roughness of the Heights and the civilized restraint of Thrushcross Grange, or between inside and outside, domestic interior and wild nature outside, beyond the window or over the wall; or between the stories of the two Catherines, or between those who read and those who scorn books as weak intermediaries, or between people of strong will like Heathcliff, who is "a fierce, pitiless, wolfish man" (I, chap. 10) and people of weak will like Lockwood.

These apparently clear oppositions have two further properties. The reader is nowhere given access to the generative unity from which the pairs are derived. The reader never sees directly, for example, the moment in childhood when Cathy and Heathcliff slept in the same bed and were joined in a union which was prior to sexual differentiation. This union was prior to any sense of separate selfhood, prior even to language, figurative or conceptual, which might express that union. As soon as Cathy can say, "I *am* Heathcliff," or "My love for Heathcliff resembles the eternal rocks beneath" (I, chap. 9), they are already divided. This division has always already occurred as soon as there is consciousness and the possibility of retrospective storytelling. Storytelling is always after the fact, and it is always constructed over a loss. What is lost in the case of *Wuthering Heights* is the "origin" which would explain everything.

Another characteristic of the oppositions follows from this loss of the explanatory source. The separated pairs, differentiations of the same rather than true opposites, have a tendency to divide further, and then subdivide again, endlessly proliferating into various nuances and subsets. Once the "primal" division has occurred, and for Brontë as soon as there is a story to tell it has already occurred, there seems to be no stopping a further division. Once this primitive cell is self-divided it divides and subdivides perpetually in an effort to achieve reunification which only multiplies it in new further-divided life cells.

The sequence of generations in *Wuthering Heights*, for example, began long before the three presented in the novel. The name Hareton Earnshaw and the date 1500 carved in stone above the front door of the Heights testify to that. The marriage of the second Cathy and the new Hareton at the end of the novel will initiate a new generation. The deaths of Heathcliff, Edgar Linton, and the first Catherine have by no means put a stop to the reproductive power of the two families. This force finds its analogue in the power of the story to reproduce itself. It is told over and over by the sequence of narrators, and it is reproduced again in each critical essay, or each time it is followed through by a new reader. The words on the page act like a genetic pattern able to program the minds of those who encounter it. It induces them to take, for a time at least, the pattern of the experience of those long-dead imaginary protagonists. The emblem for this might be that concluding scene in which Lockwood stands by the triple grave prolonging the lives of Edgar, Catherine, and Heathcliff by his meditation on the names inscribed on their tombstones. In this act and in the narration generated by it he prevents them from dying wholly. Many Victorian novels stress this double form of repetitive extension beyond the deaths of the protagonists, for example *Tess of the d'Urbervilles*, the topic of chapter 4 [of *Fiction and Repetition*]. *Wuthering Heights* gives this familiar pattern a special form by relating it to the question of whether Cathy and Heathcliff are to be thought of as surviving their deaths or whether they survive only in the narrations of those who have survived them.

Any of the oppositions which may be taken as a means of interpreting *Wuthering Heights* has this property of reproducing itself in proliferating divisions and subdivisions. Just as, for example, the name of the maiden Catherine caught between her two possible married names becomes an air "swarming" with Catherines, so the neat opposition within Christianity between good and evil, salvation and damnation, "The Helmet of Salvation" and "The Broad Way to Destruction," becomes the separation of sins into seven distinctions, and this in turn, in the Reverend Jabes Branderham's sermon, becomes a monstrous division and subdivision of sins, a dividing of the text, as Protestantism has multiplied sects and set each man's hand against his neighbor. Two becomes seven becomes seventy times seven, in a grotesque parody of a sermon: "he preached—good God! what a sermon: divided into *four hundred and ninety* parts—each fully equal to an ordinary address from the pulpit—and each discussing a separate sin!" (I, chap. 3).

Wuthering Heights is perhaps best read by taking one or more of its emblematic oppositions as an interpretative hypothesis and pushing it to the point where the initial distinction no longer clearly holds. Only by this following of a track as far as possible, until it peters out into the trackless snow, can the reader get inside this strange text and begin to understand why he cannot ever lucidly understand it or ever have rational mastery over it. The limitation of many critical essays on the novel lies not in any error in the initial interpretative hypothesis (that storm and calm are opposed in the novel, or that windows, walls, and doors are used emblematically, for example). The limitation lies rather in the failure to push the given schematic hypothesis far enough. It must be pushed to the point where it fails to hypothecate the full accounting for the novel which is demanded in the critical contract. At that point the mortgage on *Wuthering Heights* is foreclosed and the reader, it may be, confronts his mortality as reader, that vanishing of lucid understanding which his critical reason, the reason that divides and discriminates in order to master, has done everything to evade.

Why is it that, with this novel, the logical mind so conspicuously fails? What does this have to do with the gage or promissory note that both holds off death and risks death, puts one's death on the line, as a kind of mortgage insurance? Why is it that an interpretative origin, *logos* in the sense of ground, measure, chief word, or accounting reason, cannot be identified for *Wuthering*

Heights? If such an origin could be found, all obscurity could be cleared up. Everything could be brought out in the open where it might be clearly seen, added up, paid off, and evened out. What forbids this accounting?

An economic metaphor of course pervades *Wuthering Heights*. Heathcliff uses his mysteriously acquired wealth to take possession of the Heights and the Grange. He takes possession of them because each thing and person in each household reminds him of Catherine. By appropriating all and then destroying them, he can take revenge on the enemies who have stood between him and Catherine. At the same time he can reach Catherine through them, in their demolition. This is a violently incarnated way to experience a paradoxical logic of signs:

> "What is not connected with her to me? and what does not recall her? I cannot look down to this floor, but her features are shaped on the flags! In every cloud, in every tree—filling the air at night, and caught by glimpses in every object by day, I am surrounded with her image! The most ordinary faces of men and women—my own features mock me with a resemblance. The entire world is a dreadful collection of memoranda that she did exist, and that I have lost her."
>
> (II, chap. 19)

In this strange numismatics, each thing is stamped with the same image, the face of the person who is Queen to Heathcliff's Jack. In this novel no man is King or Ace. The Queen's countenance makes everything have value and pass current. There are problems with this coinage, however. For one thing, no one of these stamped images has a distinct number which indicates its worth in relation to other images or its exchange value in relation to goods or services. No orderly economic system of substitution and circulation is set up by this mint. Neither Heathcliff, nor Lockwood, nor the reader can buy anything with this money. There is, in fact, nothing left to buy, since there is nothing which is not coin stamped with the same image, of infinite value and so of no value.

The entire world is a dreadful collection of memoranda. Memoranda of what? Here is the second problem with this coinage. Each thing stands not for the presence of Catherine as the substance behind the coin, the standard guaranteeing its value, the thing both outside the money system and dispersed everywhere in delegated form within it. In this case, each thing stands rather for the absence of Catherine. All things are memoranda, written or inscribed memorials, like a note I write myself to remind me of something. They are memoranda that she did exist and that Heathcliff has lost her, that she is dead, vanished from the face of the earth. Everything in the world is a sign indicating Catherine, but also indicating, by its existence, his failure to possess her and the fact that she is dead.

Each sign is both an avenue to the desired unity with her and also the barrier standing in the way of it.

From this follows the double bind of Heathcliff's relation to Hareton and to the second Cathy, both of whom he detests and loves because they look so much like the first Catherine. From this also follows the double bind of his relation to the Heights and to the Grange. He has taken much trouble to obtain them, manipulating the property laws of Yorkshire to do this, as C. P. Sanger has shown. If he possesses the two households, he can take possession of Catherine through them, since they are her property, stamped with her image, proper to her, as much hers as her proper name. But to possess her image, like appropriating her by uttering her name ("Cathy, do come. Oh do—*once* more! Oh! my heart's darling! hear me *this* time—Catherine, at last!"; (I, chap. 3), is to possess only a sign for her, not Catherine herself. He must therefore destroy the things he has made his own in order to reach what they signify. He must destroy Hareton and the second Cathy, as well as the two houses. If he destroys them, however, he will of course reach not Catherine but her absence, the vacancy which stands behind every sign that she once existed and that he has lost her. In the same way, his goal of "dissolving with her, and being more happy still!" (II, chap. 15) is blocked, in the coffin-opening scene, by the vision of Catherine's spirit not in the grave, "not under me, but on the earth" (II, chap. 15). To merge with her body, like merging with his new possessions by destroying them, is to join only a sign and to destroy its function as sign. When Heathcliff recognizes this, he abandons his goal of destroying the Heights and the Grange. This leaves him as far from his goal as ever. He will be an infinite distance from it as long as he is alive:

> "It is a poor conclusion, is it not," he observed, having brooded a while on the scene he had just witnessed [the second Catherine and Hareton reading a book together, a sign of their growing intimacy]. "An absurd termination to my violent exertions? I get levers and mattocks to demolish the two houses, and train myself to be capable of working like Hercules, and when everything is ready, and in my power, I find the will to lift a slate off either roof has vanished! My old enemies have not beaten me—now would be the precise time to revenge myself on their representatives—I could do it; and none could hinder me—But where is the use? I don't care for striking, I can't take the trouble to raise my hand! . . . I have lost the faculty of enjoying their destruction, and I am too idle to destroy for nothing.
> (II, chap. 19)

"But where is the use?" This extraordinary passage defines a complex economy of substitution and exchange which has broken down in an infinite inflation which has made the money worthless. The manipulation of the system is therefore of no use. Each element in this system is now without value either in relation to other elements it "represents" or in relation to what it stands for outside the system, since the standard behind the system has vanished, leaving it supported by nothing. It is like a paper currency which has no gold or silver, or no more credit, behind it, and so becomes again mere paper. The two houses and their land have represented Heathcliff's enemies. His enemies are those who stood between him and Catherine, forbidding their union. To destroy the houses is to destroy the enemies. His enemies, Hindley, Earnshaw, and Edgar Linton, are now dead. He must get at them through their living representatives, Hareton and the second Catherine, the scions of the two families, last of each stock. What these have always stood for is Catherine herself. To put this more exactly, they have stood for the infinite distance between Heathcliff and Catherine. This distance always exists as long as there are still signs for her. Everything resembles her, even Heathcliff's own features, but this resemblance is the sign that she is gone. To leave these signs in existence is to be tormented by the absence they all point to, but of which they also block the filling. To destroy them is to be left with nothing, not even with any signs of the fact that Cathy once existed and that he has lost her. There is no "use" in either destroying or not destroying. Within that situation Heathcliff remains poised, destroying himself in the tension of it, so that breathing or doing any slightest act is for him "like bending back a stiff spring" (II, chap. 19).

The critic's conceptual or figurative scheme of interpretation, including my own here, is up against the same blank wall as the totalizing emblems within the novel, or up against the same impasse that blocks Heathcliff's enterprise of reaching Cathy by taking possession of everything that carries her image and then destroying it. If "something" is incompatible with any sign, if it cannot be seen, signified, or theorized about, it is, in our tradition, no "thing." It is nothing. The trace of such an absence therefore retraces nothing. It can refer only to another trace, in that relation of incongruity which leads the reader of *Wuthering Heights* from one such emblematic design to another. Each passage stands for another passage, in the way Branderham's sermon, as I have said, is a commentary on Jesus's words, themselves a commentary on an Old Testament passage, and so on. Such a movement is a constant passage from one place to another without every finding the original literal text of which the others are all figures. This missing center is the head referent which would still the wandering movement from emblem to emblem, from story to story, from generation to generation, from Catherine to Catherine, from Hareton to Hareton, from narrator to narrator. There is no way to see or name this head referent because it cannot exist as present event, as a past which once was present, or as a future which will be present. It is something which has always already occurred and been forgotten. It has become immemorial, remembered only veiled in figure, however far back one goes. In the other temporal direction, it is always about to occur, as an end which never quite comes, or when it comes comes to another, leaving only another dead sign, like the corpse of Heathcliff at the end of the novel, with its "frightful, life-like gaze of exultation" (II, chap. 20). "It" leaps suddenly from the always not yet of the future to the always already of the unremembered past. This loss leaves the theorizing spectator once more standing in meditation by a grave reading an epitaph, impelled again to tell another story, which will once more fail to bring the explanatory cause into the open. Each emblematic passage in the novel is both a seeming avenue to the desired unity and also a barrier forbidding access to it. Each means the death of experience, of consciousness, of seeing, and of theory by naming the "state" or "place" that lies always outside the words of the novel and therefore can never be experienced as such, and at the same time, in itself and in its intrinsic tendency to repeat itself, each emblematic passage holds off that death.

This "death" may be called an "it" in order not to prejudge the question of whether it is a thing, a place, a person, a state, a relationship, or a supernatural being. The various narrations and emblematic schemas of the novel presuppose an original state of unity. This ghostly glimpse is a projection outward of a oneness from a state of twoness within. This duality is within the self, within the relation of the self to another, within nature, within society, and within language. The sense that there must at some time have been an original state of unity is generated by the state of division as a haunting insight, always at the corner or at the blind center of vision, where sight fails. This insight can never be adequately expressed in language or in other signs, nor can it be "experienced directly," since experience, language, and signs exist only in one thing set against another, one thing divided from another. The insight nevertheless exists for us only in language. The sense of "something missing" is an effect of the text itself, and of the critical texts which add themselves to the primary text. This means it may be a performative effect of language, not a referential object of language. The language of narration in *Wuthering Heights* is this originating performative enacted by Lockwood, Nelly, and the rest. This narrative creates both the intuition of unitary origin and the clues, in the unresolvable heterogeneity of the narration, to the fact that the origin may be an effect of language, not some preexisting state or some "place" in or out of the world. The illusion is created by figures of one sort or another—substitutions, equivalences, representative displacements, synecdoches, emblematic invitations to totalization. The narrative sequence, in its failure ever to become transparent, in the incongruities of its not-quite-matching repetitions, demonstrates the inadequacy of any one of those figures.

Wuthering Heights, as I have said, is an example of a special form of repetition in realistic fiction. This form is controlled by the invitation to believe that some invisible or transcendent cause, some origin, end, or underlying ground, would explain all the enigmatic incongruities of what is visible. Conrad's *Heart of Darkness* is another example of such a repetitive form, as is *Lord Jim*, discussed in chapter 2 [of *Fiction and Repetition*]. It is by no means the case that all realistic fiction takes this form. . . . The special form of "undecidability" in *Wuthering Heights* or in other narratives in which repetition takes this form lies in the impossibility, in principle, of determining whether there is some extralinguistic explanatory cause or whether the sense that there is one is generated by the linguistic structure itself. Nor is this a trivial issue. It is the most important question the novel raises, the one thing about which we ought to be able to make a decision, and yet a thing about which the novel forbids the reader to make a decision. In this *Wuthering Heights* justifies being called an "uncanny" text. To alter Freud's formulas a little, the uncanny in *Wuthering Heights* is the constant bringing into the open of something which seems familiar and which one feels ought to have been kept secret, not least because it is impossible to tell whether there is any secret at all hidden in the depths, or whether the sense of familiarity and of the unveiling of a secret may not be an effect of the repetition in difference of one part of the text by another, on the surface. In the oscillation between the invitation to expect the novel to be an example of the first, grounded form of repetition and the constant frustration of that expectation, *Wuthering Heights* is a special case of the intertwining of two forms of repetition described in chapter 1 [of *Fiction and Repetition*].

I have suggested that the narration in *Wuthering Heights* somehow involves the reader's innocence or guilt. It may now be seen how this is the case. Any repetitive structure of the "uncanny" sort, whether in real life or in words, tends to generate an irrational sense of guilt in the one who experiences it. I have not done anything (or have I?), and yet what I witness makes demands on me which I cannot fulfill. The mere fact of passive looking or of reading may make one guilty of the crime of seeing what ought not to have been seen. What I see or what I read repeats or seems to repeat something earlier, something deeper in. That something hidden is brought back out into the open in a disguised repetition by what I see. It should be brought out now into full clarity. At the same time perhaps it should be kept secret, since it may possibly be one of those things which, to paraphrase Winnie Verloc in Conrad's *The Secret Agent*, does not stand much looking into. One way or the other I am forced to do something for which I will feel guilty. I am guilty if I reveal what ought to have been kept secret. I am guilty if I refuse the demand it makes on me to "get in," to penetrate all the way to the bottom of the mystery. The situation of the reader of *Wuthering Heights* is inscribed within the novel in the situations of all those characters who are readers, tellers of tales, most elaborately in Lockwood. The lesson for the reader is to make him aware that he has by reading the novel incurred a responsibility like that of the other spectator-interpreters.

"Thou art the man!"—this applies as much to the reader as to Lockwood or to the other narrators. The double guilt of Lockwood's narration as of any critic's discourse is the following. If he does not penetrate all the way to the innermost core of the story he tells, he keeps the story going, repeating itself interminably in its incompletion. This is like the guilt of the one who keeps a grave open, or like the guilt of a sexual failure. On the other hand, to pierce all the way in is to be guilty of the desecration of a grave, to be guilty, like Heathcliff when he opens Cathy's grave, of necrophilia. The punishment for that is to be condemned to go where the vanished protagonists are. Really to penetrate, to get inside the events, rather than seeing them safely from the outside, would be to join Cathy and Heathcliff wherever they now are. The reader's sense of guilt is systematically connected to the swarm of other emotions aroused in any good reader of *Wuthering Heights* as he makes his way through the book: affection for the two Catherines, though in a different way for each, and mixed with some fear of her intransigence in the case of the first Catherine; scorn for Lockwood, but some pity for his limitations; awe of Heathcliff's suffering; and so on.

The line of witnesses who feel one or another form of this complex of emotions goes from the reader-critic to Charlotte Brontë to Emily Brontë to that pseudonymous author "Ellis Bell" to Lockwood to Nelly to Heathcliff to Cathy, the inside of the inside, or it moves the other way around, from Cathy out to the reader. The reader is the last surviving consciousness enveloping all these other consciousnesses, one inside the other. The reader is condemned, like all the others, to be caught by a double contradictory demand: to bring it all out in the open and at the same time to give it decent burial, to keep the book open and at the same time to close its covers once and for all, so it may be forgotten, or so it may be read once more, this time definitively. The guilt of the reader is the impossibility of doing either of these things, once he has opened the book and begun to read: "1801—I have just returned from a visit to my landlord" (I, chap. 1).

The reading of the first present-tense words of the novel performs a multiple act of resurrection, an opening of graves or a raising of ghosts. In reading those first words and then all the ones that follow to the end, the reader brings back from the grave first the fictive "I" who is supposed to have written them or spoken them, that Lockwood who has and had no existence outside the covers of the book. With that "I" the reader brings back also the moment in the fall of 1801 when his "I have just returned" is supposed to have been written or spoken. By way of that first "I" and first present moment the reader then resurrects from the dead, with Lockwood's help, in one direction Hindley, Nelly, Joseph, Hareton, the two Catherines, Heathcliff, and the rest, so that they walk the moors once again and live once again at the Heights and the Grange. In the other direction are also evoked first Ellis Bell, the pseudonymous author, who functions as a ghostly name on the title page. Ellis Bell is a male name veiling the female author, but it is also the name of a character in the book: someone who has survived Lockwood, an "editor" into whose hands Lockwood's diary has fallen and who presents it to the public, or, more likely, the consciousness surrounding Lockwood's consciousness, overhearing what he says to himself, what he thinks, feels, sees, and presenting it again to the reader as though it were entirely the words of Lockwood. In doing this Ellis Bell effaces himself, but he is present as a ghostly necessity of the narrative behind Lockwood's words. The name Ellis Bell functions to name a spectator outside Lockwood, who is the primary spectator. Ellis Bell is another representative of the reader, overhearing, overseeing, overthinking, and overfeeling what Lockwood says, sees, thinks, feels, and writing it down so we can in our turns evoke Lockwood again and raise also that thin and almost invisible ghost, effaced presupposition of the words of the novel, Ellis Bell himself. Behind Ellis Bell, finally, is Brontë, who, the reader knows, actually wrote down those words, "1801—I have just returned . . ." at Haworth on some day probably in 1846. Brontë too, in however indirect fashion, is brought back to life in the act of reading.

If in Lockwood's dream the air swarms with Catherines, so does this book swarm with ghosts who walk the Yorkshire moors inside the covers of any copy of *Wuthering Heights*, waiting to be brought back from the grave by anyone who chances to open the book and read. The most powerful form of repetition in fiction, it may be, is not the echoes of one part of the book by another, but the way even the simplest, most representational words in a novel ("1801—I have just returned . . .") present themselves as already a murmuring repetition, something which has been repeating itself incessantly there in the words on the page waiting for me to bring it back to life as the meaning of the words forms itself in my mind. Fiction is possible only because of an intrinsic capacity possessed by ordinary words in grammatical order. Words no different from those we use in everyday life, "I have just returned," may detach themselves or be detached from any present moment, any living "I," any immediate perception of reality, and go on functioning as the creators of the fictive world repeated into existence, to use the verb transitively, whenever the act of reading those words is performed. The words themselves, there on the page, both presuppose the deaths of that long line of personages and at the same time keep them from dying wholly, as long as a single copy of *Wuthering Heights* survives to be reread.

Chronology

1812   The Reverend Patrick Brontë marries Maria Branwell.

1814   Maria Brontë, their first child, born.

1815   Elizabeth Brontë born.

1816   Charlotte Brontë born on April 21.

1817   Patrick Branwell Brontë, the only son, born in June.

1818   Emily Jane Brontë born on July 30.

1820   Anne Brontë born on January 17. The Brontë family moves to the parsonage at Haworth, near Bradford, Yorkshire.

1821   Mrs. Brontë dies of cancer in September. Her sister, Elizabeth Branwell, takes charge of the household.

1824   Maria and Elizabeth attend the Clergy Daughters' School at Cowan Bridge. Charlotte follows them in August, and Emily in November.

1825   The two oldest girls, Maria and Elizabeth, contract tuberculosis at school. Maria dies on May 6; Elizabeth dies June 15. Charlotte and Emily are withdrawn from the school on June 1. Charlotte and Emily do not return to school until they are in their teens; in the meantime they are educated at home.

1826   Rev. Brontë brings home a box of wooden soldiers for his son; this is the catalyst for the creation of the Brontës' juvenile fantasy worlds and writings. Charlotte and Branwell begin the "Angrian" stories and magazines; Emily and Anne work on the "Gondal" saga.

1831   Charlotte attends Miss Wooler's school. She leaves the school seven months later, to tend to her sisters' education. In 1835, however, she returns as governess. She is accompanied by Emily.

1835   After only three months, Emily leaves Miss Wooler's school because of homesickness. Anne arrives in January 1836 and remains until December 1837.

1837   In September, Emily becomes a governess at Miss Patchett's school, near Halifax.

1838   In May, Charlotte leaves her position at Miss Wooler's school.

1839   Anne becomes governess for the Ingram family at Blake Hall, Mirfield. She leaves in December. Charlotte becomes governess in the Sidwick family, at Stonegappe Hall, near Skipton. She leaves after two months (July).

1840   All three sisters live at Haworth.

1841   Anne becomes governess in the Robinson family, near York. Charlotte becomes governess in the White family and moves to Upperwood House, Rawdon. She leaves in December. The sisters plan to start their own school. The scheme, attempted several years later, fails for lack of inquiries.

1842   Charlotte and Emily travel to Brussels to study in the Pensionnat Héger. Here, Charlotte suffers unrequited love for the master of the school, M. Héger. Upon the death of their aunt in November, they return to Haworth.

1843   Branwell joins Anne in York as tutor to the Robinson family. Charlotte returns to Brussels and remains until January 1844.

1845   Charlotte discovers Emily's poetry and suggests that a selection be published along with the poetry of herself and Anne.

1846   *Poems, by Currer, Ellis, and Acton Bell* published by Aylott & Jones. Two copies are sold. Charlotte's *The Professor,* Emily's *Wuthering Heights,* and Anne's *Agnes Grey* are all completed. The latter two are accepted by T. C. Newby, but *The Professor* is rejected. Charlotte's *Jane Eyre* is begun in August and immediately accepted by Smith, Elder & Co. upon its completion in August 1847.

1847   *Jane Eyre* published. *Wuthering Heights* and *Agnes Grey* published by T. C. Newby.

1848   Anne's *The Tenant of Wildfell Hall* published by T. C. Newby, which tries to sell it to an American publisher as a new book by Currer Bell, author of the immensely popular *Jane Eyre.* Smith, Elder & Co.

requests that Charlotte bring her sisters to London to prove that there are three Bells. Charlotte and Anne visit London. Branwell dies of tuberculosis, September 24. Emily dies of the same, December 19.

1849   Anne dies of tuberculosis, May 28. Charlotte's *Shirley* published by Smith, Elder & Co. Charlotte meets Thackeray and Harriet Martineau in London.

1850   Charlotte meets G. H. Lewes and Mrs. Gaskell in London. Edits her sisters' work. Smith, Elder & Co. publishes a new edition of *Wuthering Heights* and *Agnes Grey*, along with some of Anne's and Emily's poetry, and a "Biographical Notice" of her sisters' lives by Charlotte.

1852   The Reverend A. B. Nicholls proposes marriage to Charlotte. Her father objects, and Nicholls is rejected. Eventually, Rev. Brontë yields, and Charlotte marries in June, 1854.

1853   Charlotte's *Villette* published in January.

1855   Charlotte dies of toxemia of pregnancy, March 31.

1857   Charlotte's *The Professor* published posthumously with a preface written by her husband. Mrs. Gaskell's *Life of Charlotte Brontë* published in March.

1860   "Emma," a fragment of a story by Charlotte, published in *The Cornhill Magazine* with an introduction by Thackeray.

1861   The Reverend Patrick Brontë, having survived all his children, dies.

Contributors

HAROLD BLOOM, Sterling Professor of the Humanities at Yale University, is the author of *The Anxiety of Influence, Poetry and Repression*, and many other volumes of literary criticism. His forthcoming study, *Freud: Transference and Authority*, attempts a full-scale reading of all of Freud's major writings. A MacArthur Prize Fellow, he is general editor of five series of literary criticism published by Chelsea House.

INGA-STINA EWBANK is Professor of English Literature at the University of Leeds. She is the author of *Their Proper Sphere*, a study of the Brontës, and the editor of a study of Shakespeare.

W. A. CRAIK is Senior Lecturer at the University of Aberdeen and the author of *The Brontë Novels* and *Jane Austen: The Six Novels*.

RAYMOND WILLIAMS is Judith E. Wilson Professor of Drama at Cambridge University. The most influential of British Marxist critics of literature, his books include *Culture and Society, The Long Revolution*, and *The Country and the City*.

ROSALIND MILES lectures in English at Lanchester Polytechnic, Coventry. Her books include *The Fiction of Sex* and studies of *Measure for Measure*.

MARGARET HOMANS is Associate Professor of English at Yale University. Among her publications is *Women Writers and Poetic Identity: Dorothy Wordsworth, Emily Brontë, and Emily Dickinson*.

SANDRA M. GILBERT is Professor of English at Princeton University. SUSAN GUBAR is Professor of English at Indiana University. Together they have written *The Madwoman in the Attic: The Woman Writer and the Nineteenth-Century Literary Imagination* and edited *The Norton Anthology of Women's Literature* and *Shakespeare's Sisters: Feminist Essays on Women Poets*.

JANICE CARLISLE teaches at Washington University, St. Louis. Her publications include *Sense of an Audience: Dickens, Thackeray, and George Eliot at Mid-Century.*

ROSEMARIE BODENHEIMER is Associate Professor of English at Boston College.

J. HILLIS MILLER is Frederick W. Hilles Professor of English and Comparative Literature at Yale University. Among his many volumes of criticism are *The Disappearance of God: Five Nineteenth-Century Writers, Poets of Reality: Six Twentieth-Century Writers, Fiction and Repetition: Seven English Novels,* and, most recently, *The Linguistic Moment.*

Bibliography

Allott, Miriam, ed. *The Brontës: The Critical Heritage*. London and Boston: Routledge & Kegan Paul, 1974.

———, ed. Wuthering Heights: *A Casebook*. London: Macmillan & Co., 1970.

Auerbach, Nina. "Charlotte Brontë: The Two Countries." *University of Toronto Quarterly* 42 (1972–73): 328–42.

———. "This Changeful Life: Emily Brontë's Anti-Romance." In *Shakespeare's Sisters: Feminist Essays on Women Poets*, edited by Sandra M. Gilbert and Susan Gubar. Bloomington: Indiana University Press, 1979.

Benvenuto, Richard. "The Child of Nature, the Child of Grace, and the Unresolved Conflict of *Jane Eyre*." *ELH* 39 (1972): 620–38.

———. *Emily Brontë*. Boston: Twayne, 1982.

Bledsoe, Robert. "Snow beneath Snow: A Reconsideration of the Virgin of *Villette*." In *Gender and Literary Voice*, edited by Janet Todd. New York: Holmes & Meier, 1980.

Blom, M. A. "*Jane Eyre*: Mind as Law Unto Itself." *Criticism* 15 (1973): 350–64.

Blondel, Jacques. *Emily Brontë: Experience Spirituelle et Creation Poetique*. Paris: Presses Universitaires de France, 1955.

Burkhart, Charles. *Charlotte Brontë: A Psychosexual Study of Her Novels*. London: Victor Gollancz, 1973.

Cecil, David. *Victorian Novelists: Essays in Revaluation*. London: Constable, 1948.

Chase, Richard. "The Brontës, or, Myth Domesticated." In *Forms of Modern Fiction: Essays Collected in Honor of Joseph Warren Beach*, edited by William Van O'Connor. Bloomington: Indiana University Press, 1962.

Craik, W. A. *The Brontë Novels*. London: Methuen, 1968.

Crosby, Christina. "Charlotte Brontë's Haunted Text." *Studies in English Literature 1500–1900* 24, no. 4 (Autumn 1984): 701–15.

Cunningham, Valentine. *Everywhere Spoken Against: Dissent in the Victorian Novel*. Oxford: Oxford University Press, 1975.

Daiches, David. "Introduction." In *Wuthering Heights*. London: Penguin Books, 1965.

De Grazia, Emilio. "The Ethical Dimension of *Wuthering Heights*." *Midwest Quarterly* 19 (Winter 1978): 178–95.

Dingle, Herbert. *The Mind of Emily Brontë*. London: Martin Brian & O'Keeffe, 1974.

Dodds, Madeleine Hope. "Gondaliand." *Modern Language Review* 18 (January 1923): 9–21.

Donoghue, Denis. "Emily Brontë: On the Latitude of Interpretation." In *The Interpretation of Narrative: Theory and Practice*, Harvard English Studies 1, edited by Morton W. Bloomfield, 105–33. Cambridge: Harvard University Press, 1970.

Drew, David P. "Emily Brontë and Emily Dickinson as Mystical Poets." *Brontë Society Transactions* 15 (1968): 227–32.

Dry, Florence Swinton. *The Sources of* Wuthering Heights. Cambridge, England: W. Heffer & Sons, 1937.

Dunn, Richard J., ed. *Charlotte Brontë: Jane Eyre*. A Norton Critical Edition. New York: Norton, 1971.

Eagleton, Terry. *Myths of Power: A Marxist Study of the Brontës*. London: Macmillan, 1975.

Ewbank, Inga-Stina. *Their Proper Sphere: A Study of the Brontë Sisters as Early-Victorian Female Novelists*. London: Edward Arnold, 1966.

Gaskell, Elizabeth. *The Life of Charlotte Brontë*. London: J. M. Dent, 1960.

Gerin, Winifred. *Charlotte Brontë: The Evolution of Genius*. London: Oxford University Press, 1967.

Gilbert, Sandra M., and Susan Gubar. *The Madwoman in the Attic: The Woman Writer and the Nineteenth-Century Literary Imagination*. New Haven: Yale University Press, 1979.

Gregor, Ian, ed. *The Brontës: A Collection of Critical Essays*. Englewood Cliffs, N.J.: Prentice-Hall, 1970.

Hardy, Barbara. *The Appropriate Form: An Essay on the Novel*. London: Athlone, 1964.

Heilman, Robert B. "Charlotte Brontë, Reason, and the Moon." *Nineteenth-Century Fiction* 14, no. 4 (March 1960): 283–302.

———. "Charlotte Brontë's 'New Gothic.' " In *From Jane Austen to Joseph Conrad*, edited by Robert C. Rathburn and Martin Steinmann, Jr., 118–32. Minneapolis: University of Minnesota Press, 1958.

Hewish, John. *Emily Brontë: A Critical and Biographical Study*. London: Macmillan, 1969.

Hinkley, Laura L. *The Brontës: Charlotte and Emily*. London: Hammond, Hammond & Co., 1947.

Homans, Margaret. "Dreaming of Children: Literalization in *Jane Eyre* and *Wuthering Heights*." In *The Female Gothic*, edited by Judith E. Fleenor, 257–79. Montreal: Eden, 1983.

Horne, Margot. "Portrait of the Artist as a Young Woman: The Dualism of Heroine and Anti-Heroine in *Villette*." *Dutch Quarterly Review of Anglo-American Letters* 6, no. 3 (1976): 216–32.

Jackson, Arlene M. "The Question of Credibility in Anne Brontë's *The Tenant of Wildfell Hall*." *English Studies* 63, no. 3 (June 1982): 198–206.

Jacobus, Mary. "The Buried Letter: Feminism and Romanticism in *Villette*. In *Women Writing and Writing About Women*, edited by Mary Jacobus, 42–60. London and Sydney: Croom Helm, 1984.

Kettle, Arnold. *An Introduction to the English Novel*. Vol. 1. London: Hutchinson University Library, 1951.

Kiely, Robert. *The Romantic Novel in England*. Cambridge: Harvard University Press, 1972.

Knoepflmacher, U. C. *Laughter and Despair: Reading in Ten Novels of the Victorian Era*. Berkeley and Los Angeles: University of California Press, 1971.

Krupat, Arnold. "The Strangeness of *Wuthering Heights.*" *Nineteenth-Century Fiction* 25 (December 1970): 269–80.

Leavis, Q. D. "A Fresh Approach to *Wuthering Heights.*" In *Lectures in America*, by F. R. and Q. D. Leavis. New York: Pantheon, 1969.

Lenta, Margaret. "The Tone of Protest: An Interpretation of Charlotte Brontë's *Villette.*" *English Studies* 64, no. 5 (October 1983): 422–32.

Martin, Robert. *The Accents of Persuasion: Charlotte Brontë's Novels.* London: Faber & Faber, 1966.

Mathison, John K. "Nelly Dean and the Power of *Wuthering Heights.*" *Nineteenth-Century Fiction* 11 (September 1956): 106–29.

McKibben, Robert C. "The Image of the Book in *Wuthering Heights.*" *Nineteenth-Century Fiction* 15 (September 1960): 159–69.

Miller, J. Hillis. *The Disappearance of God: Five Nineteenth-Century Writers.* New York: Schocken, 1965.

———. *The Form of Victorian Fiction.* Notre Dame: University of Notre Dame Press, 1968.

Moglen, Helene. *Charlotte Brontë: The Self Conceived.* New York: Norton, 1976.

Moser, Thomas. "What is the Matter with Emily Jane? Conflicting Impulses in *Wuthering Heights.*" *Nineteenth-Century Fiction* 17 (June 1962): 1–19.

Ohmann, Carol. *Charlotte Brontë: The Limits of Her Feminism.* Old Westbury, N.Y.: The Feminist Press, 1972.

———. "Emily Brontë in the Hands of Male Critics." *College English* 32 (May 1971): 906–13.

Paden, W. D. *An Investigation of Gondal.* New York: Bookman Associates, 1958.

Peters, Margot. *Charlotte Brontë: Style in the Novel.* Madison: University of Wisconsin Press, 1973.

———. *Unquiet Soul: A Biography of Charlotte Brontë.* New York: Doubleday, 1975.

Pinion, F. B. *A Brontë Companion: Literary Assessment, Background, and Reference.* London: Macmillan, 1975.

Ratchford, Fannie Elizabeth. *The Brontës' Web of Childhood.* New York: Columbia University Press, 1941.

———, ed. *Gondal's Queen: A Novel in Verse by Emily Jane Brontë.* Austin: University of Texas Press, 1955.

Sale, William M., Jr. ed. *Emily Brontë:* Wuthering Heights. A Norton Critical Edition. New York: Norton, 1963.

Schorer, Mark. "Fiction and the 'Matrix of Analogy.'" *The Kenyon Review* 11, no. 4 (Autumn 1949): 539–60.

Sinclair, May. *The Three Brontës.* Boston and New York: Houghton Mifflin, 1912.

Smith, Anne. *The Art of Emily Brontë.* London: Vision Press, 1976.

Sonstroem, David. "*Wuthering Heights* and the Limits of Vision." *PMLA* 86 (January 1971): 51–62.

Spark, Muriel, and Derek Stanford. *Emily Brontë: Her Life and Work.* New York: Coward-McCann, 1966.

Starzyk, Lawrence J. "Emily Brontë: Poetry in a Mingled Tone." *Criticism* 14 (Spring 1972): 119–36.

Stevenson, W. H. "*Wuthering Heights*: The Facts." *Essays in Criticism* 14, no. 2 (April 1985): 149–66.

Stone, Donald D. *The Romantic Impulse in Victorian Fiction.* Cambridge: Harvard University Press, 1980.

Tillotson, Kathleen. *Novels of the 1840s.* Oxford: Clarendon Press, 1954.

Van Ghent, Dorothy. *Form and Function in the English Novel.* New York: Harper & Row, 1961.

Visick, Mary. *The Genesis of* Wuthering Heights. Hong Kong: Hong Kong University Press, 1958.

Winnifrith, Tom. *The Brontës and Their Background: Romance and Reality.* London: Macmillan, 1973.

Acknowledgments

"Artistic Truth in the Novels of Charlotte Brontë" (originally entitled "Charlotte Brontë: The Woman Writer as an Author Only") by Inga-Stina Ewbank from *Their Proper Sphere: A Study of the Brontë Sisters as Early Victorian Female Novelists* by Inga-Stina Ewbank, © 1966 by Inga-Stina Ewbank. Reprinted by permission of the author and Edward Arnold Ltd.

"*The Tenant of Wildfell Hall*" by W. A. Craik from *The Brontë Novels* by W. A. Craik, © 1968 by W. A. Craik. Reprinted by permission of the author and Methuen & Co. Ltd.

"Charlotte and Emily Brontë" by Raymond Williams from *The English Novel: From Dickens to Lawrence* by Raymond Williams, © 1970 by Raymond Williams. Reprinted by permission of the author and Chatto & Windus Ltd.

"A Baby God: The Creative Dynamism of Emily Brontë's Poetry" by Rosalind Miles from *The Art of Emily Brontë*, edited by Anne Smith, © 1976 by Vision Press. Reprinted by permission.

"Repression and Sublimation of Nature in *Wuthering Heights*" by Margaret Homans from *PMLA* 93, no. 1 (January 1978), © 1978 by the Modern Language Association of America. Reprinted by permission of the Modern Language Association of America.

"The Genesis of Hunger According to *Shirley*" by Sandra M. Gilbert and Susan Gubar from *The Madwoman in the Attic: The Woman Writer and the Nineteenth-Century Literary Imagination* by Sandra M. Gilbert and Susan Gubar, © 1979 by Yale University. Reprinted by permission. A version of this essay originally appeared in *Feminist Studies* 3, nos. 3 and 4 (Spring/Summer 1976).

"The Face in the Mirror: *Villette* and the Conventions of Autobiography" by Janice Carlisle from *ELH* 46, no. 2 (Summer 1979), © 1979 by the Johns Hopkins University Press. Reprinted by permission of the Johns Hopkins University Press.

"Jane Eyre in Search of Her Story" by Rosemarie Bodenheimer from *Papers on Language and Literature* 16, no. 3 (Summer 1980), © 1980 by the Board of Trustees, Southern Illinois University. Reprinted by permission.

"*Wuthering Heights*: Repetition and the 'Uncanny' " by J. Hillis Miller from *Fiction and Repetition: Seven English Novels* by J. Hillis Miller, © 1982 by J. Hillis Miller. Reprinted by permission of the author and Harvard University Press.

Index

X